what did you eat yesterday? 9
fumi yoshinaga

VERTICAL.

#65

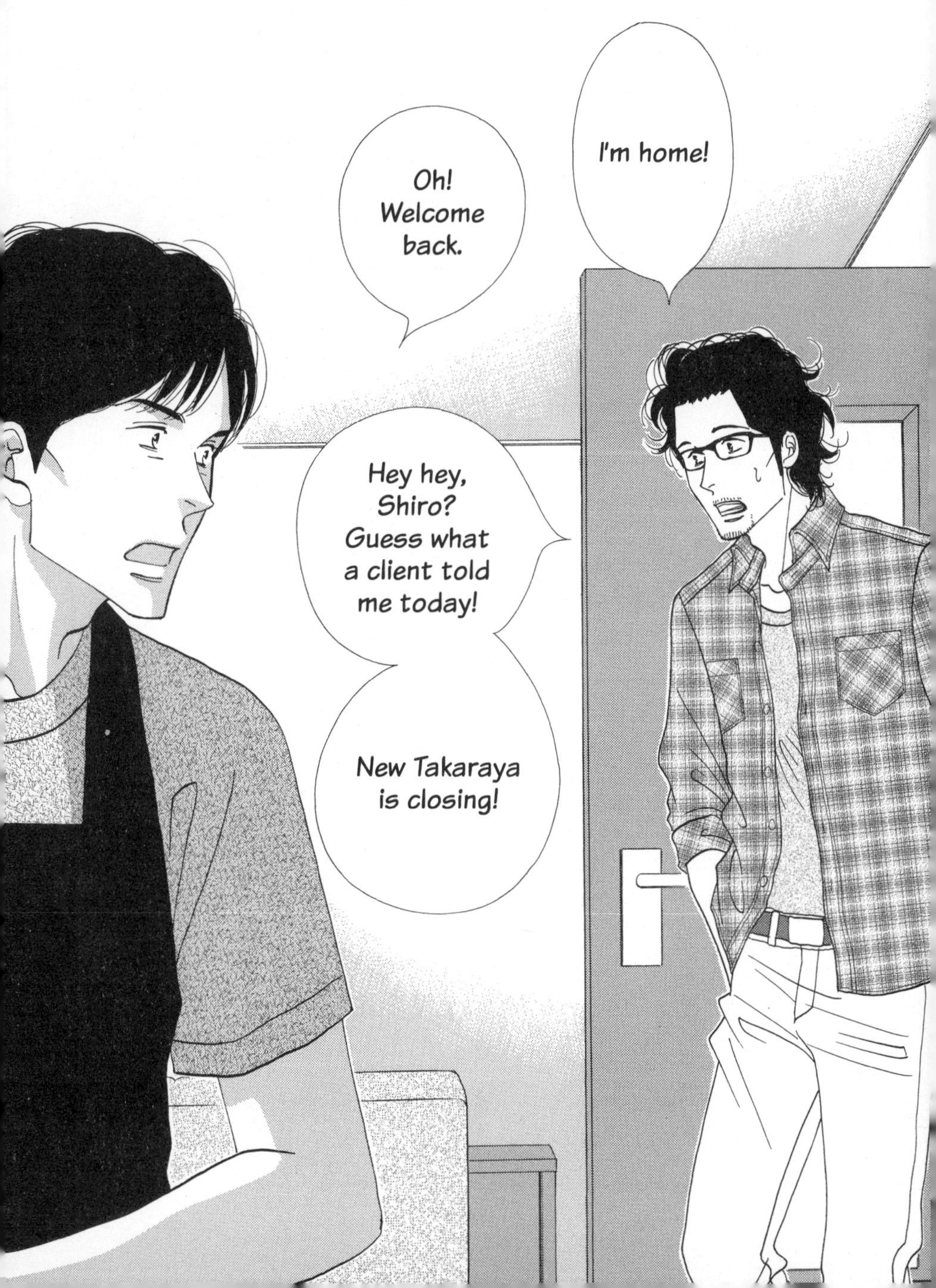
I'm home!
Oh! Welcome back.
Hey hey, Shiro? Guess what a client told me today!
New Takaraya is closing!

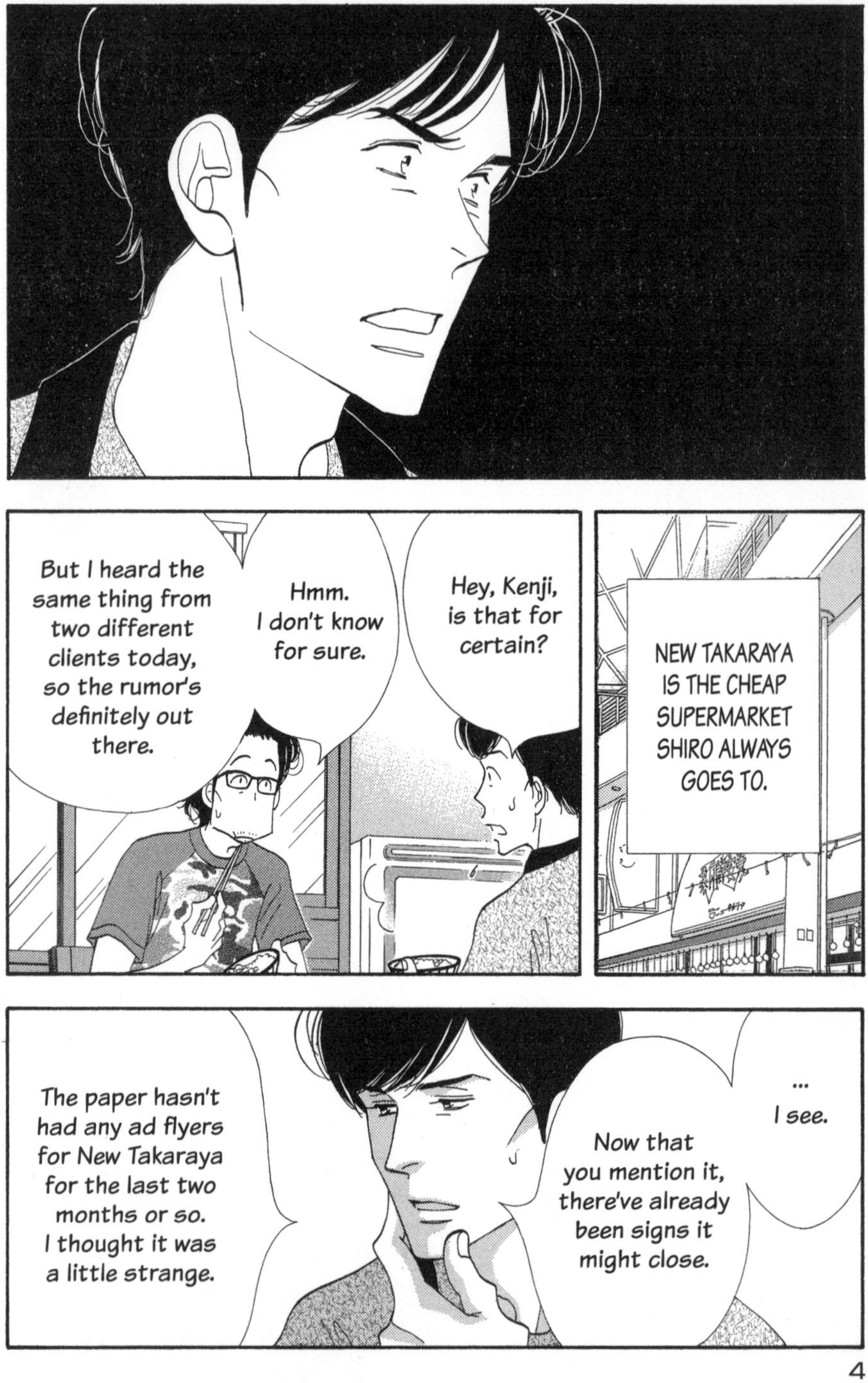
NEW TAKARAYA IS THE CHEAP SUPERMARKET SHIRO ALWAYS GOES TO.
Hey, Kenji, is that for certain?
Hmm. I don't know for sure.
But I heard the same thing from two different clients today, so the rumor's definitely out there.
... I see.
Now that you mention it, there've already been signs it might close.
The paper hasn't had any ad flyers for New Takaraya for the last two months or so. I thought it was a little strange.

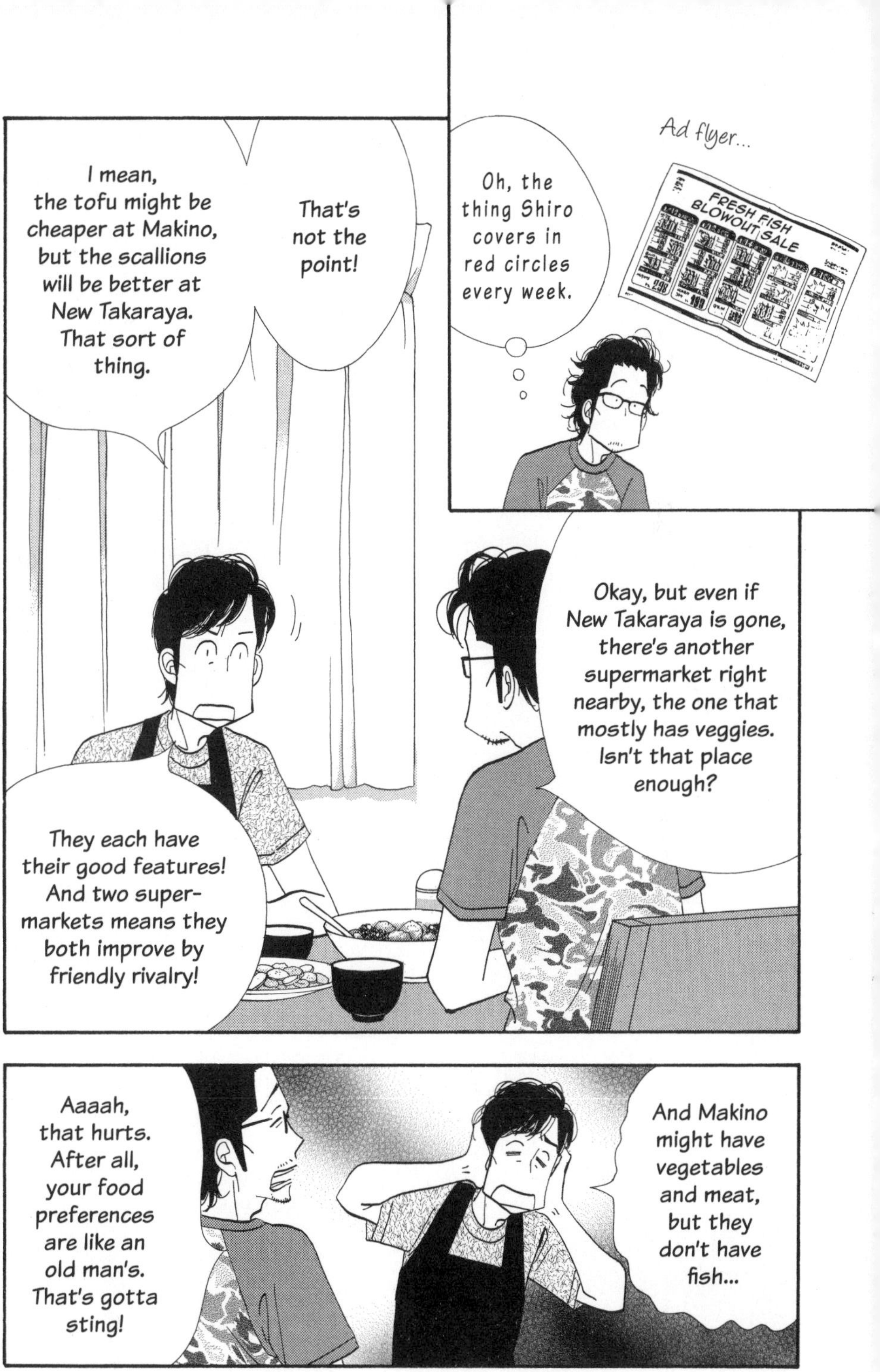
Ad flyer...
FRESH FISH BLOWOUT SALE
Oh, the thing Shiro covers in red circles every week.
That's not the point!
I mean, the tofu might be cheaper at Makino, but the scallions will be better at New Takaraya. That sort of thing.
Okay, but even if New Takaraya is gone, there's another supermarket right nearby, the one that mostly has veggies. Isn't that place enough?
They each have their good features! And two super-markets means they both improve by friendly rivalry!
And Makino might have vegetables and meat, but they don't have fish...
Aaaah, that hurts. After all, your food preferences are like an old man's. That's gotta sting!

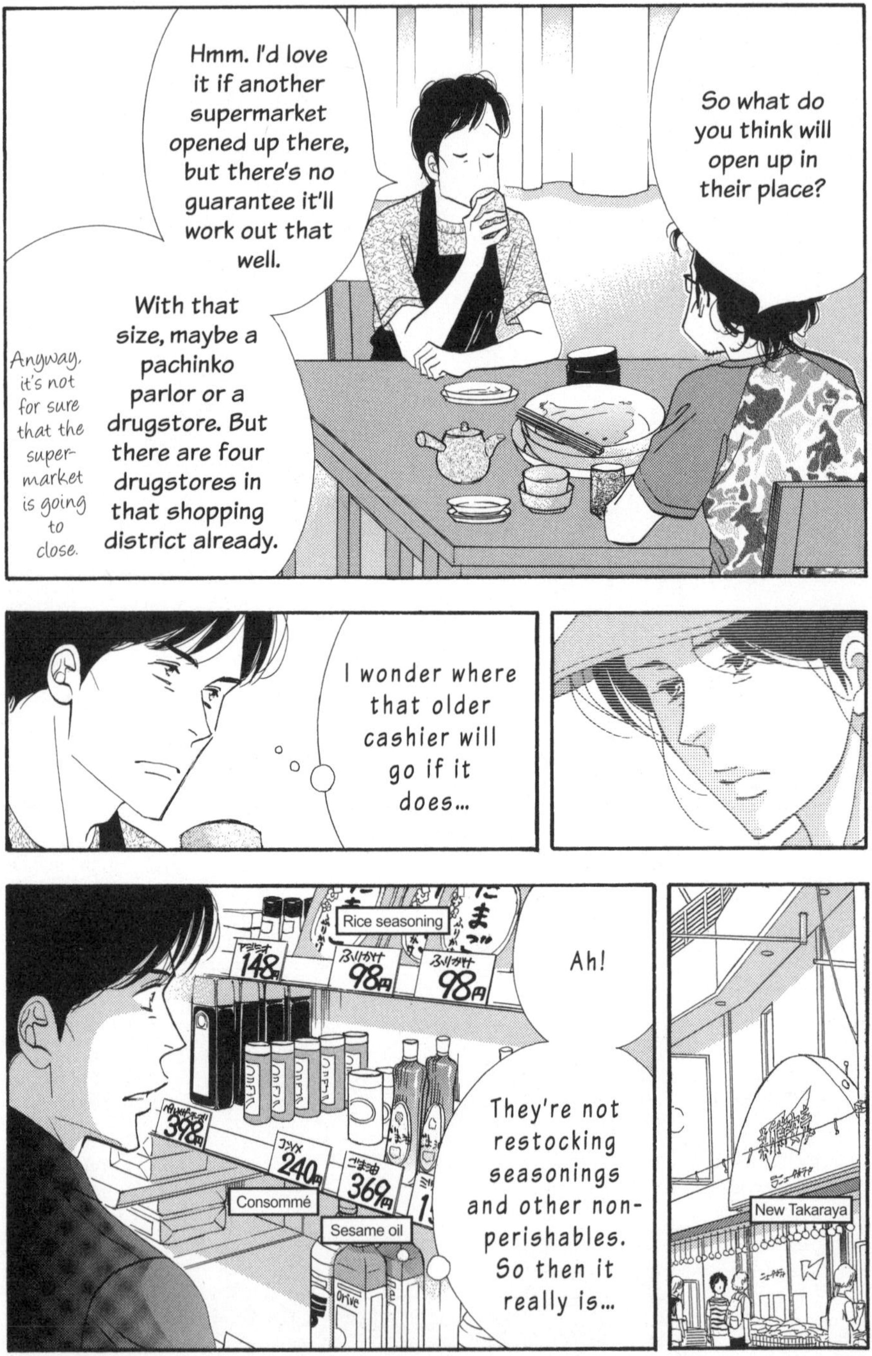
So what do you think will open up in their place?
Hmm. I'd love it if another supermarket opened up there, but there's no guarantee it'll work out that well.
With that size, maybe a pachinko parlor or a drugstore. But there are four drugstores in that shopping district already.
Anyway, it's not for sure that the supermarket is going to close.
I wonder where that older cashier will go if it does...
New Takaraya
Ah!
Rice seasoning
They're not restocking seasonings and other non-perishables. So then it really is...
Consommé
Sesame oil

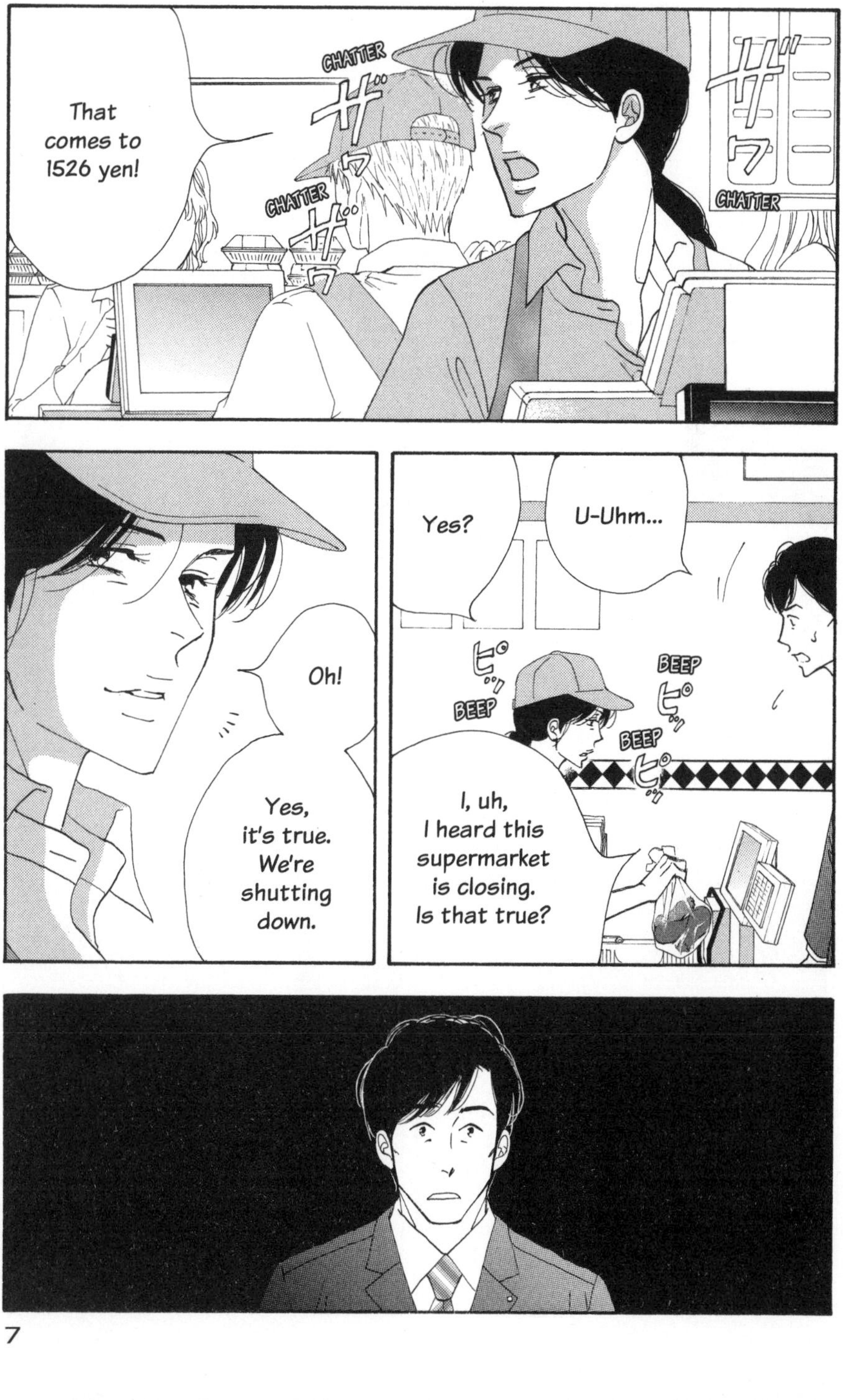
ザワ
CHATTER
CHATTER
ザワ
That comes to 1526 yen!
CHATTER
ザワ
U-Uhm...
Yes?
BEEP
ピッ
BEEP
ピッ
BEEP
ピッ
I, uh, I heard this supermarket is closing. Is that true?
Oh!
Yes, it's true. We're shutting down.

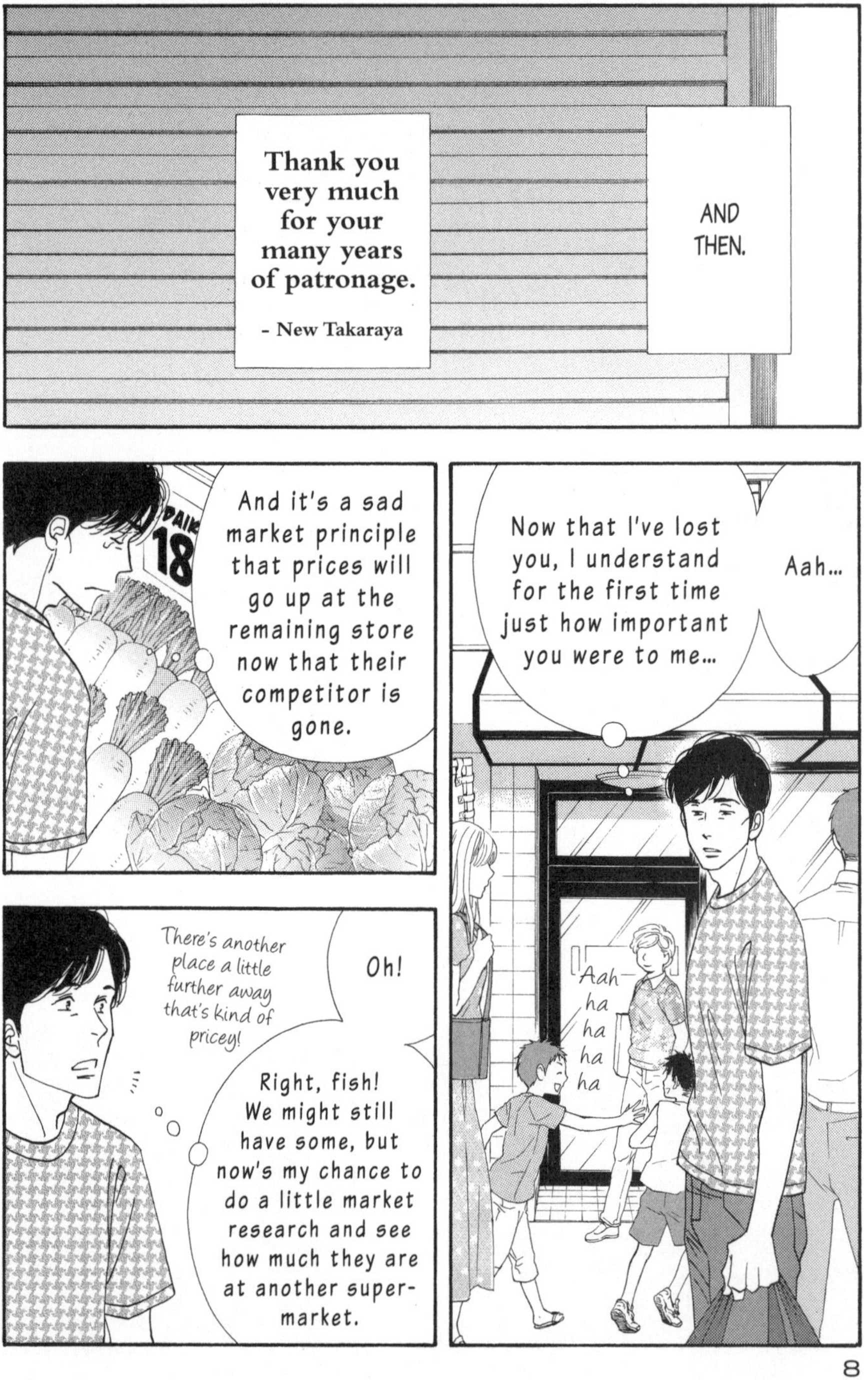
Thank you very much for your many years of patronage.
- New Takaraya
AND THEN.
Aah...
Now that I've lost you, I understand for the first time just how important you were to me...
Aah ha ha ha ha
And it's a sad market principle that prices will go up at the remaining store now that their competitor is gone.
Oh!
There's another place a little further away that's kind of pricey!
Right, fish! We might still have some, but now's my chance to do a little market research and see how much they are at another super-market.

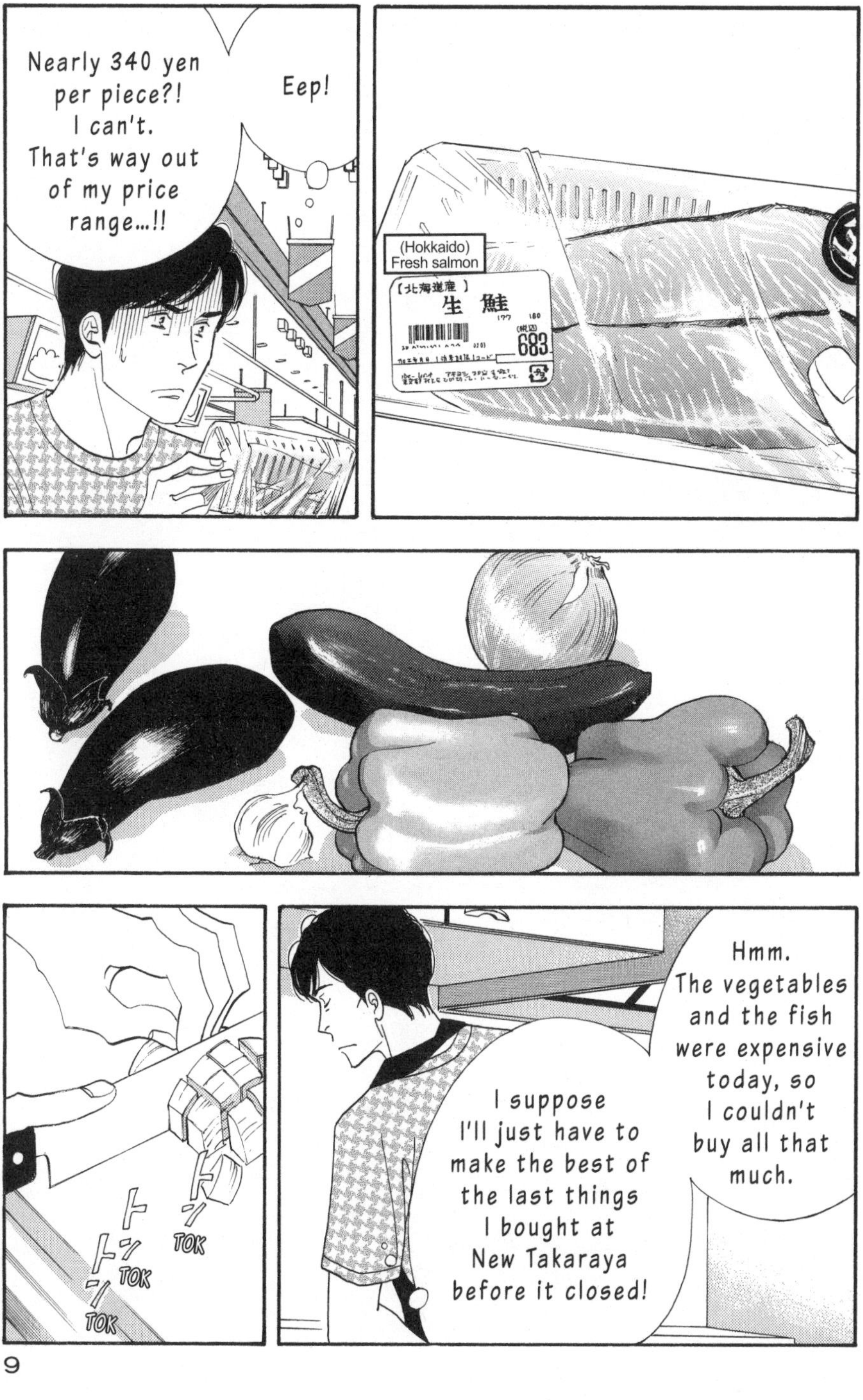
(Hokkaido)
Fresh salmon
【北海道産】
生 鮭
683
Eep!
Nearly 340 yen per piece?! I can't. That's way out of my price range...!!
Hmm. The vegetables and the fish were expensive today, so I couldn't buy all that much.
I suppose I'll just have to make the best of the last things I bought at New Takaraya before it closed!
トン
TOK
トン
TOK
トン
TOK

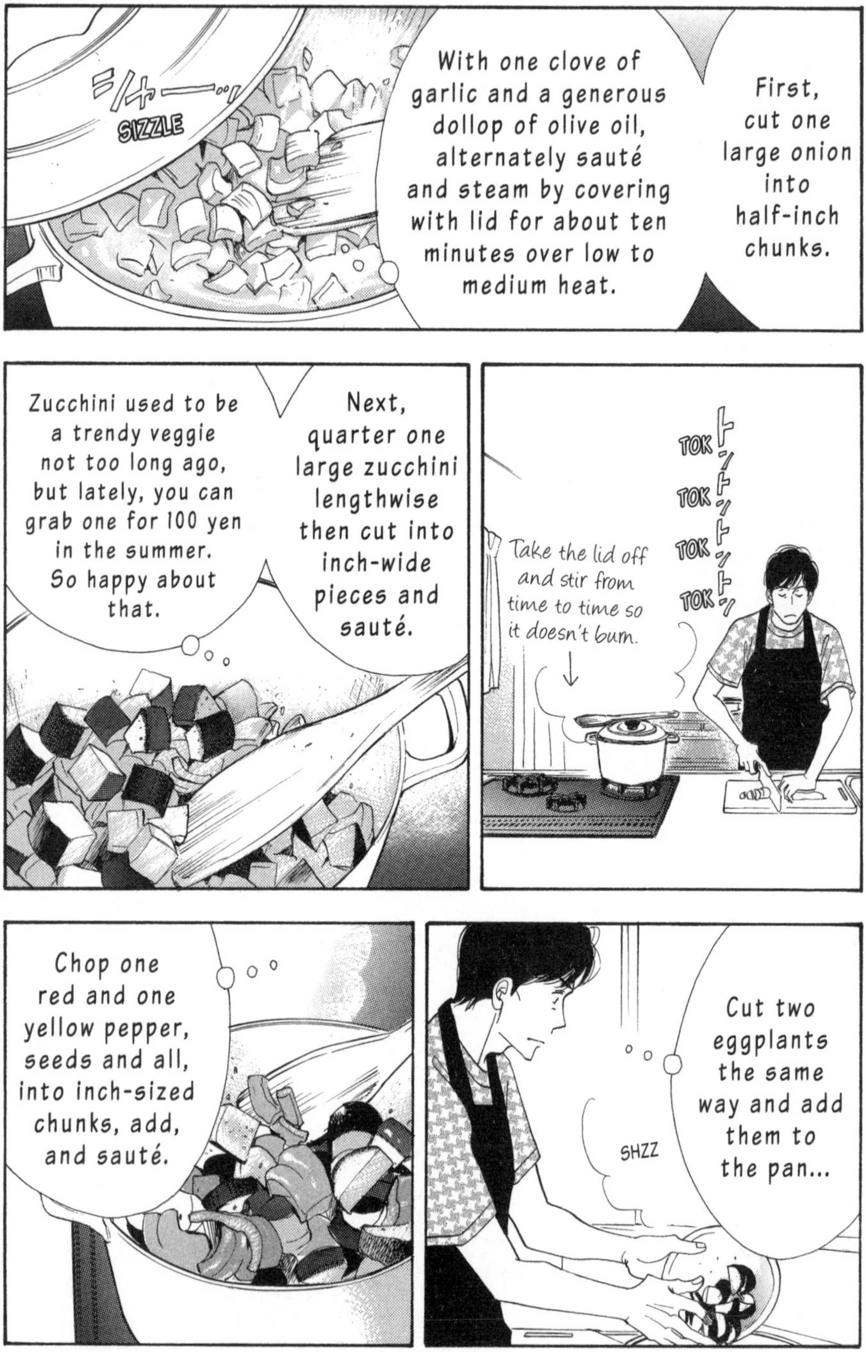
First, cut one large onion into half-inch chunks.
With one clove of garlic and a generous dollop of olive oil, alternately sauté and steam by covering with lid for about ten minutes over low to medium heat.
SIZZLE
TOK TOK TOK TOK
Take the lid off and stir from time to time so it doesn't burn.
Next, quarter one large zucchini lengthwise then cut into inch-wide pieces and sauté.
Zucchini used to be a trendy veggie not too long ago, but lately, you can grab one for 100 yen in the summer. So happy about that.
Cut two eggplants the same way and add them to the pan...
SHZZ
Chop one red and one yellow pepper, seeds and all, into inch-sized chunks, add, and sauté.

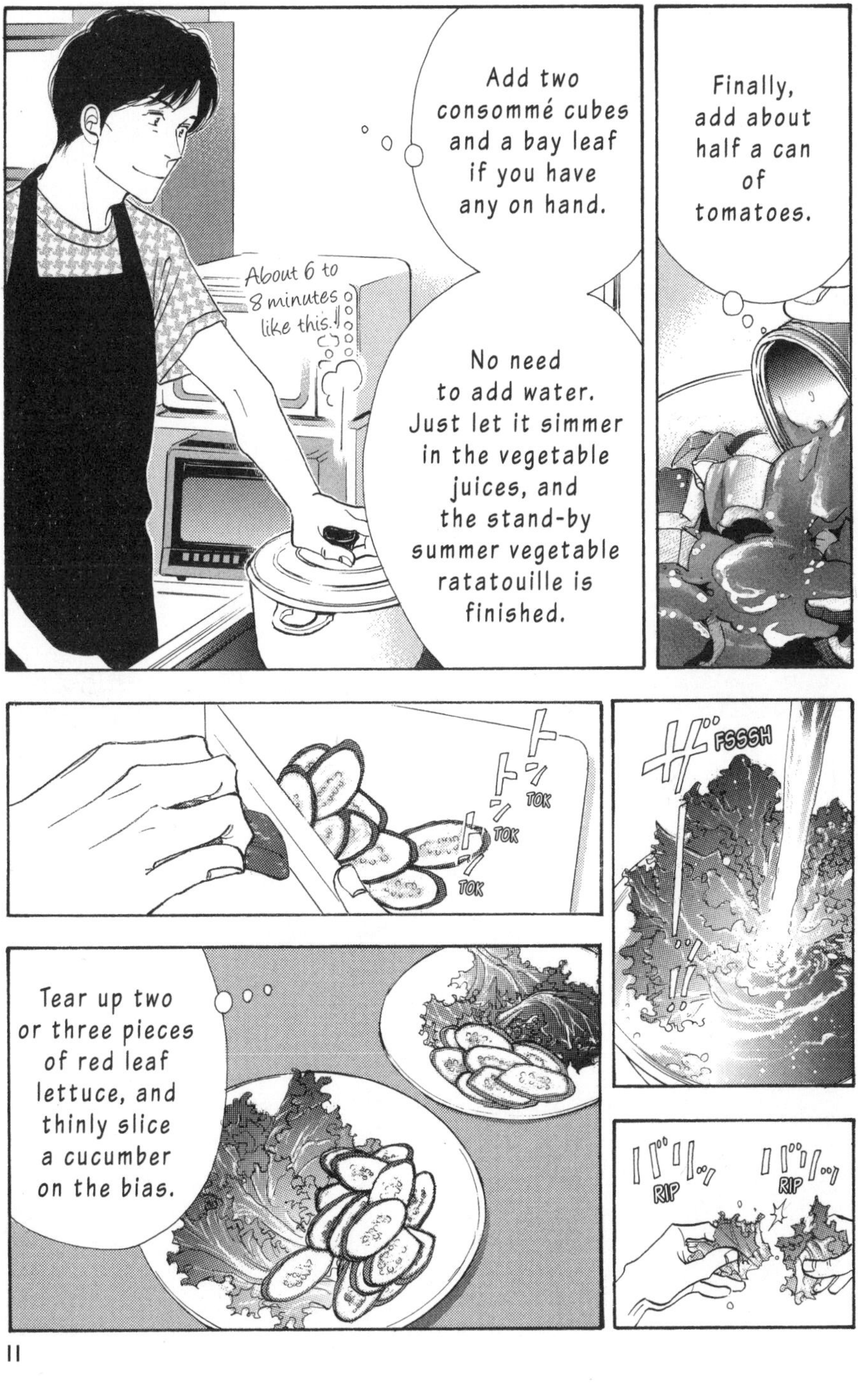
Finally, add about half a can of tomatoes.
Add two consommé cubes and a bay leaf if you have any on hand.
About 6 to 8 minutes like this.
No need to add water. Just let it simmer in the vegetable juices, and the stand-by summer vegetable ratatouille is finished.
FSSSH
TOK
TOK
TOK
RIP
RIP
Tear up two or three pieces of red leaf lettuce, and thinly slice a cucumber on the bias.

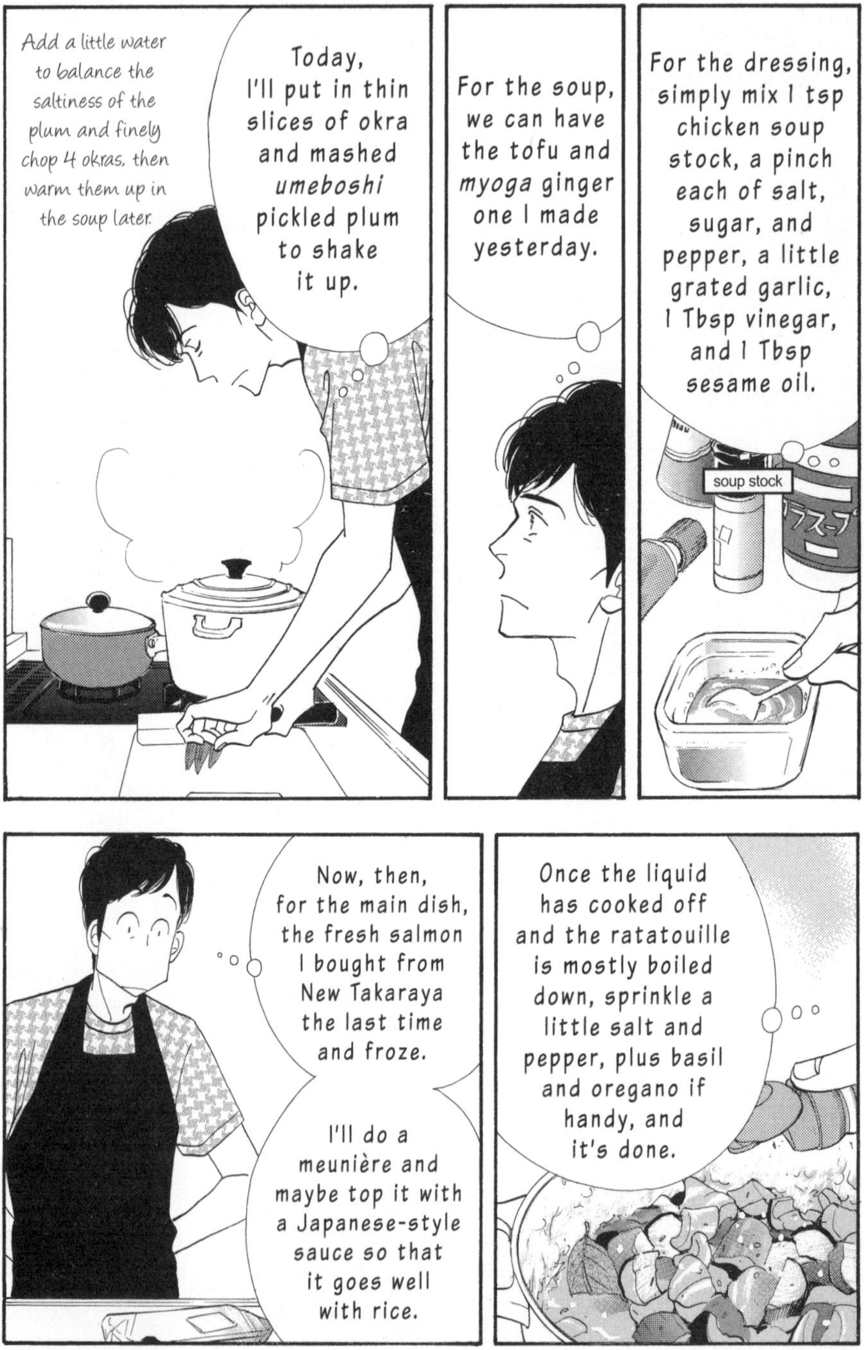
For the dressing, simply mix 1 tsp chicken soup stock, a pinch each of salt, sugar, and pepper, a little grated garlic, 1 Tbsp vinegar, and 1 Tbsp sesame oil.
soup stock
For the soup, we can have the tofu and *myoga* ginger one I made yesterday.
Today, I'll put in thin slices of okra and mashed *umeboshi* pickled plum to shake it up.
Add a little water to balance the saltiness of the plum and finely chop 4 okras, then warm them up in the soup later.
Once the liquid has cooked off and the ratatouille is mostly boiled down, sprinkle a little salt and pepper, plus basil and oregano if handy, and it's done.
Now, then, for the main dish, the fresh salmon I bought from New Takaraya the last time and froze.
I'll do a meunière and maybe top it with a Japanese-style sauce so that it goes well with rice.

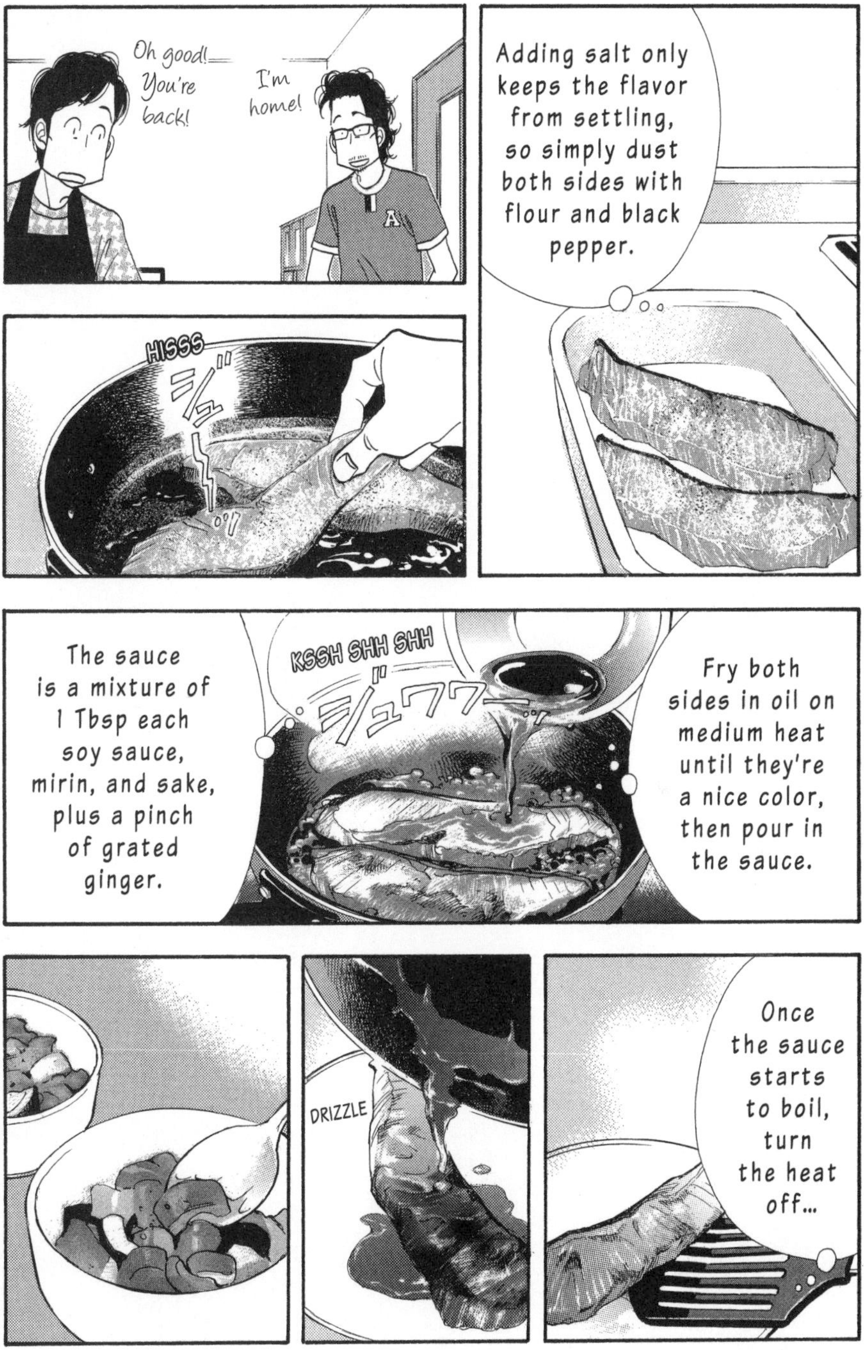

Adding salt only keeps the flavor from settling, so simply dust both sides with flour and black pepper.
I'm home!
Oh good! You're back!
HISSS
Fry both sides in oil on medium heat until they're a nice color, then pour in the sauce.
KSSH SHH SHH
The sauce is a mixture of 1 Tbsp each soy sauce, mirin, and sake, plus a pinch of grated ginger.
Once the sauce starts to boil, turn the heat off...
DRIZZLE

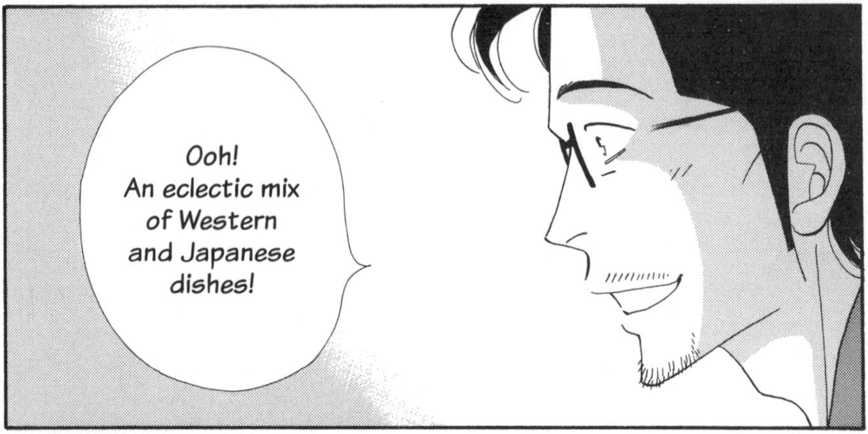
Ooh! An eclectic mix of Western and Japanese dishes!

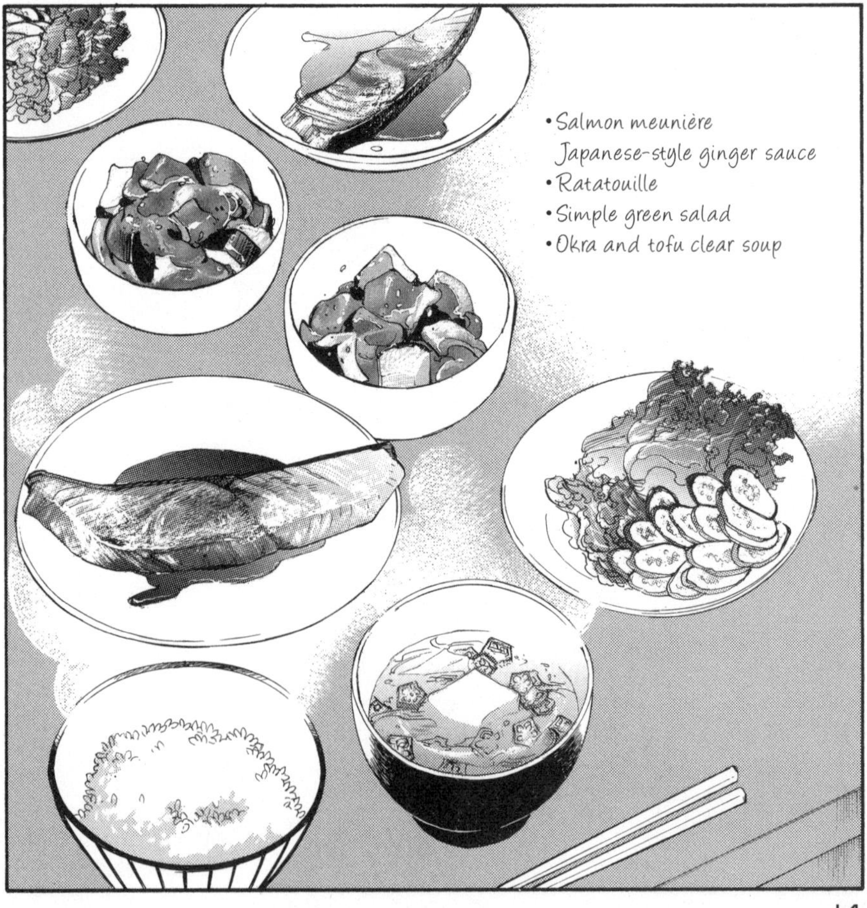
•Salmon meunière
Japanese-style ginger sauce
•Ratatouille
•Simple green salad
•Okra and tofu clear soup

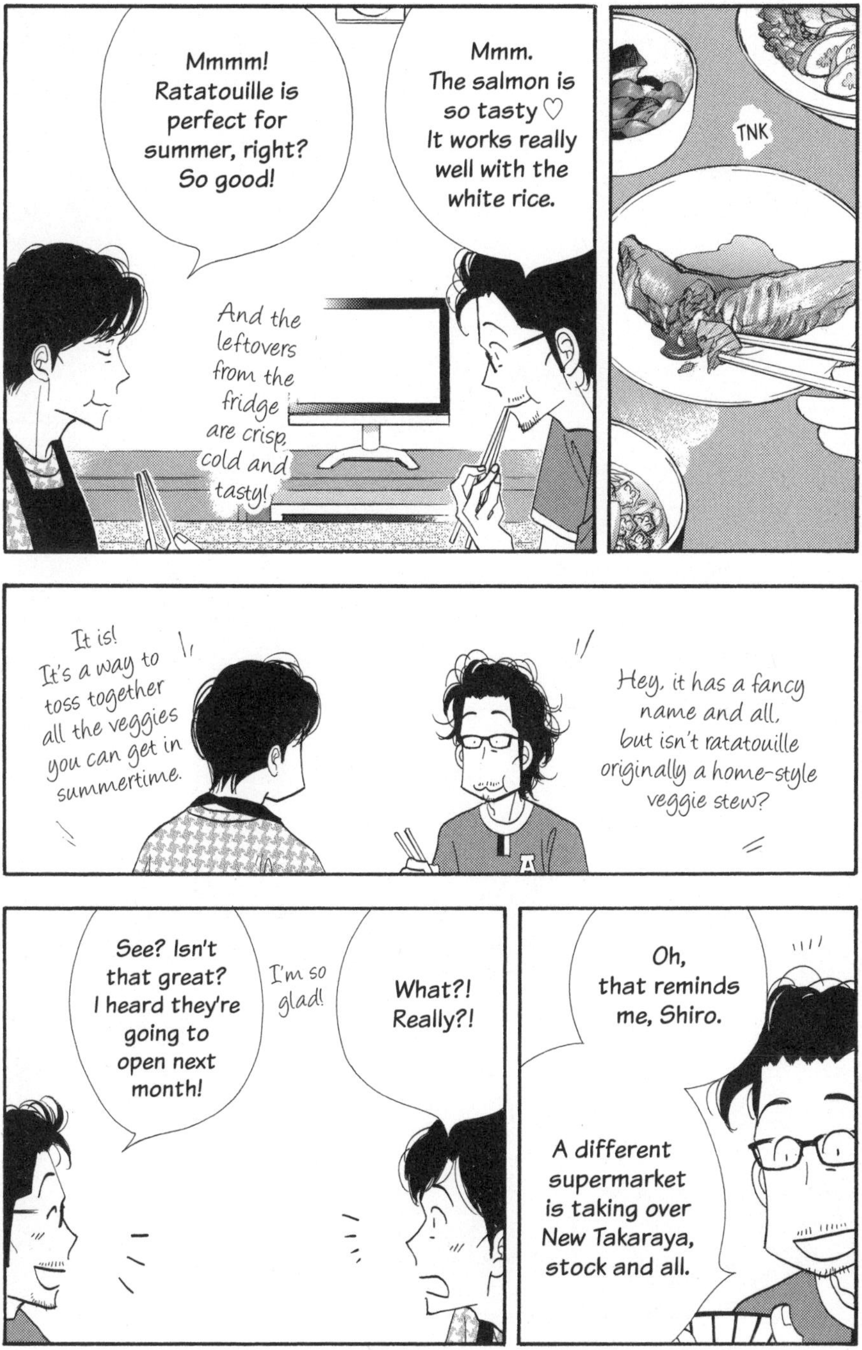
TNK
Mmm. The salmon is so tasty♡ It works really well with the white rice.
Mmmm! Ratatouille is perfect for summer, right? So good!
And the leftovers from the fridge are crisp, cold and tasty!
Hey, it has a fancy name and all, but isn't ratatouille originally a home-style veggie stew?
It is! It's a way to toss together all the veggies you can get in summertime.
Oh, that reminds me, Shiro.
A different supermarket is taking over New Takaraya, stock and all.
What?! Really?!
I'm so glad!
See? Isn't that great? I heard they're going to open next month!

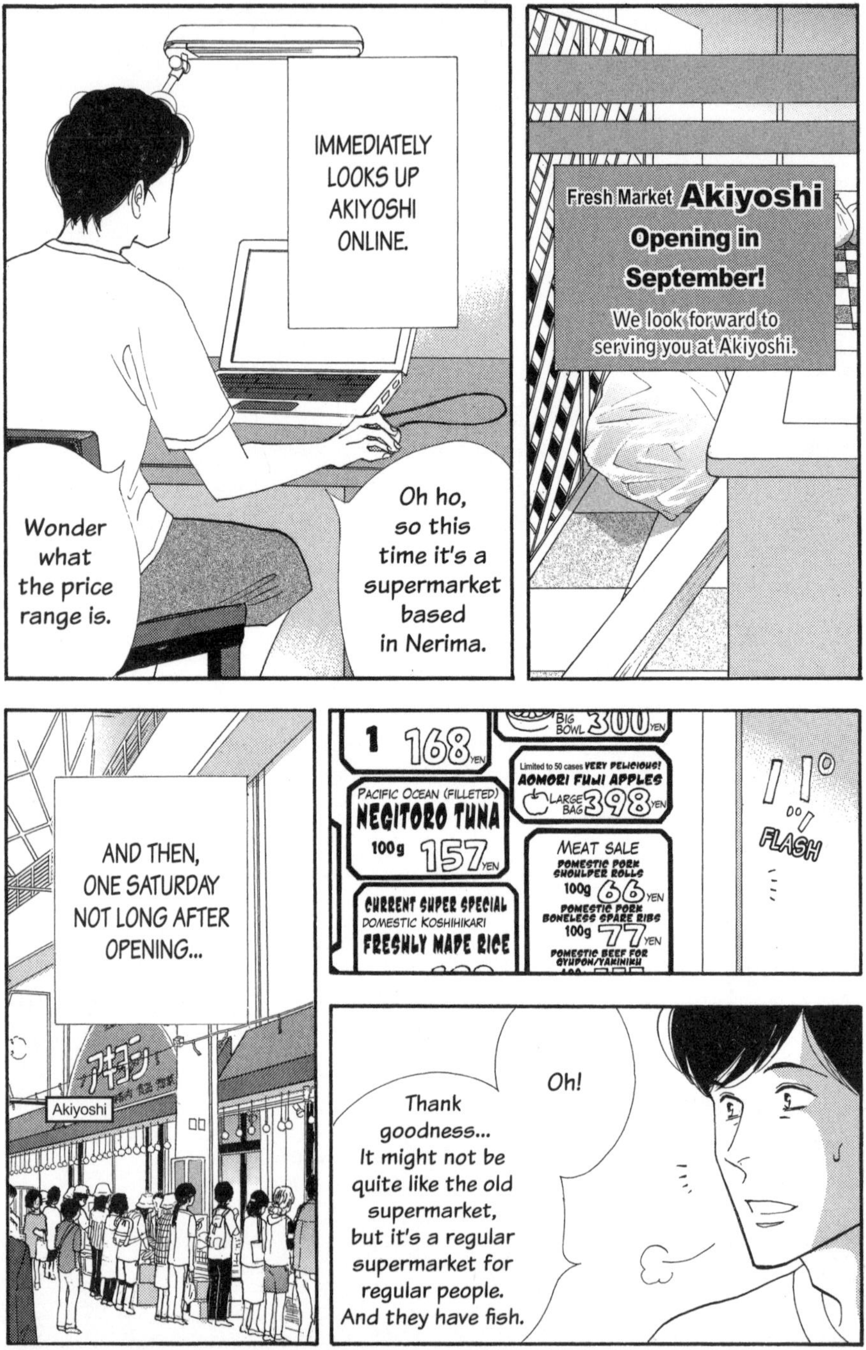
Fresh Market Akiyoshi
Opening in September!
We look forward to serving you at Akiyoshi.
IMMEDIATELY LOOKS UP AKIYOSHI ONLINE.
Oh ho, so this time it's a supermarket based in Nerima.
Wonder what the price range is.
BIG BOWL 300 YEN
1 168 YEN
Limited to 50 cases VERY DELICIOUS!
AOMORI FUJI APPLES
LARGE BAG 398 YEN
PACIFIC OCEAN (FILLETED)
NEGITORO TUNA
100g 157 YEN
MEAT SALE
DOMESTIC PORK SHOULDER ROLLS
100g 66 YEN
DOMESTIC PORK BONELESS SPARE RIBS
100g 77 YEN
DOMESTIC BEEF FOR GYUDON/YAKINIKU
CURRENT SUPER SPECIAL
DOMESTIC KOSHIHIKARI
FRESHLY MADE RICE
FLASH
Oh!
Thank goodness... It might not be quite like the old supermarket, but it's a regular supermarket for regular people. And they have fish.
AND THEN, ONE SATURDAY NOT LONG AFTER OPENING...
Akiyoshi

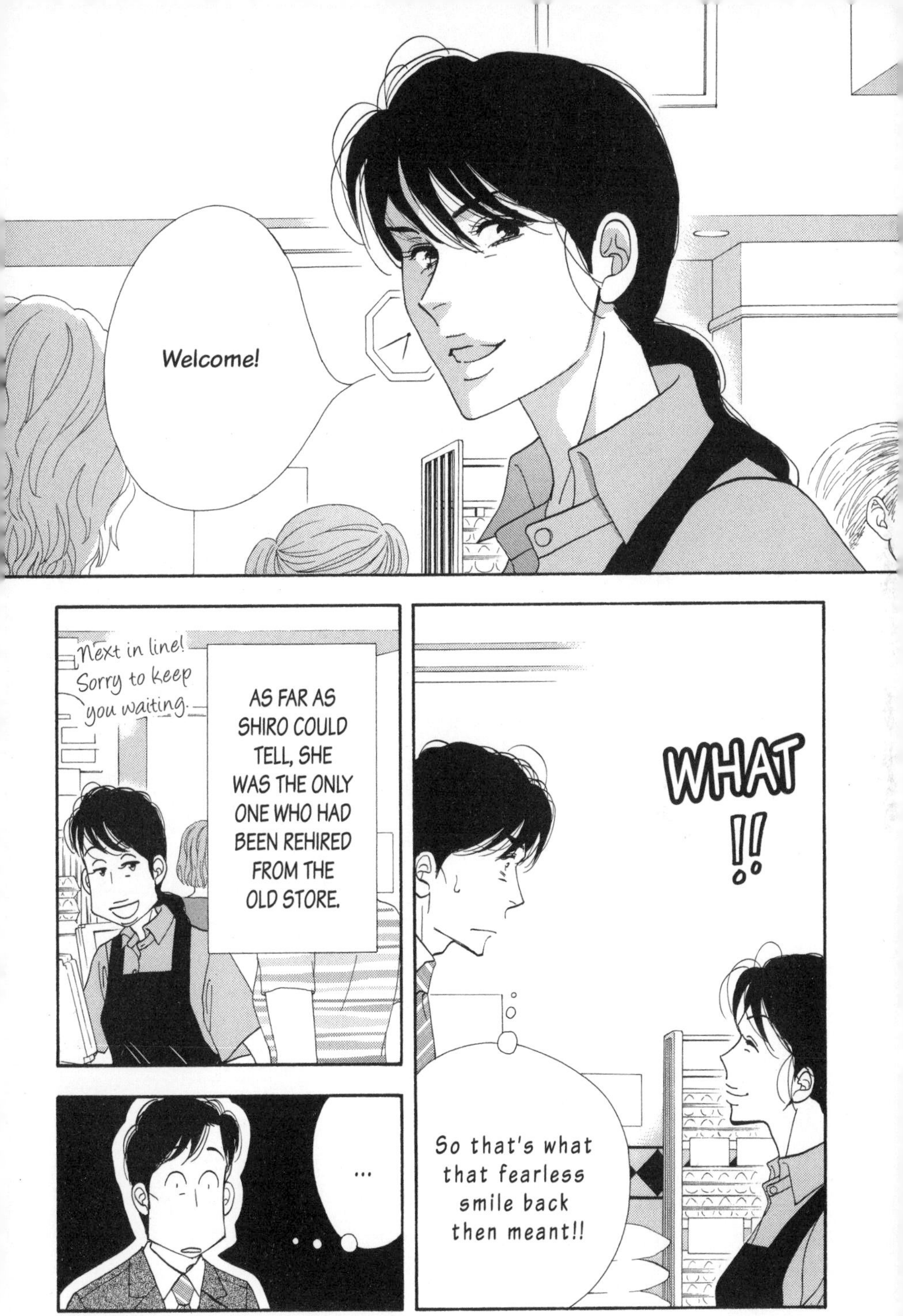
Welcome!
WHAT!!
So that's what that fearless smile back then meant!!
AS FAR AS SHIRO COULD TELL, SHE WAS THE ONLY ONE WHO HAD BEEN REHIRED FROM THE OLD STORE.
Next in line! Sorry to keep you waiting.
...

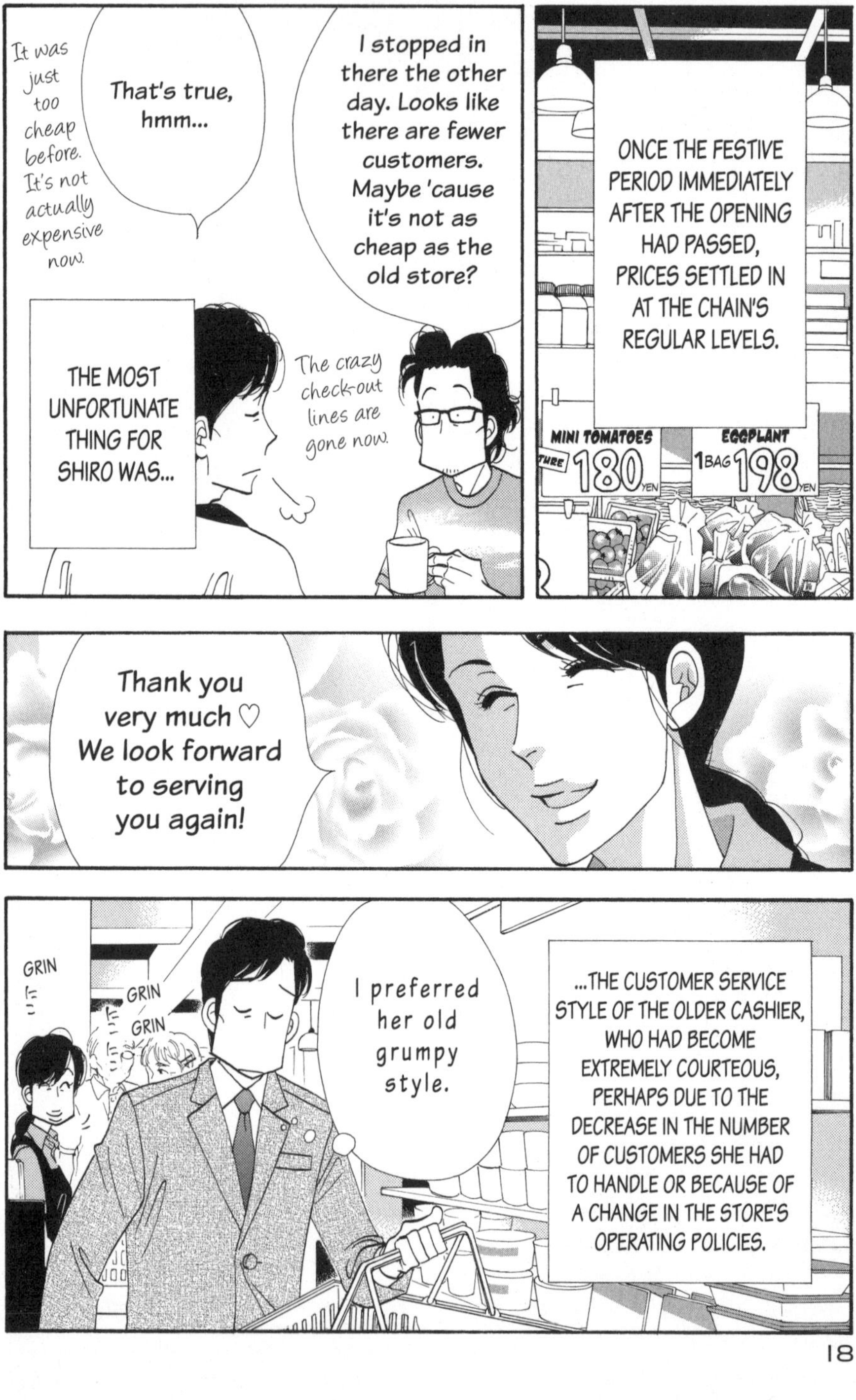
ONCE THE FESTIVE PERIOD IMMEDIATELY AFTER THE OPENING HAD PASSED, PRICES SETTLED IN AT THE CHAIN'S REGULAR LEVELS.
EGGPLANT
1BAG 198 YEN
MINI TOMATOES
180 YEN
I stopped in there the other day. Looks like there are fewer customers. Maybe 'cause it's not as cheap as the old store?
That's true, hmm...
It was just too cheap before. It's not actually expensive now.
The crazy check-out lines are gone now.
THE MOST UNFORTUNATE THING FOR SHIRO WAS...
Thank you very much ♡ We look forward to serving you again!
...THE CUSTOMER SERVICE STYLE OF THE OLDER CASHIER, WHO HAD BECOME EXTREMELY COURTEOUS, PERHAPS DUE TO THE DECREASE IN THE NUMBER OF CUSTOMERS SHE HAD TO HANDLE OR BECAUSE OF A CHANGE IN THE STORE'S OPERATING POLICIES.
I preferred her old grumpy style.
GRIN
GRIN
GRIN

Ratatouille will keep in the refrigerator for three or four days.
(You can freeze it too, although the texture will get a little softer.)
You can also use it in omelets or pasta sauce.

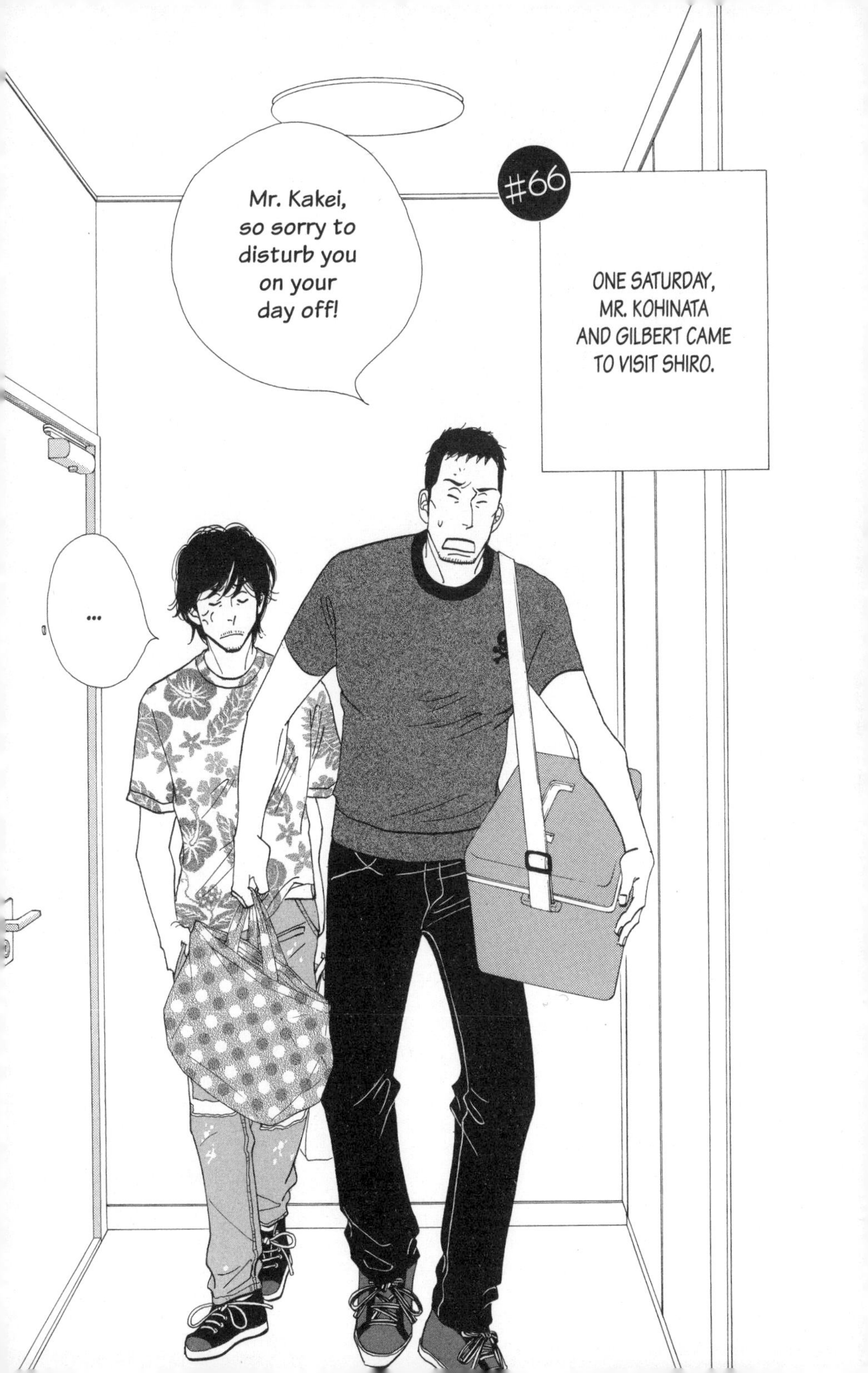
#66
ONE SATURDAY, MR. KOHINATA AND GILBERT CAME TO VISIT SHIRO.
Mr. Kakei, so sorry to disturb you on your day off!
...

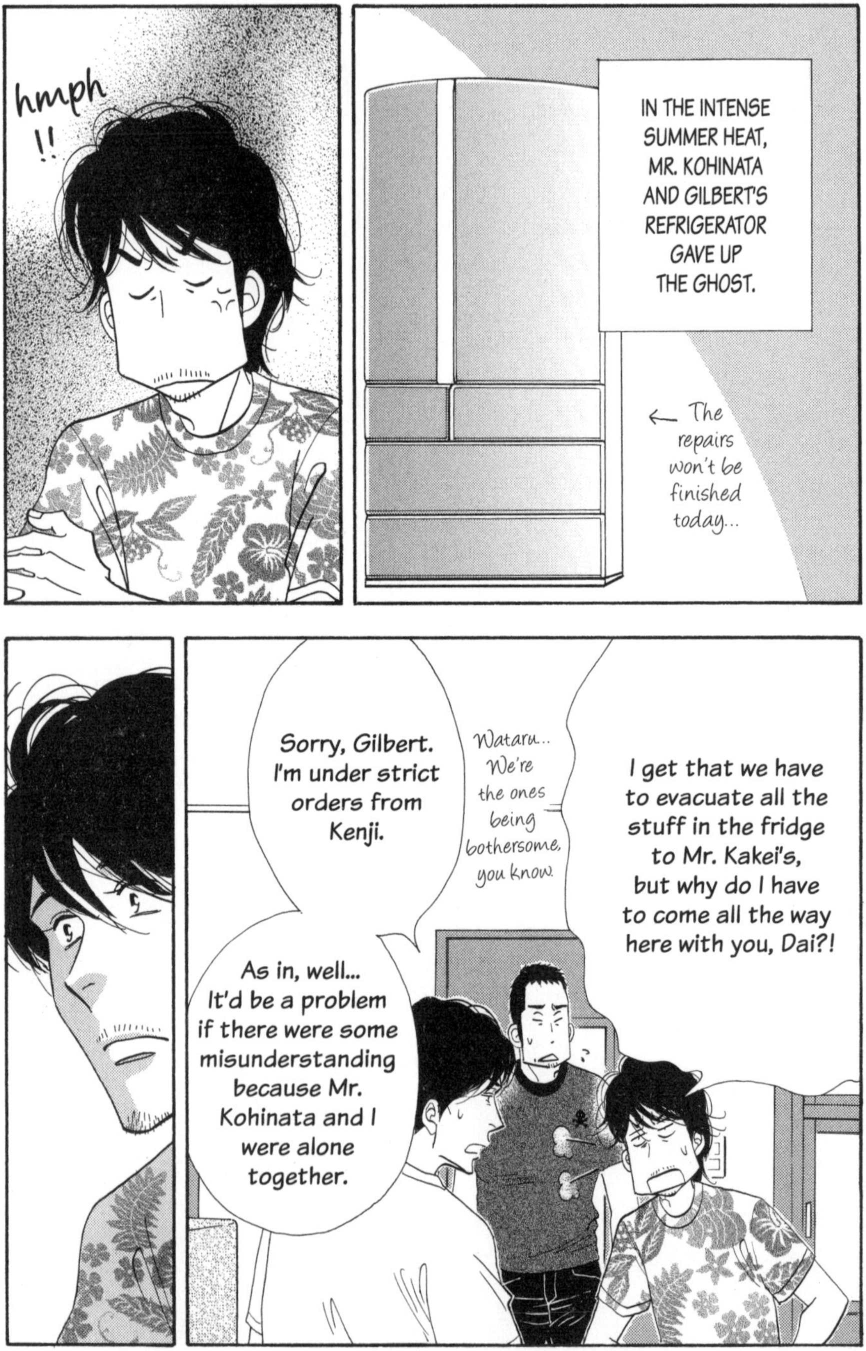
IN THE INTENSE SUMMER HEAT, MR. KOHINATA AND GILBERT'S REFRIGERATOR GAVE UP THE GHOST.
← The repairs won't be finished today...
hmph !!
I get that we have to evacuate all the stuff in the fridge to Mr. Kakei's, but why do I have to come all the way here with you, Dai?!
Wataru... We're the ones being bothersome, you know.
Sorry, Gilbert. I'm under strict orders from Kenji.
As in, well... It'd be a problem if there were some misunderstanding because Mr. Kohinata and I were alone together.

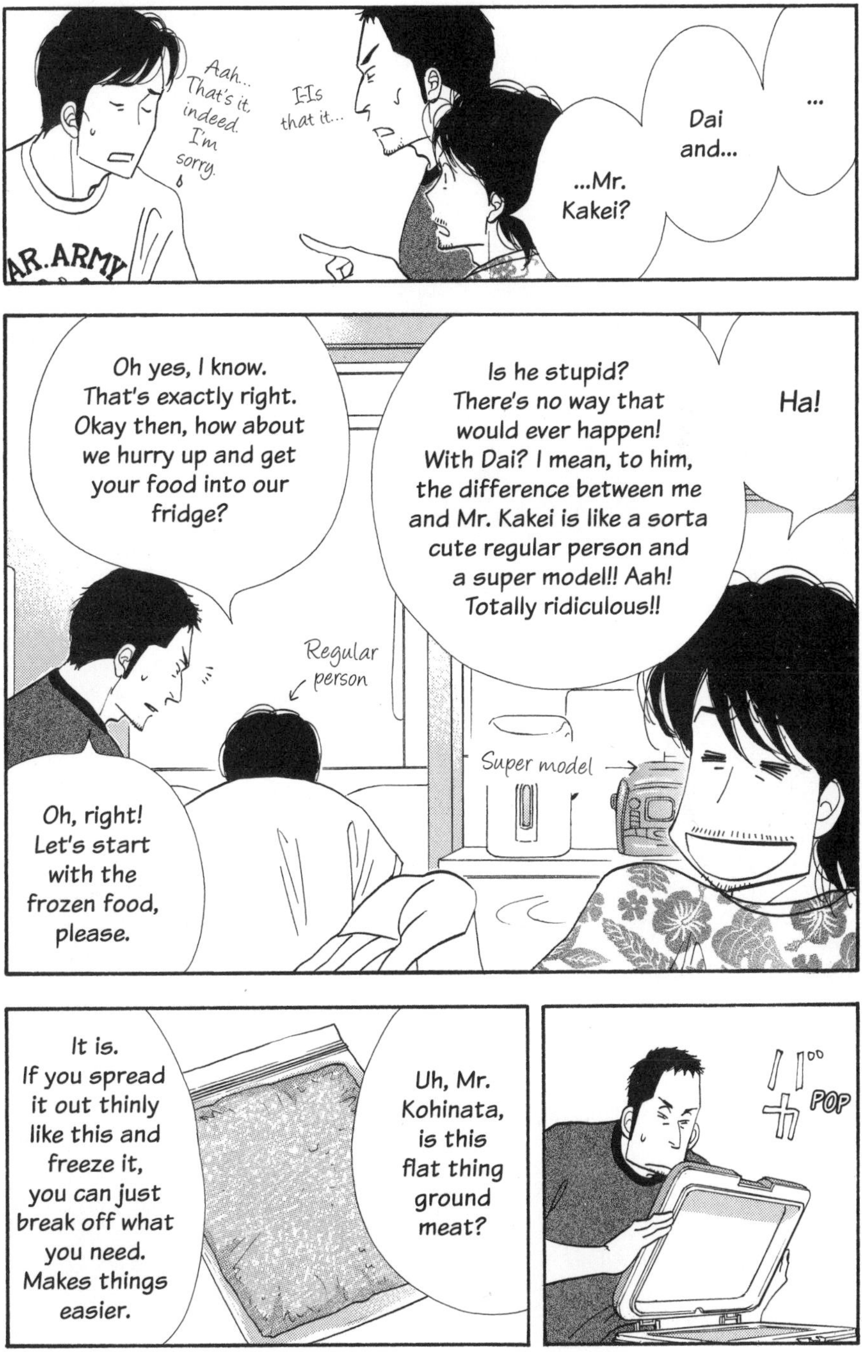
...
Dai and...
...Mr. Kakei?
I-Is that it...
Aah... That's it, indeed. I'm sorry.
Ha!
Is he stupid? There's no way that would ever happen! With Dai? I mean, to him, the difference between me and Mr. Kakei is like a sorta cute regular person and a super model!! Aah! Totally ridiculous!!
Oh yes, I know. That's exactly right. Okay then, how about we hurry up and get your food into our fridge?
Regular person
Super model
Oh, right! Let's start with the frozen food, please.
POP
Uh, Mr. Kohinata, is this flat thing ground meat?
It is. If you spread it out thinly like this and freeze it, you can just break off what you need. Makes things easier.

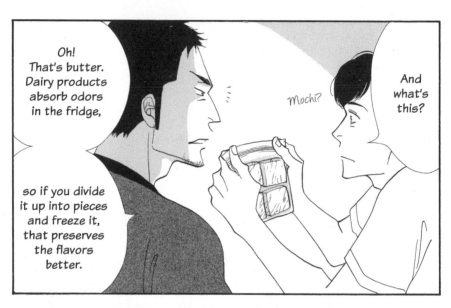

And what's this?
Mochi?
Oh! That's butter. Dairy products absorb odors in the fridge,
so if you divide it up into pieces and freeze it, that preserves the flavors better.
Ha ha! You really are methodical, Mr. Kohinata. Even your frozen rice is in neat squares—
Hmm?
BAM
BAM
...Mr. Kohinata.
Yes...
Uhm, look.
It appears that you have some rather large food items that we are quite unable to store, given that our average-capacity fridge tends to be on the full side to begin with...

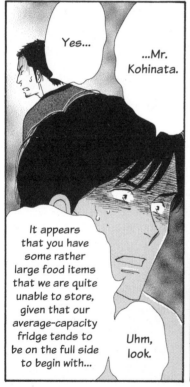

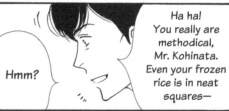

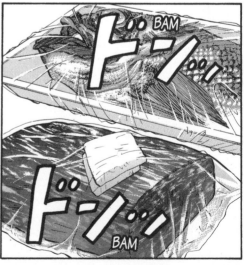

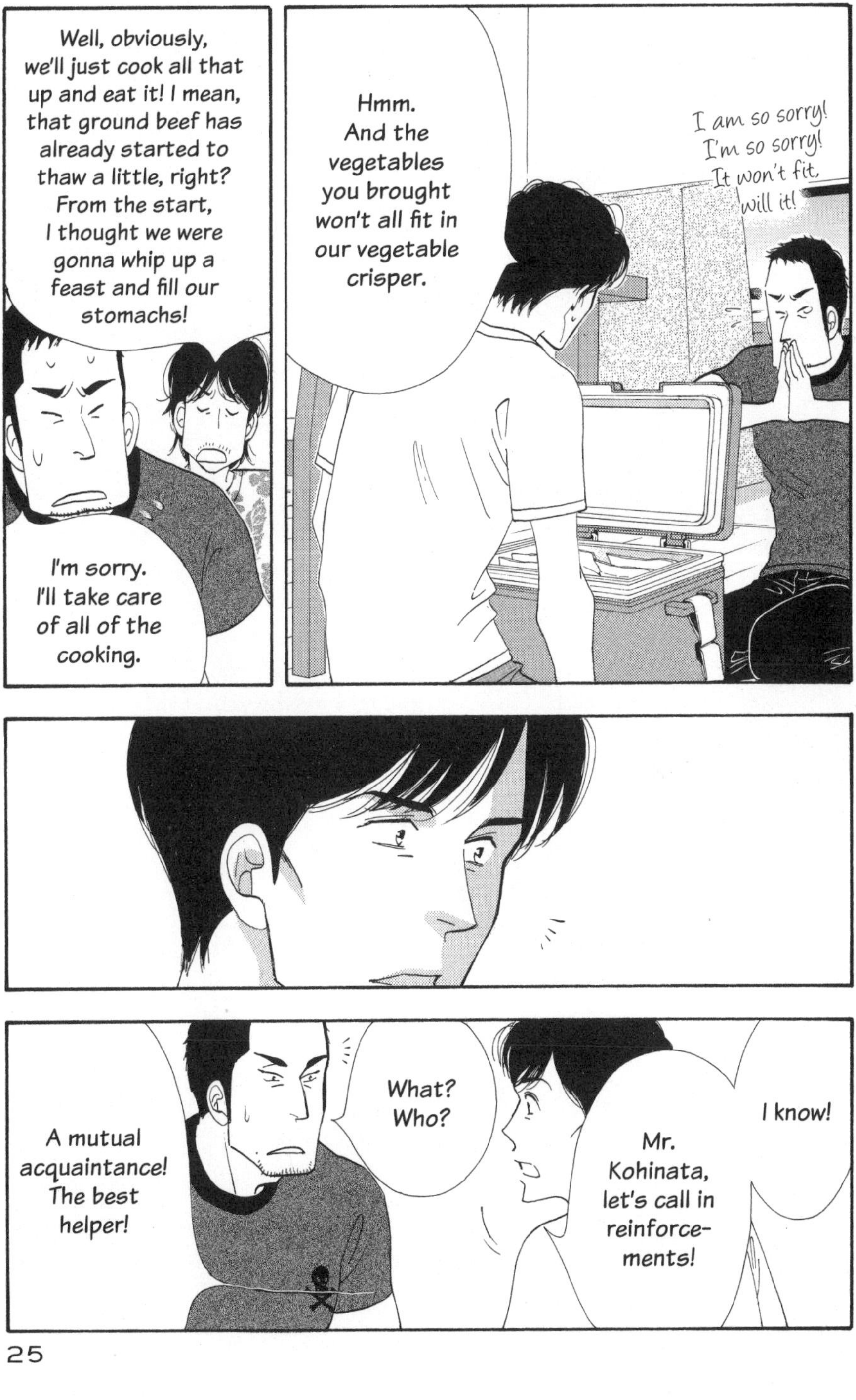
I am so sorry! I'm so sorry! It won't fit, will it!
Hmm. And the vegetables you brought won't all fit in our vegetable crisper.
Well, obviously, we'll just cook all that up and eat it! I mean, that ground beef has already started to thaw a little, right? From the start, I thought we were gonna whip up a feast and fill our stomachs!
I'm sorry. I'll take care of all of the cooking.
I know!
Mr. Kohinata, let's call in reinforce-ments!
What? Who?
A mutual acquaintance! The best helper!

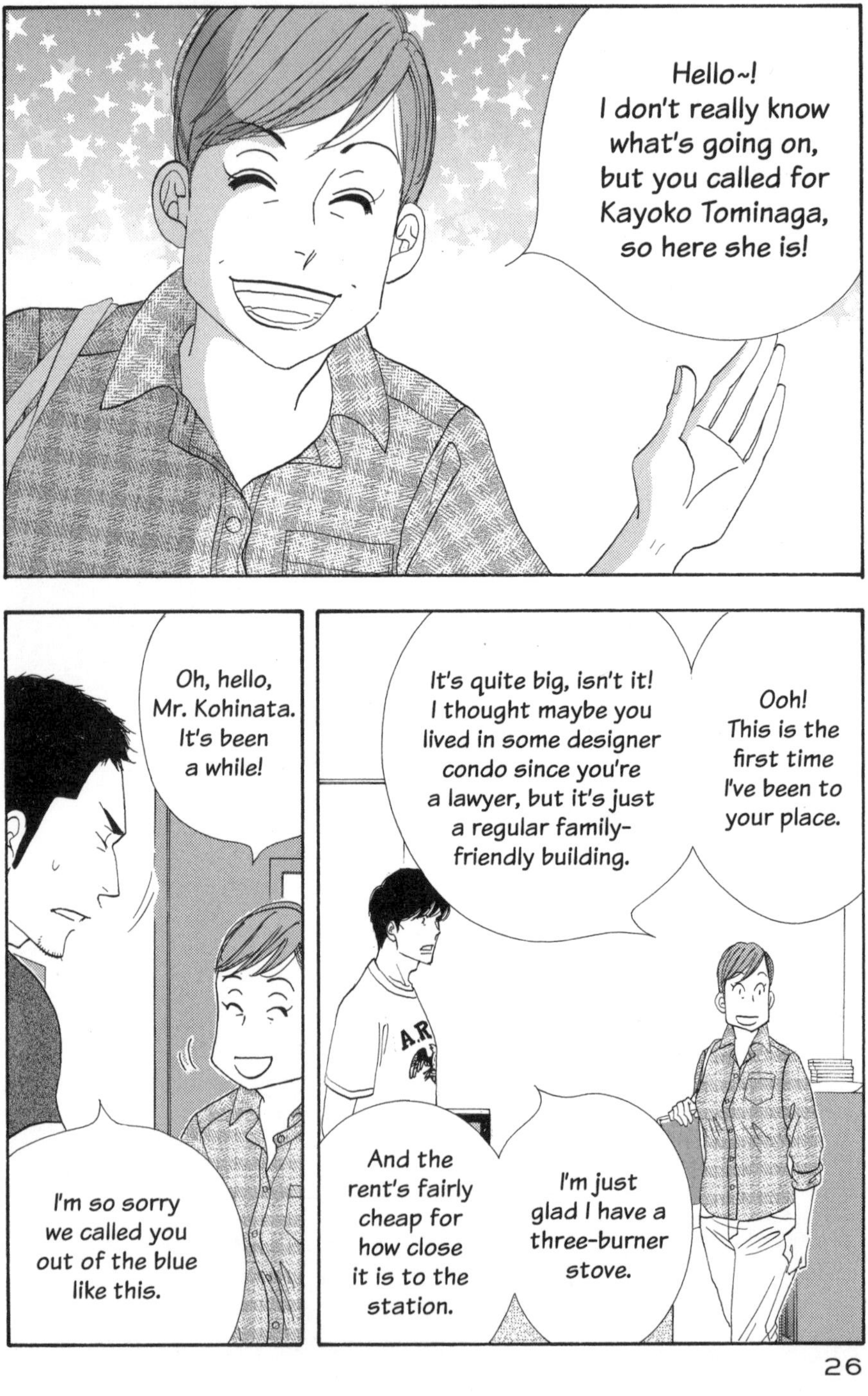
Hello~! I don't really know what's going on, but you called for Kayoko Tominaga, so here she is!
Ooh! This is the first time I've been to your place.
It's quite big, isn't it! I thought maybe you lived in some designer condo since you're a lawyer, but it's just a regular family-friendly building.
I'm just glad I have a three-burner stove.
And the rent's fairly cheap for how close it is to the station.
Oh, hello, Mr. Kohinata. It's been a while!
I'm so sorry we called you out of the blue like this.

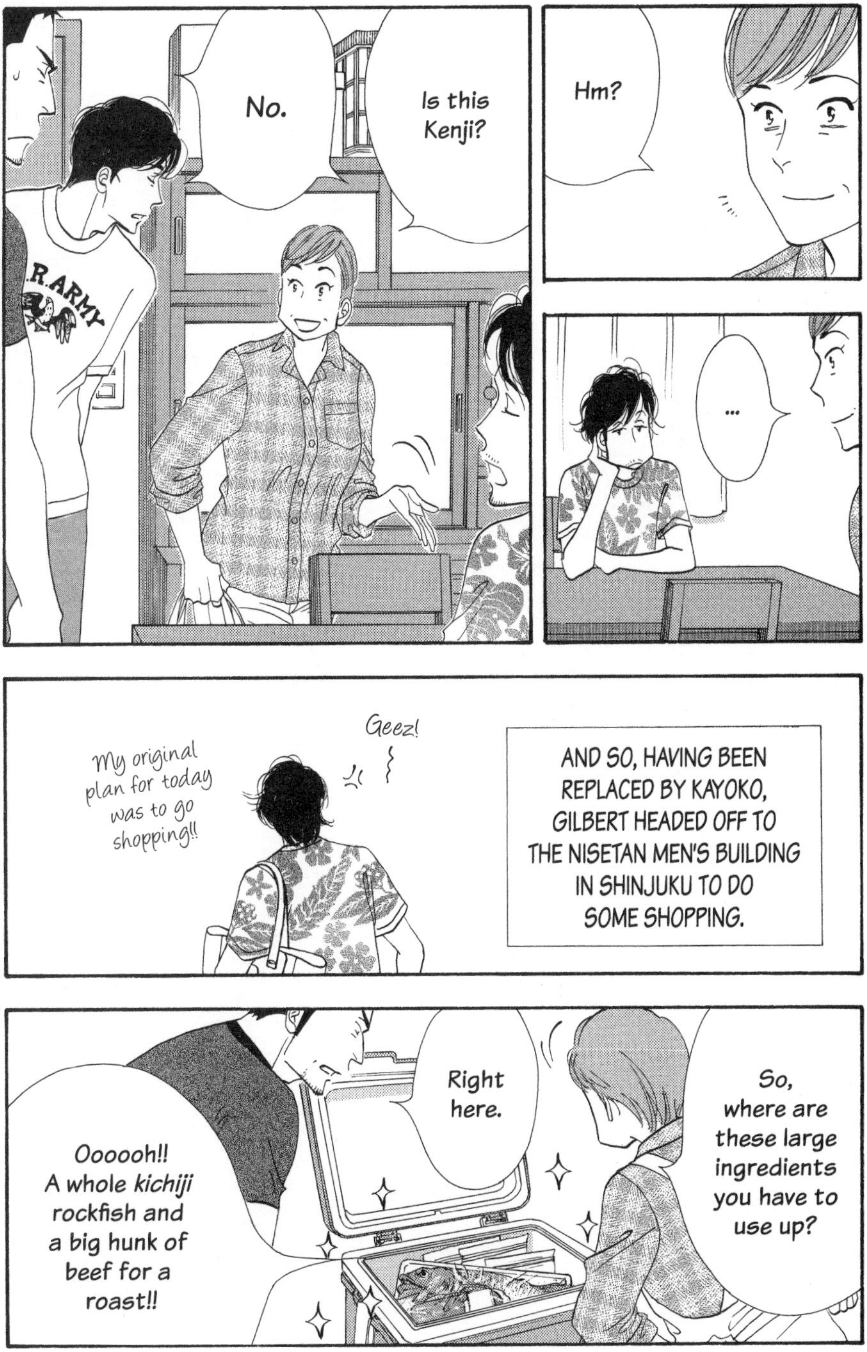
Hm?
...
Is this Kenji?
No.
AND SO, HAVING BEEN REPLACED BY KAYOKO, GILBERT HEADED OFF TO THE NISETAN MEN'S BUILDING IN SHINJUKU TO DO SOME SHOPPING.
Geez!
My original plan for today was to go shopping!!
So, where are these large ingredients you have to use up?
Right here.
Oooooh!! A whole *kichiji* rockfish and a big hunk of beef for a roast!!

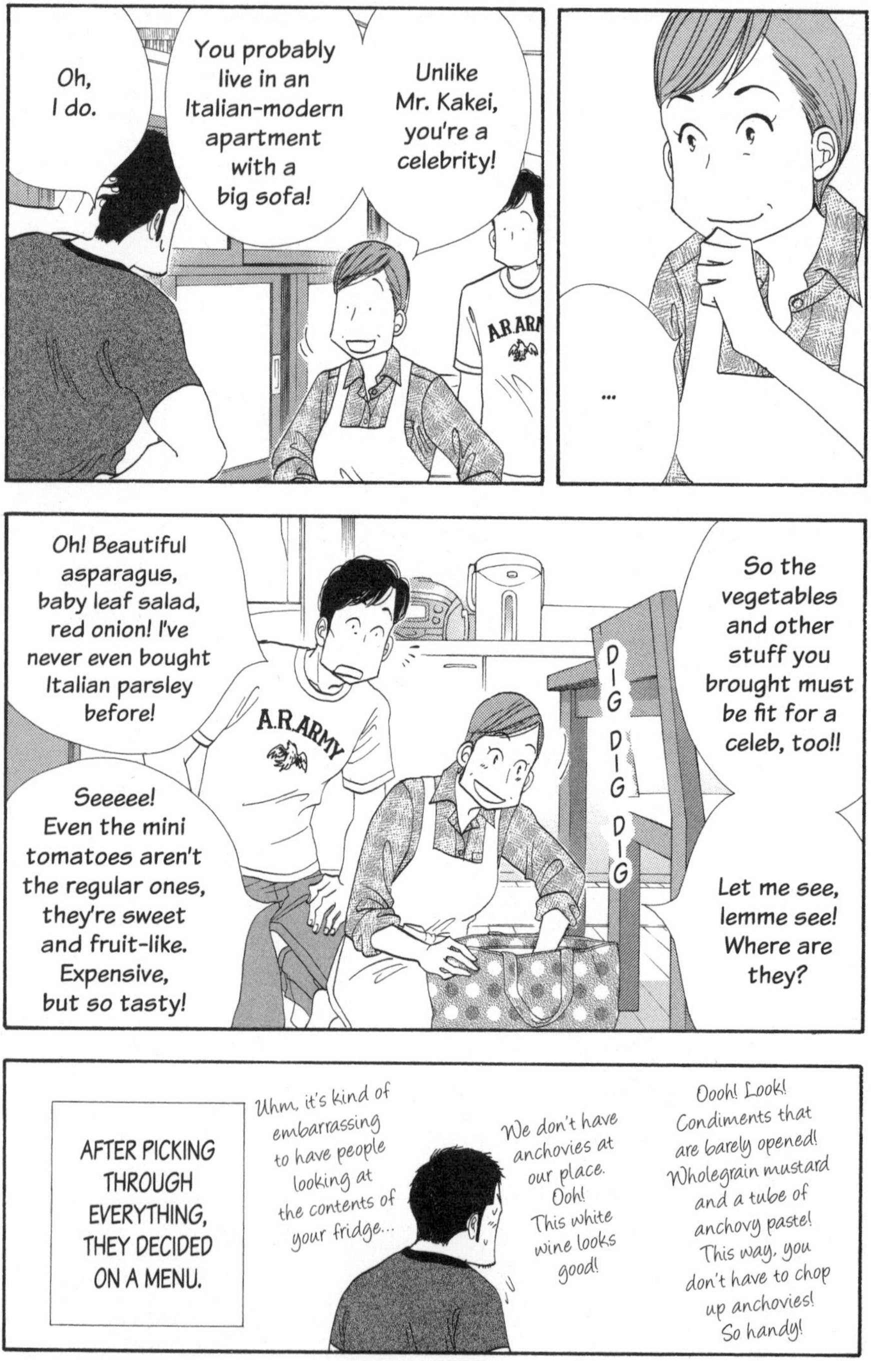
...
Unlike Mr. Kakei, you're a celebrity!
You probably live in an Italian-modern apartment with a big sofa!
Oh, I do.
So the vegetables and other stuff you brought must be fit for a celeb, too!!
Let me see, lemme see! Where are they?
DIG DIG DIG DIG
Oh! Beautiful asparagus, baby leaf salad, red onion! I've never even bought Italian parsley before!
Seeeee! Even the mini tomatoes aren't the regular ones, they're sweet and fruit-like. Expensive, but so tasty!
Oooh! Look! Condiments that are barely opened! Wholegrain mustard and a tube of anchovy paste! This way, you don't have to chop up anchovies! So handy!
We don't have anchovies at our place. Ooh! This white wine looks good!
Uhm, it's kind of embarrassing to have people looking at the contents of your fridge...
AFTER PICKING THROUGH EVERYTHING, THEY DECIDED ON A MENU.

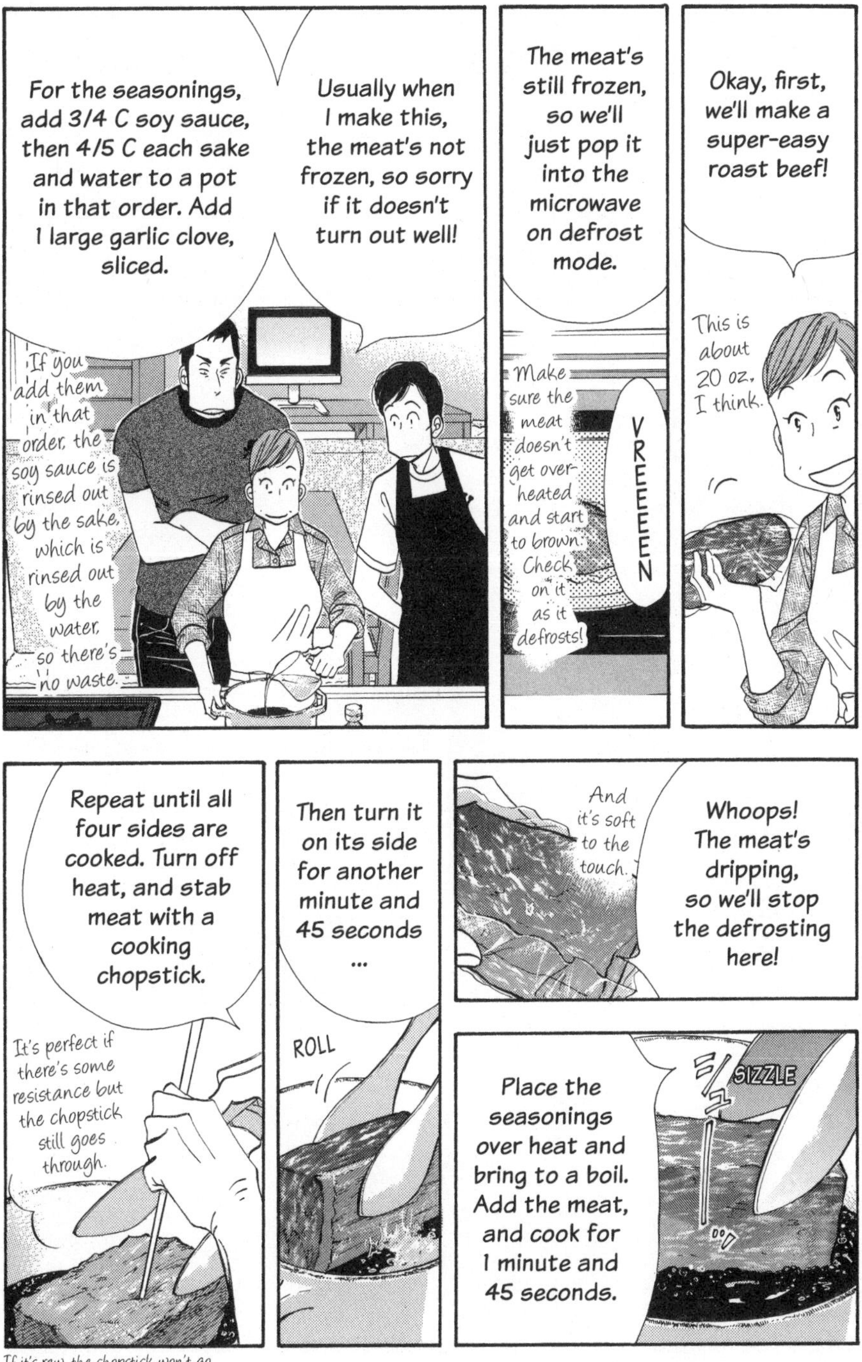
Okay, first, we'll make a super-easy roast beef!
This is about 20 oz. I think.
The meat's still frozen, so we'll just pop it into the microwave on defrost mode.
Make sure the meat doesn't get overheated and start to brown. Check on it as it defrosts!
VREEEEN
Usually when I make this, the meat's not frozen, so sorry if it doesn't turn out well!
For the seasonings, add 3/4 C soy sauce, then 4/5 C each sake and water to a pot in that order. Add 1 large garlic clove, sliced.
If you add them in that order, the soy sauce is rinsed out by the sake, which is rinsed out by the water, so there's no waste.
Whoops! The meat's dripping, so we'll stop the defrosting here!
And it's soft to the touch.
Place the seasonings over heat and bring to a boil. Add the meat, and cook for 1 minute and 45 seconds.
SIZZLE
Then turn it on its side for another minute and 45 seconds ...
ROLL
Repeat until all four sides are cooked. Turn off heat, and stab meat with a cooking chopstick.
It's perfect if there's some resistance but the chopstick still goes through.

If it's raw, the chopstick won't go in at all, and if it slips through easily, then it's overcooked.

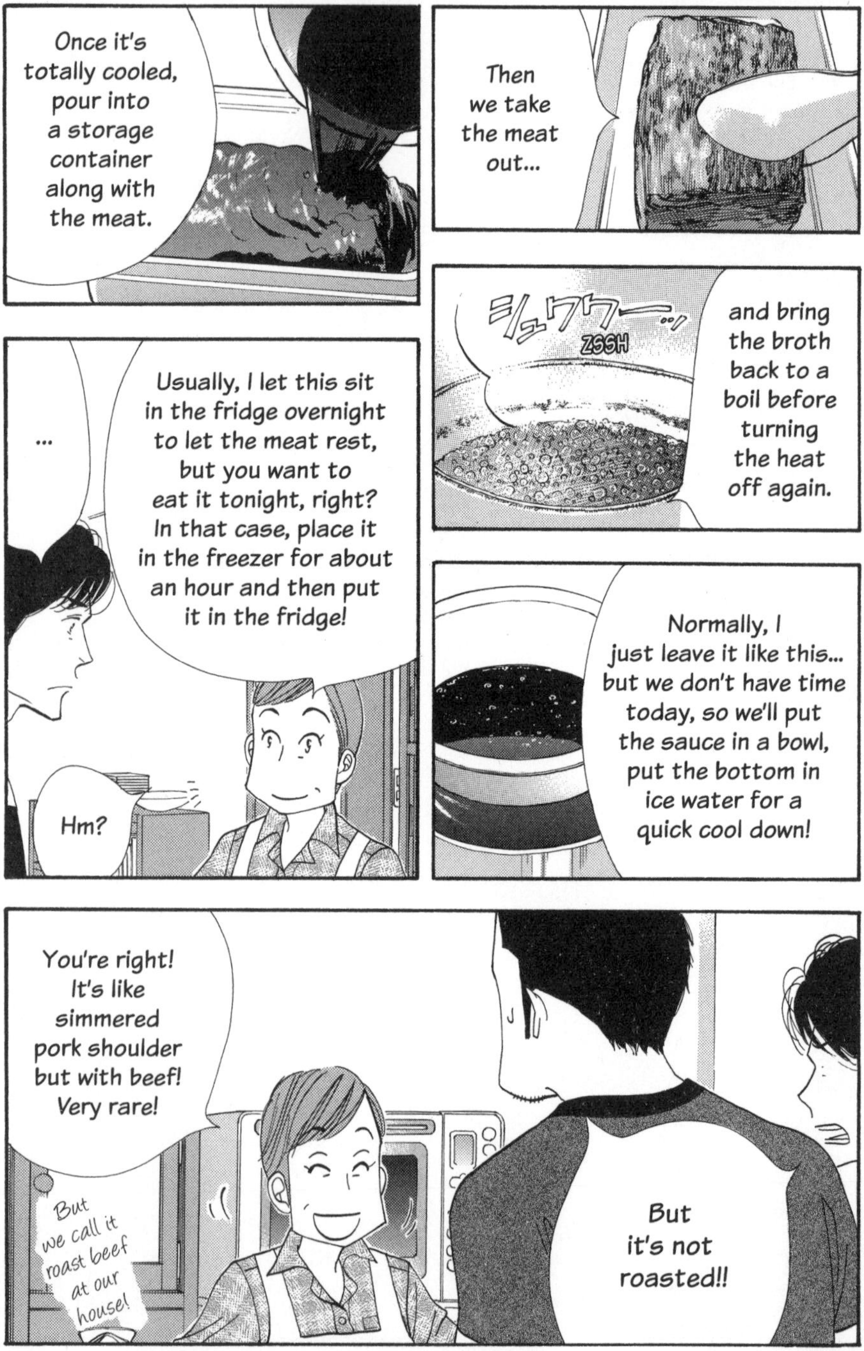
Then we take the meat out...
ZSSH
and bring the broth back to a boil before turning the heat off again.
Normally, I just leave it like this... but we don't have time today, so we'll put the sauce in a bowl, put the bottom in ice water for a quick cool down!
Once it's totally cooled, pour into a storage container along with the meat.
Usually, I let this sit in the fridge overnight to let the meat rest, but you want to eat it tonight, right? In that case, place it in the freezer for about an hour and then put it in the fridge!
...
Hm?
You're right! It's like simmered pork shoulder but with beef! Very rare!
But it's not roasted!!
But we call it roast beef at our house!

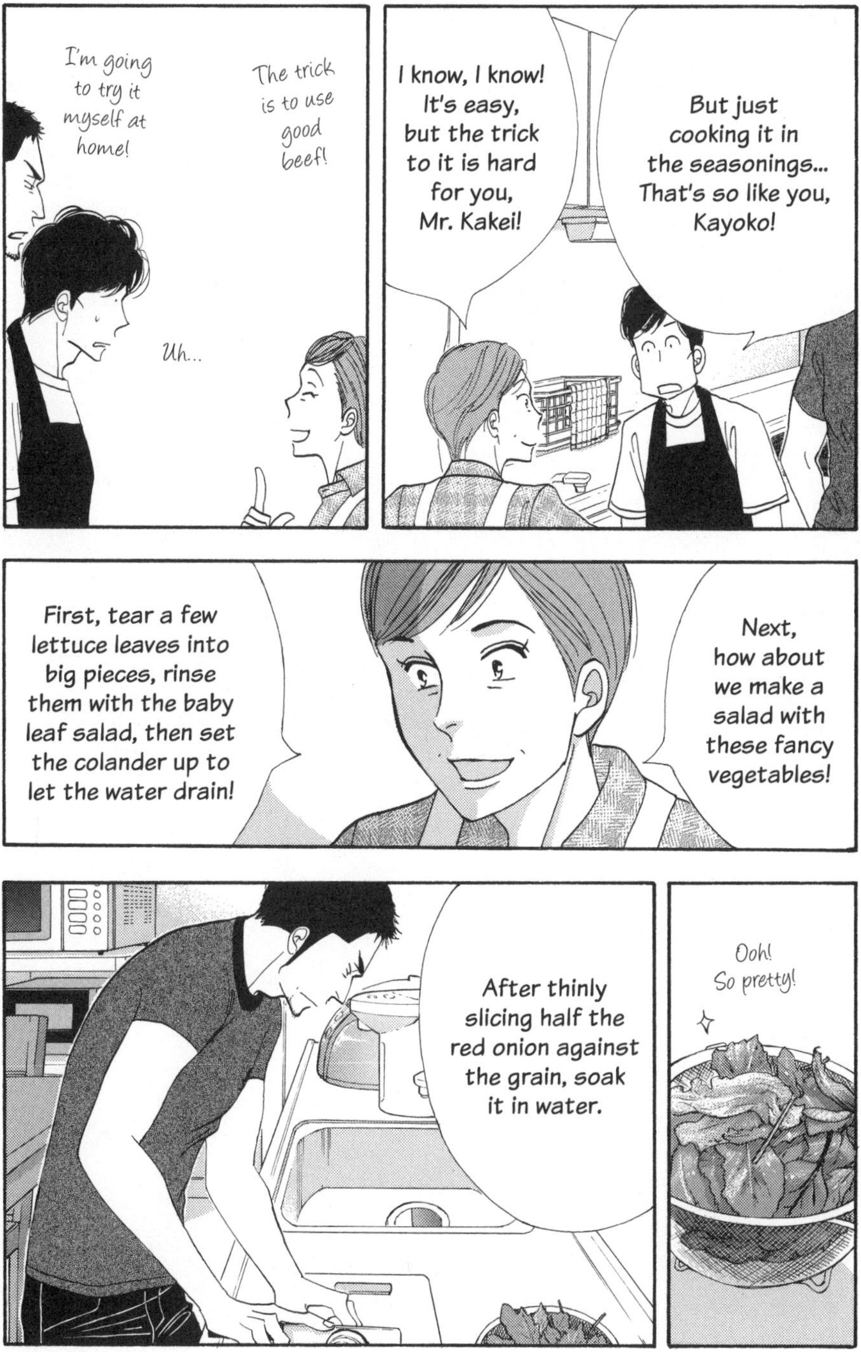
But just cooking it in the seasonings... That's so like you, Kayoko!
I know, I know! It's easy, but the trick to it is hard for you, Mr. Kakei!
The trick is to use good beef!
I'm going to try it myself at home!
Uh...
Next, how about we make a salad with these fancy vegetables!
First, tear a few lettuce leaves into big pieces, rinse them with the baby leaf salad, then set the colander up to let the water drain!
Ooh! So pretty!
After thinly slicing half the red onion against the grain, soak it in water.

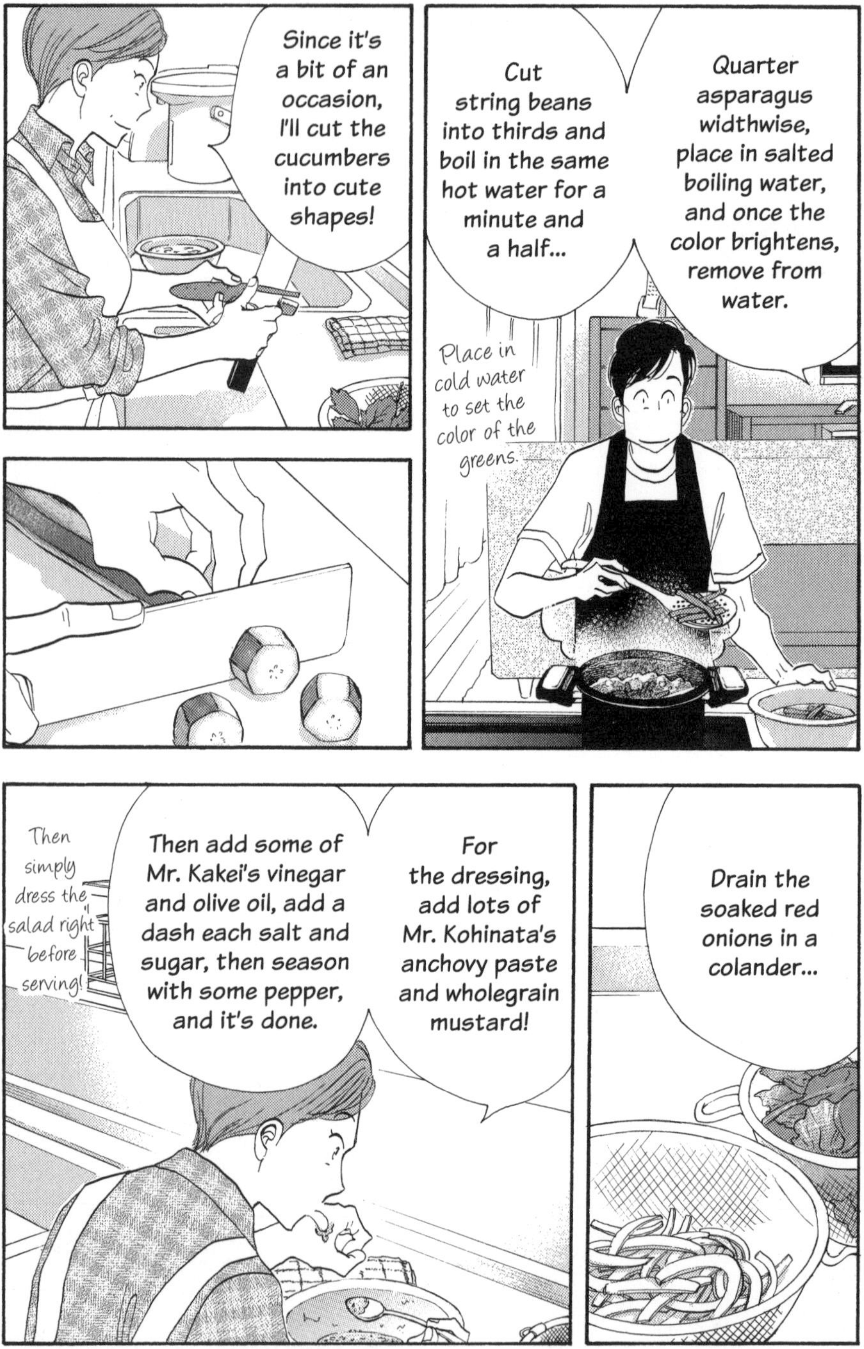
Quarter asparagus widthwise, place in salted boiling water, and once the color brightens, remove from water.
Cut string beans into thirds and boil in the same hot water for a minute and a half...
Place in cold water to set the color of the greens.
Since it's a bit of an occasion, I'll cut the cucumbers into cute shapes!
Drain the soaked red onions in a colander...
For the dressing, add lots of Mr. Kohinata's anchovy paste and wholegrain mustard!
Then add some of Mr. Kakei's vinegar and olive oil, add a dash each salt and sugar, then season with some pepper, and it's done.
Then simply dress the salad right before serving!

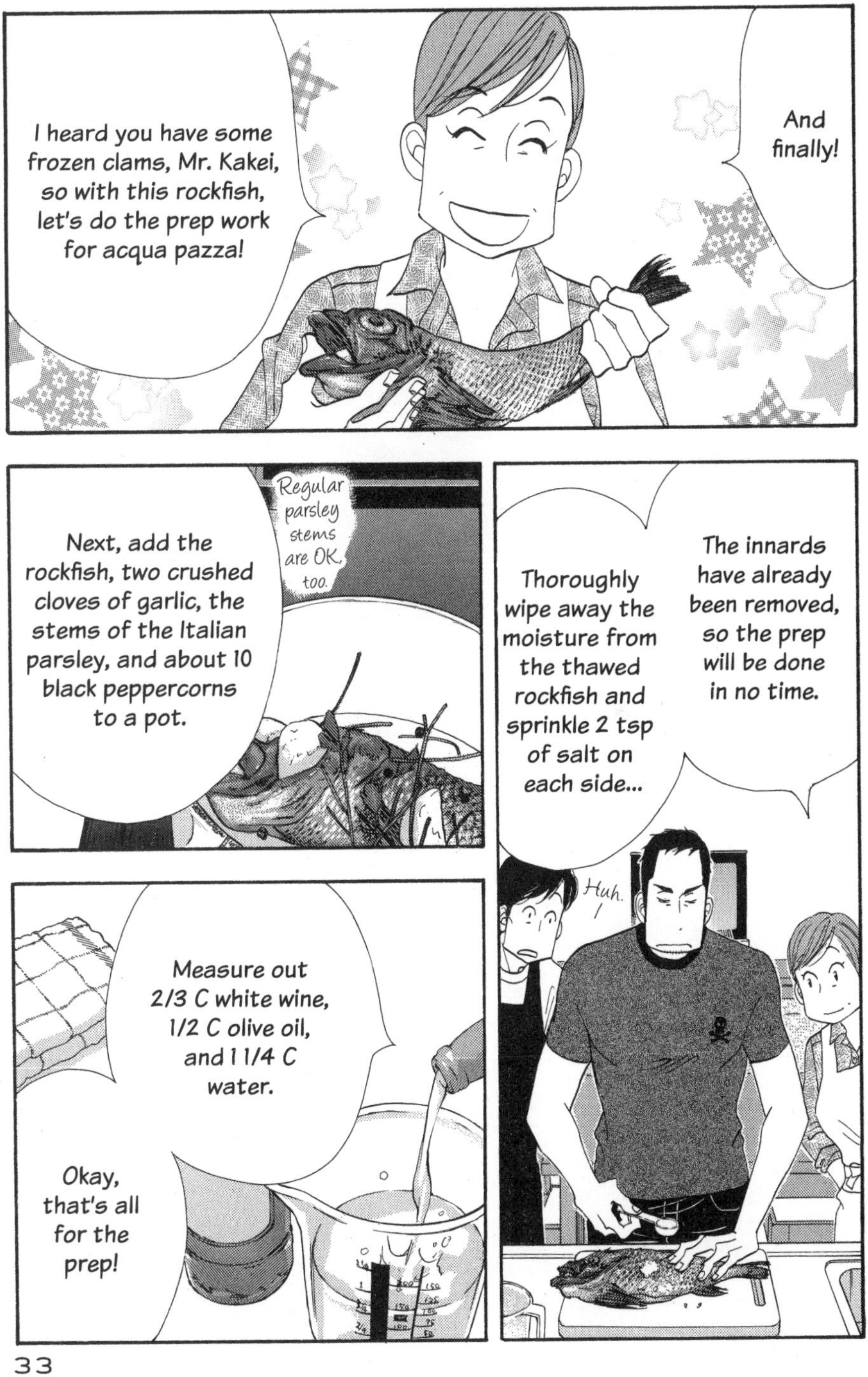
And finally!
I heard you have some frozen clams, Mr. Kakei, so with this rockfish, let's do the prep work for acqua pazza!
The innards have already been removed, so the prep will be done in no time.
Thoroughly wipe away the moisture from the thawed rockfish and sprinkle 2 tsp of salt on each side...
Huh.
Regular parsley stems are OK, too.
Next, add the rockfish, two crushed cloves of garlic, the stems of the Italian parsley, and about 10 black peppercorns to a pot.
Measure out 2/3 C white wine, 1/2 C olive oil, and 1 1/4 C water.
Okay, that's all for the prep!

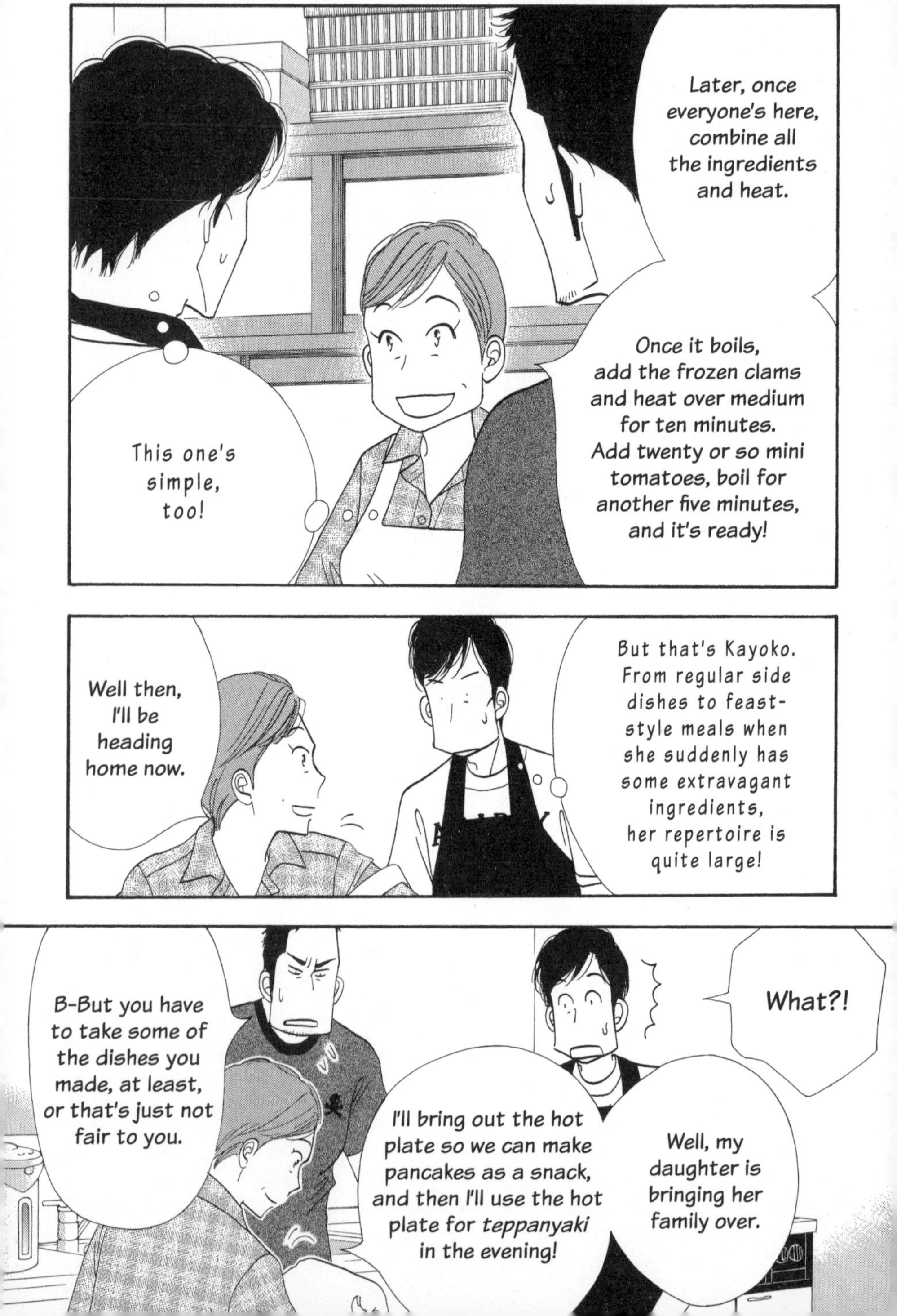
Later, once everyone's here, combine all the ingredients and heat.
Once it boils, add the frozen clams and heat over medium for ten minutes. Add twenty or so mini tomatoes, boil for another five minutes, and it's ready!
This one's simple, too!
But that's Kayoko. From regular side dishes to feast-style meals when she suddenly has some extravagant ingredients, her repertoire is quite large!
Well then, I'll be heading home now.
What?!
Well, my daughter is bringing her family over.
I'll bring out the hot plate so we can make pancakes as a snack, and then I'll use the hot plate for teppanyaki in the evening!
B-But you have to take some of the dishes you made, at least, or that's just not fair to you.

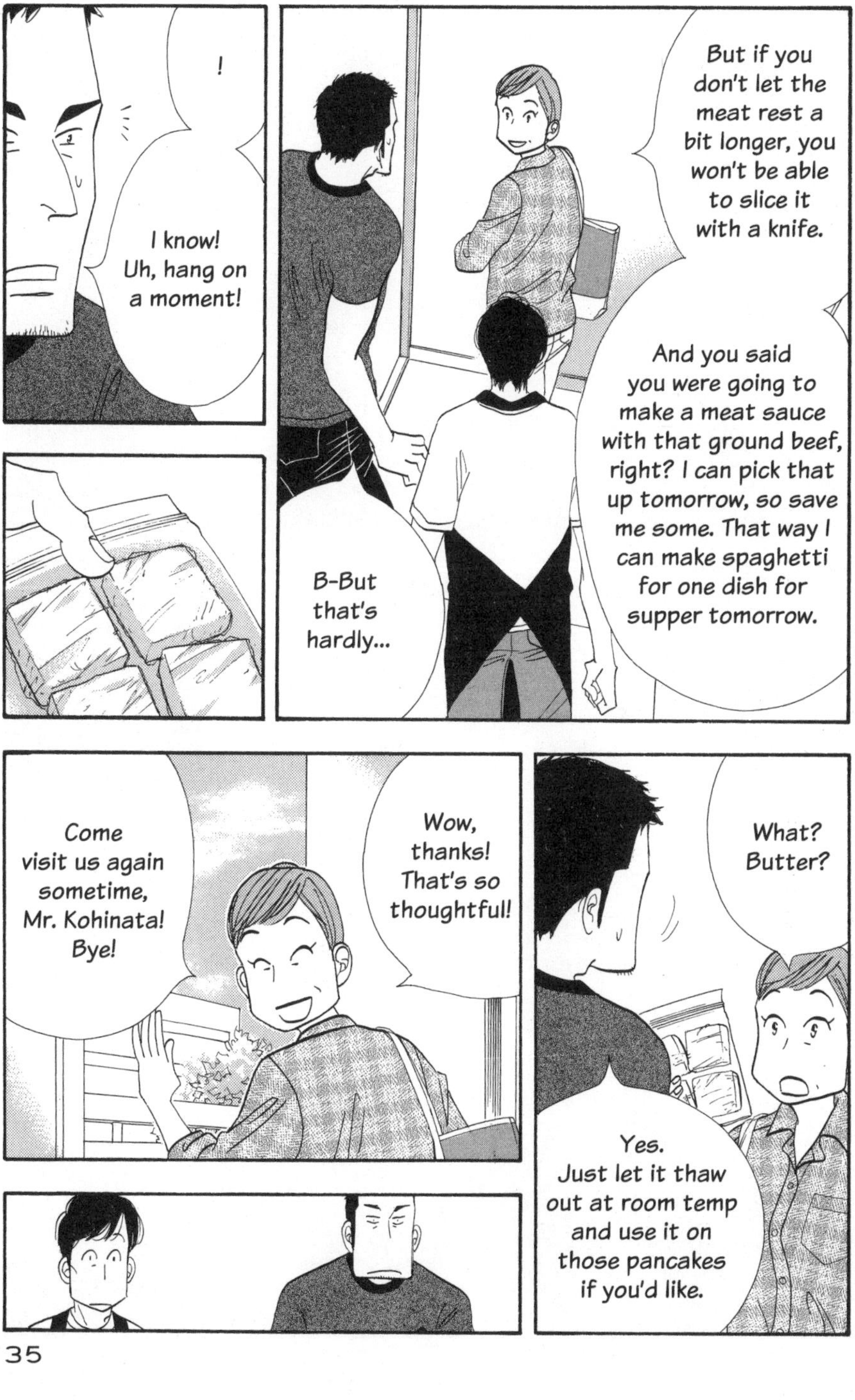
But if you don't let the meat rest a bit longer, you won't be able to slice it with a knife.
And you said you were going to make a meat sauce with that ground beef, right? I can pick that up tomorrow, so save me some. That way I can make spaghetti for one dish for supper tomorrow.
B-But that's hardly...
!
I know! Uh, hang on a moment!
What? Butter?
Yes. Just let it thaw out at room temp and use it on those pancakes if you'd like.
Wow, thanks! That's so thoughtful!
Come visit us again sometime, Mr. Kohinata! Bye!

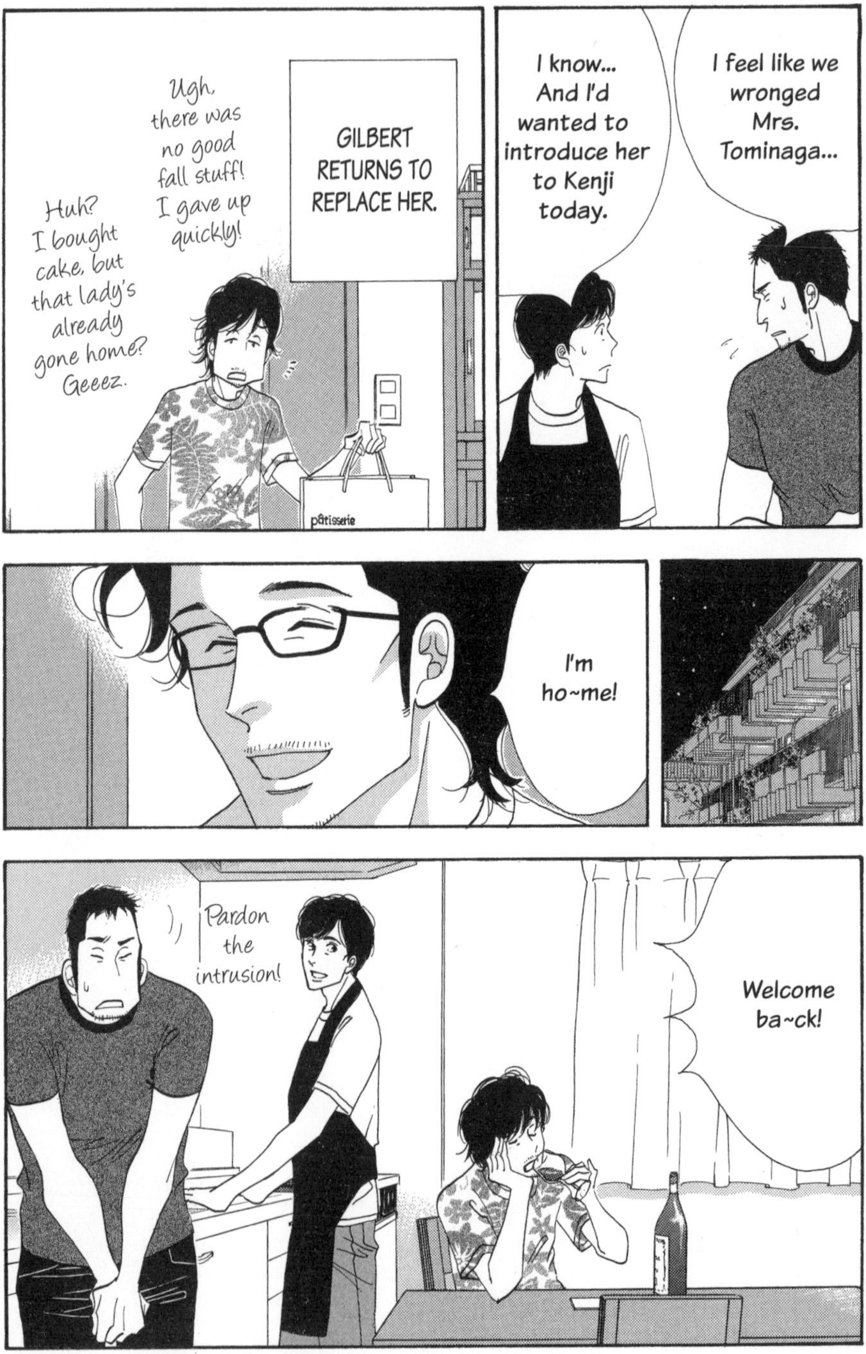
I feel like we wronged Mrs. Tominaga...
I know... And I'd wanted to introduce her to Kenji today.
GILBERT RETURNS TO REPLACE HER.
Ugh, there was no good fall stuff! I gave up quickly!
Huh? I bought cake, but that lady's already gone home? Geeez.
pâtisserie
I'm ho~me!
Welcome ba~ck!
Pardon the intrusion!

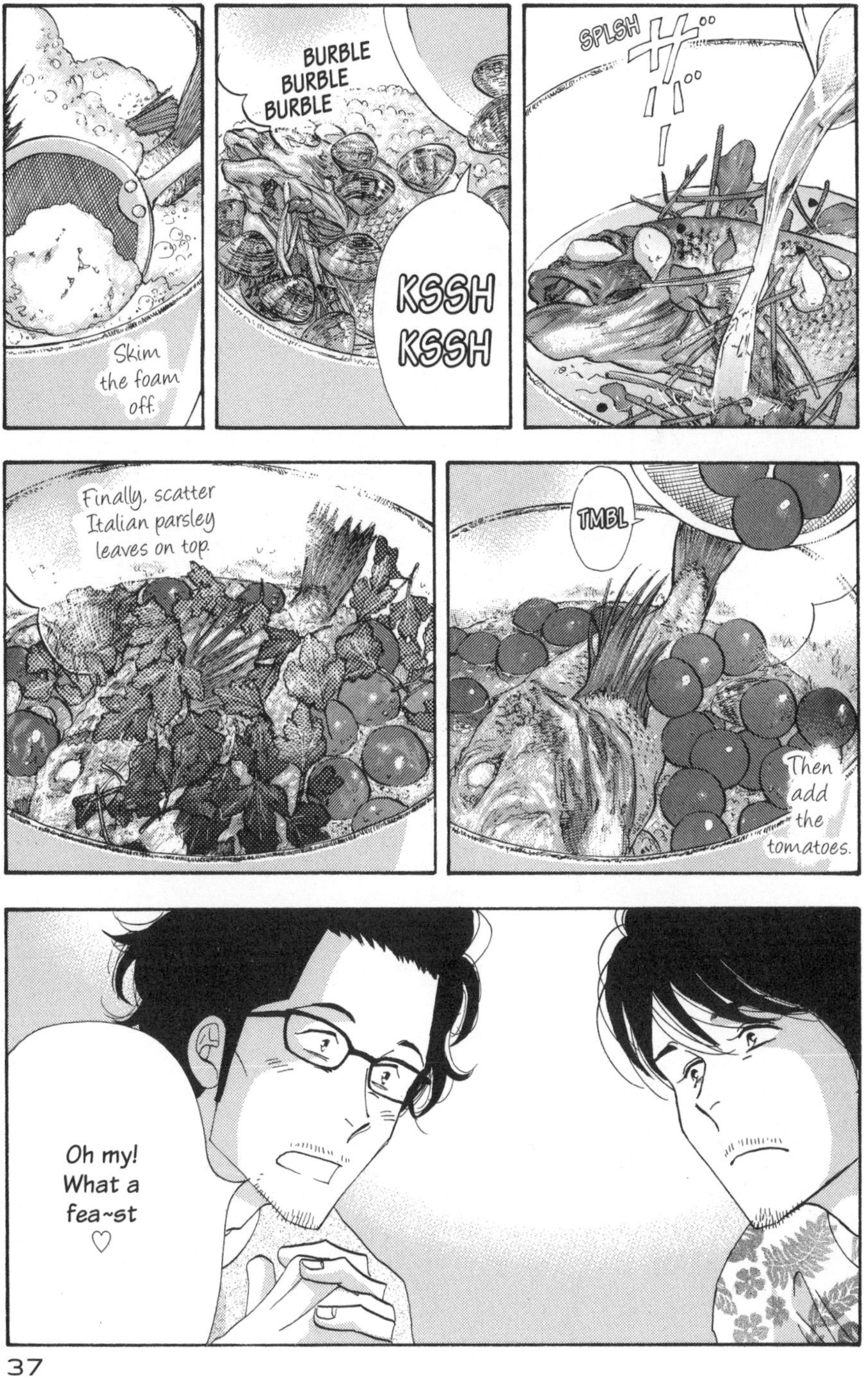
SPLSH
BURBLE BURBLE BURBLE
KSSH KSSH
Skim the foam off.
TMBL
Then add the tomatoes.
Finally, scatter Italian parsley leaves on top.
Oh my! What a fea~st ♡

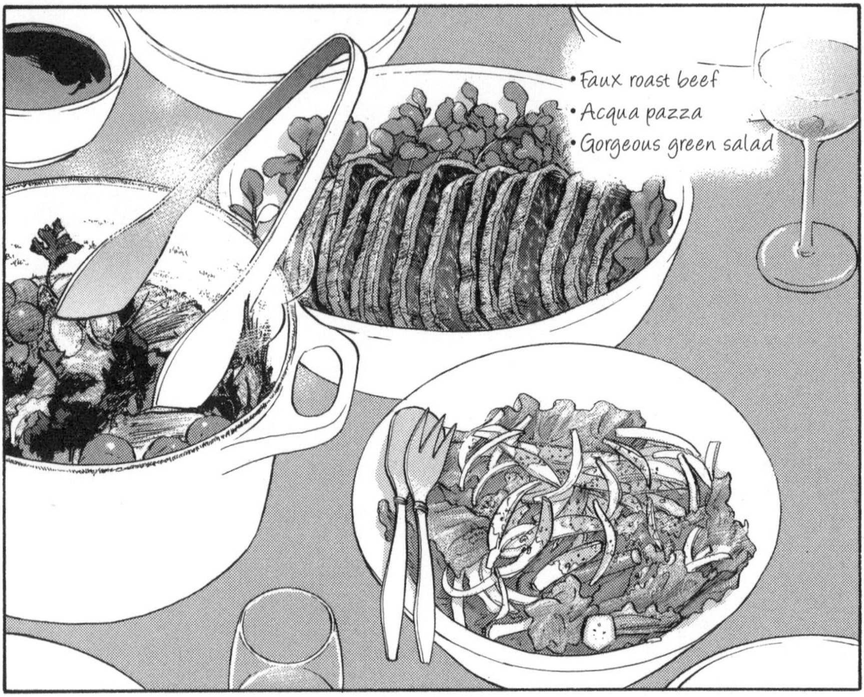
•Faux roast beef
•Acqua pazza
•Gorgeous green salad

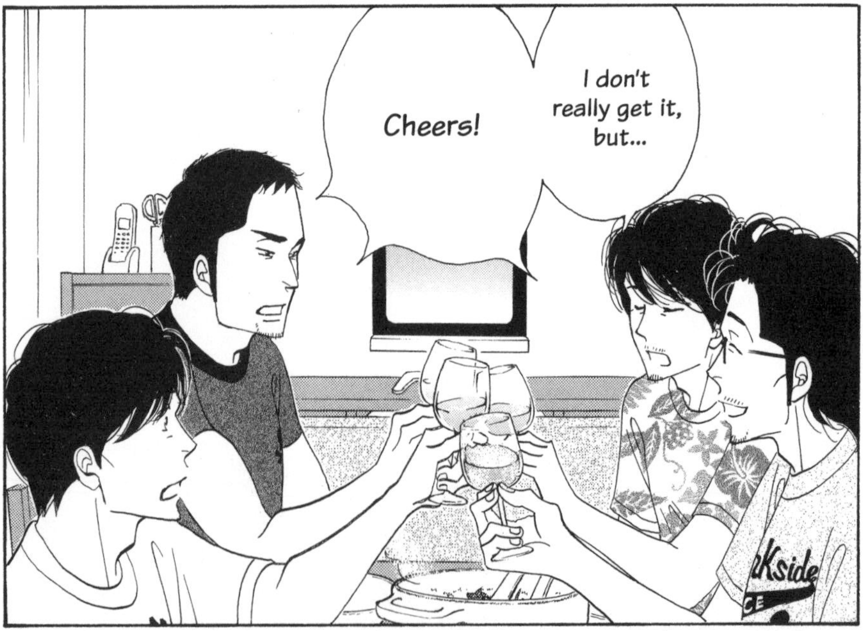
I don't really get it, but...
Cheers!

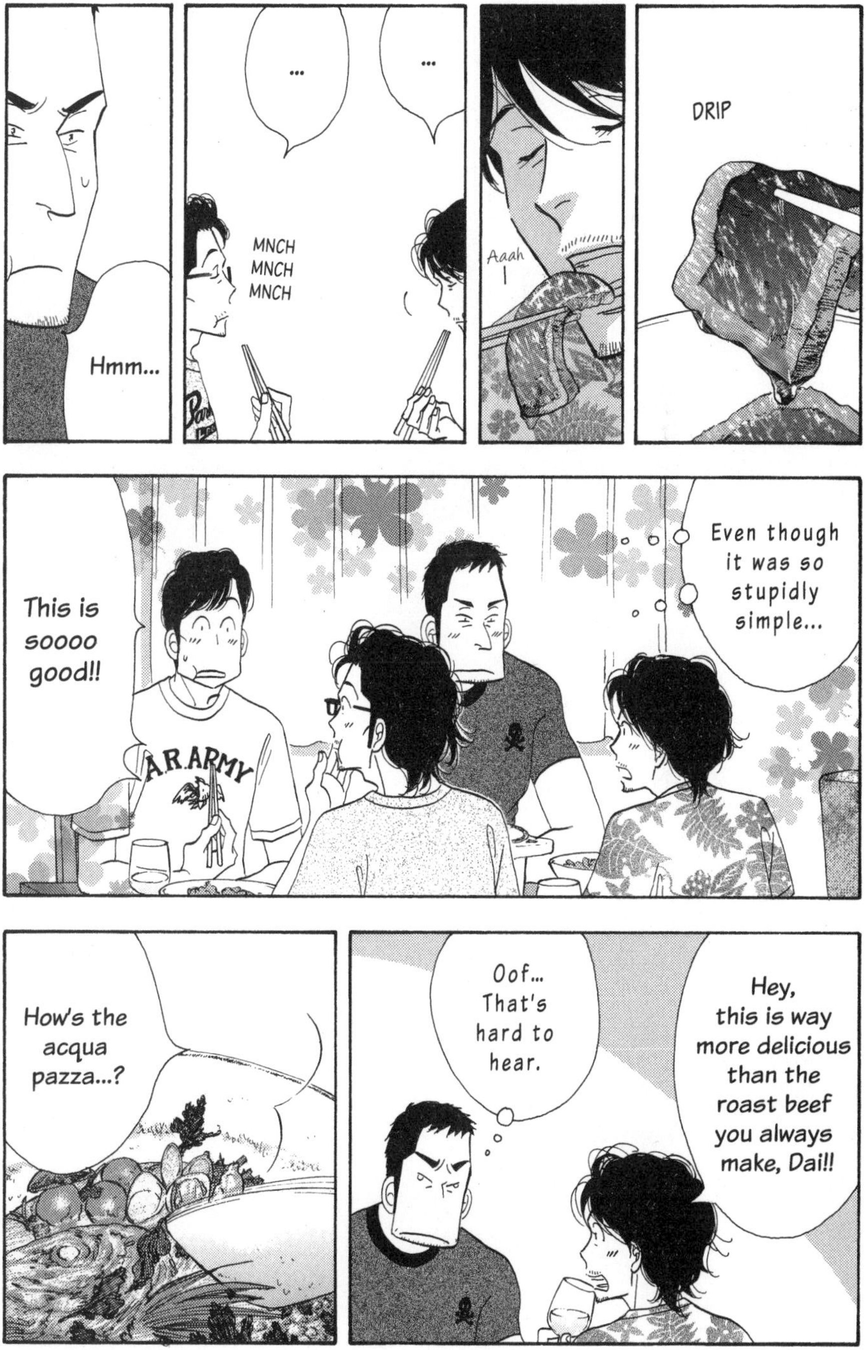
DRIP
Aaah
...
...
MNCH MNCH MNCH
Hmm...
Even though it was so stupidly simple...
This is soooo good!!
Hey, this is way more delicious than the roast beef you always make, Dai!!
Oof... That's hard to hear.
How's the acqua pazza...?

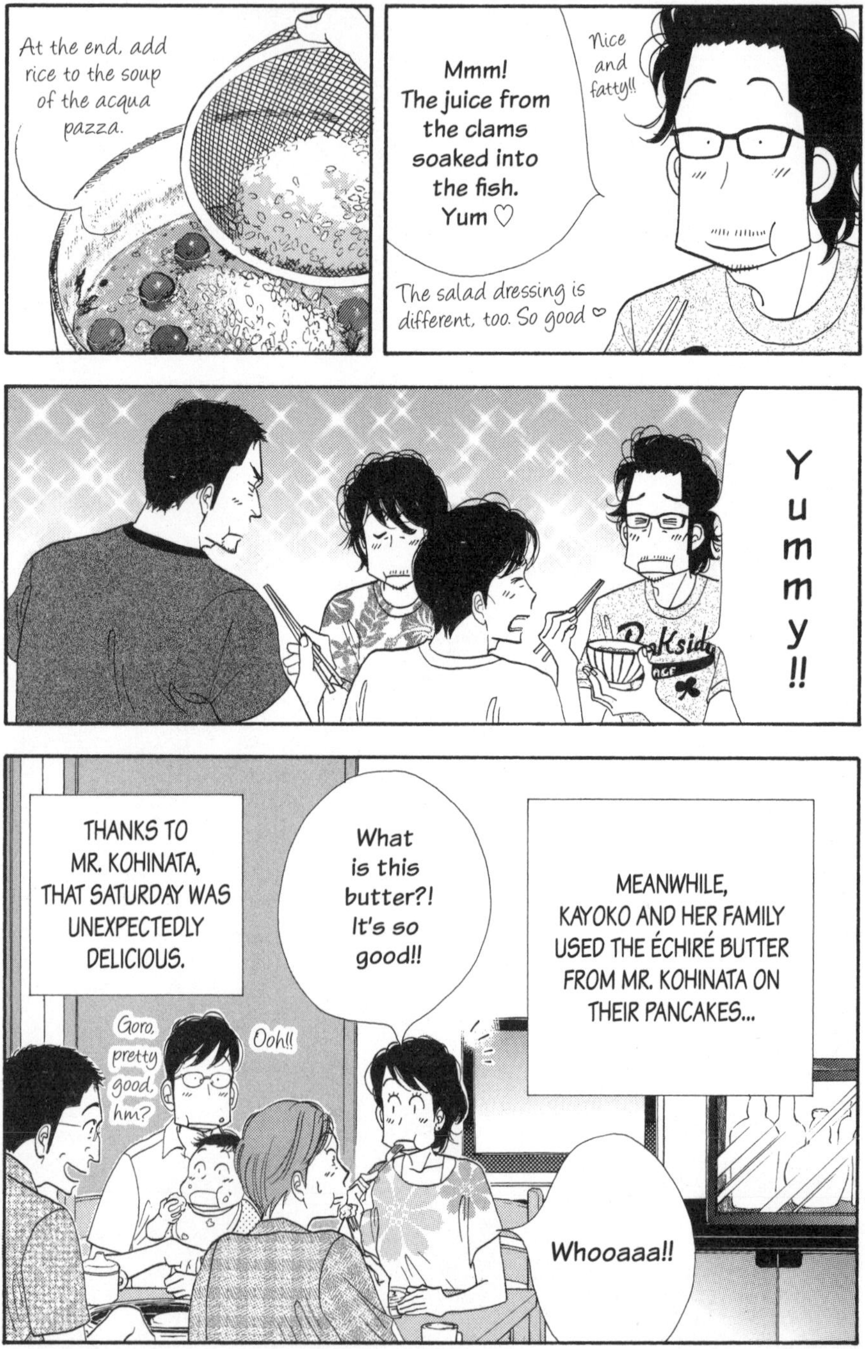
Mmm! The juice from the clams soaked into the fish. Yum ♡
Nice and fatty!!
The salad dressing is different, too. So good ♡
At the end, add rice to the soup of the acqua pazza.
Yummy!!
MEANWHILE, KAYOKO AND HER FAMILY USED THE ÉCHIRÉ BUTTER FROM MR. KOHINATA ON THEIR PANCAKES...
What is this butter?! It's so good!!
Whooaaa!!
THANKS TO MR. KOHINATA, THAT SATURDAY WAS UNEXPECTEDLY DELICIOUS.
Ooh!!
Goro, pretty good, hm?

It's better to make the **roast beef** with fresh meat
that hasn't been frozen the day before you serve it.
In that case you'll be able to cut thin slices of the
completely chilled meat so it's easier to eat.
All you have to do is slice it up the day of,
so it's really the perfect meal for entertaining.

I think pretty much any white-meat fish
works in **acqua pazza**, like red snapper,
sea bass, chicken grunt, or red bream.
You can also make it with filets for single servings
or more.

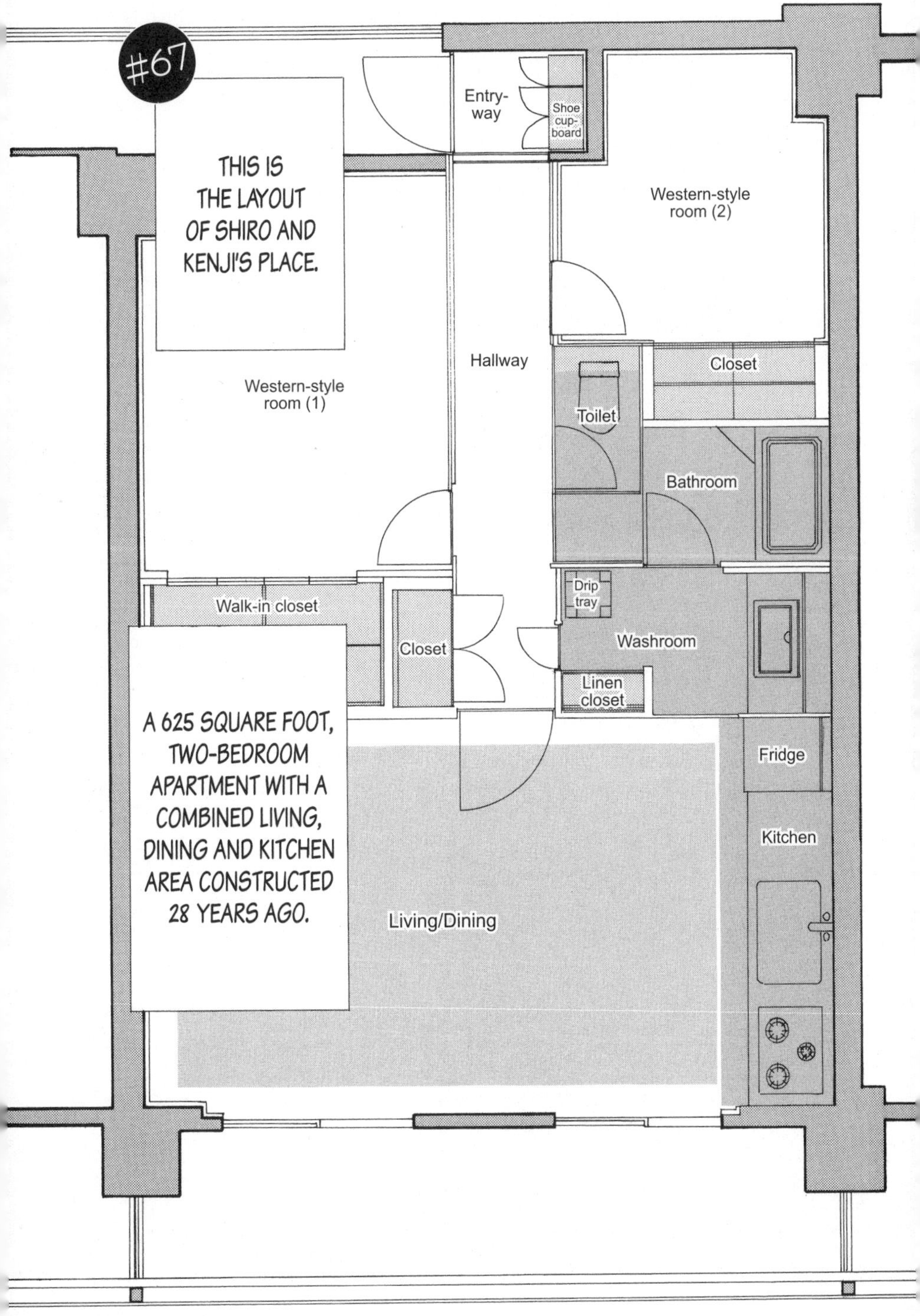
#67
THIS IS THE LAYOUT OF SHIRO AND KENJI'S PLACE.
A 625 SQUARE FOOT, TWO-BEDROOM APARTMENT WITH A COMBINED LIVING, DINING AND KITCHEN AREA CONSTRUCTED 28 YEARS AGO.
Entry-way
Shoe cup-board
Western-style room (2)
Hallway
Closet
Western-style room (1)
Toilet
Bathroom
Drip tray
Walk-in closet
Washroom
Closet
Linen closet
Fridge
Kitchen
Living/Dining

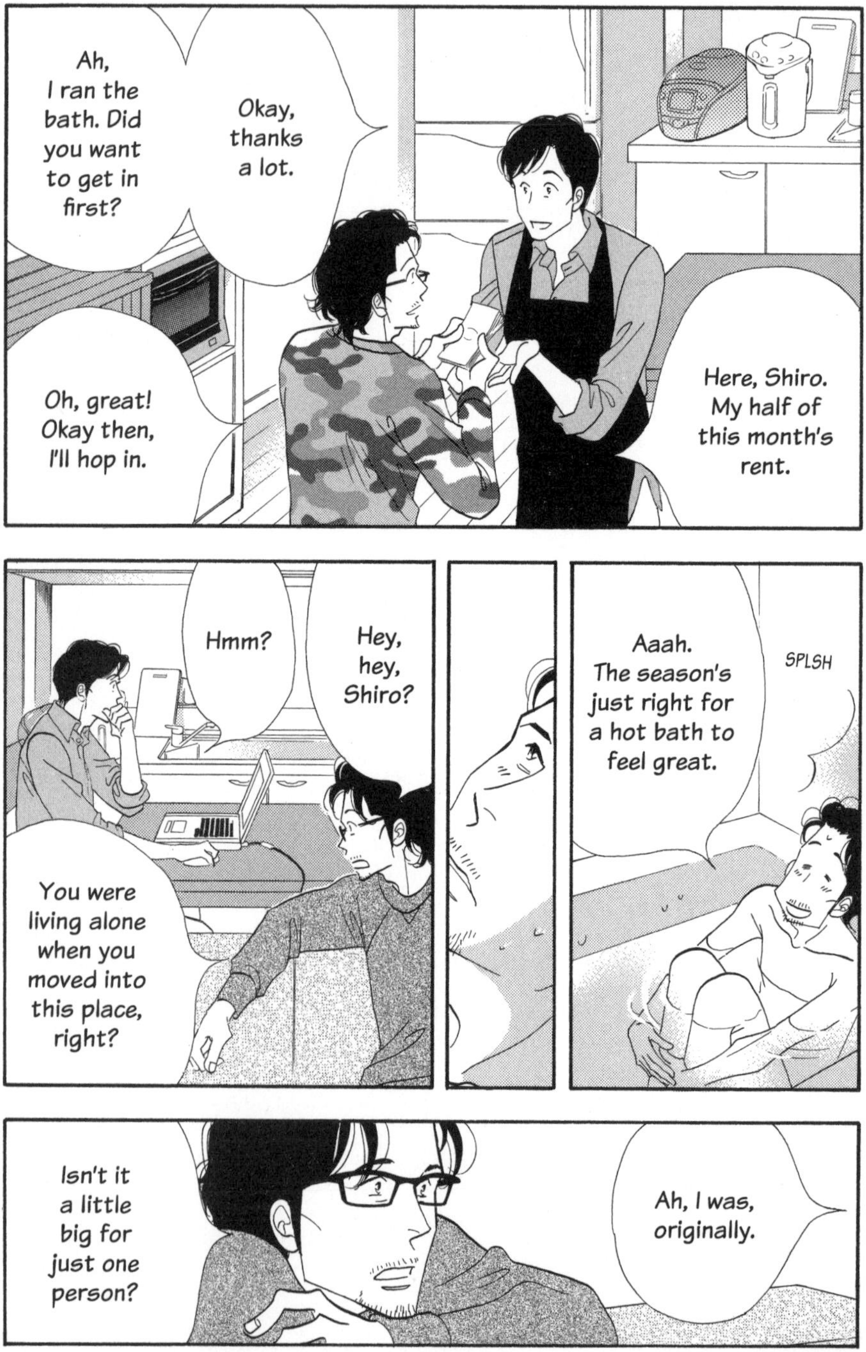
Here, Shiro. My half of this month's rent.
Okay, thanks a lot.
Ah, I ran the bath. Did you want to get in first?
Oh, great! Okay then, I'll hop in.
SPLSH
Aaah. The season's just right for a hot bath to feel great.
Hey, hey, Shiro?
Hmm?
You were living alone when you moved into this place, right?
Ah, I was, originally.
Isn't it a little big for just one person?

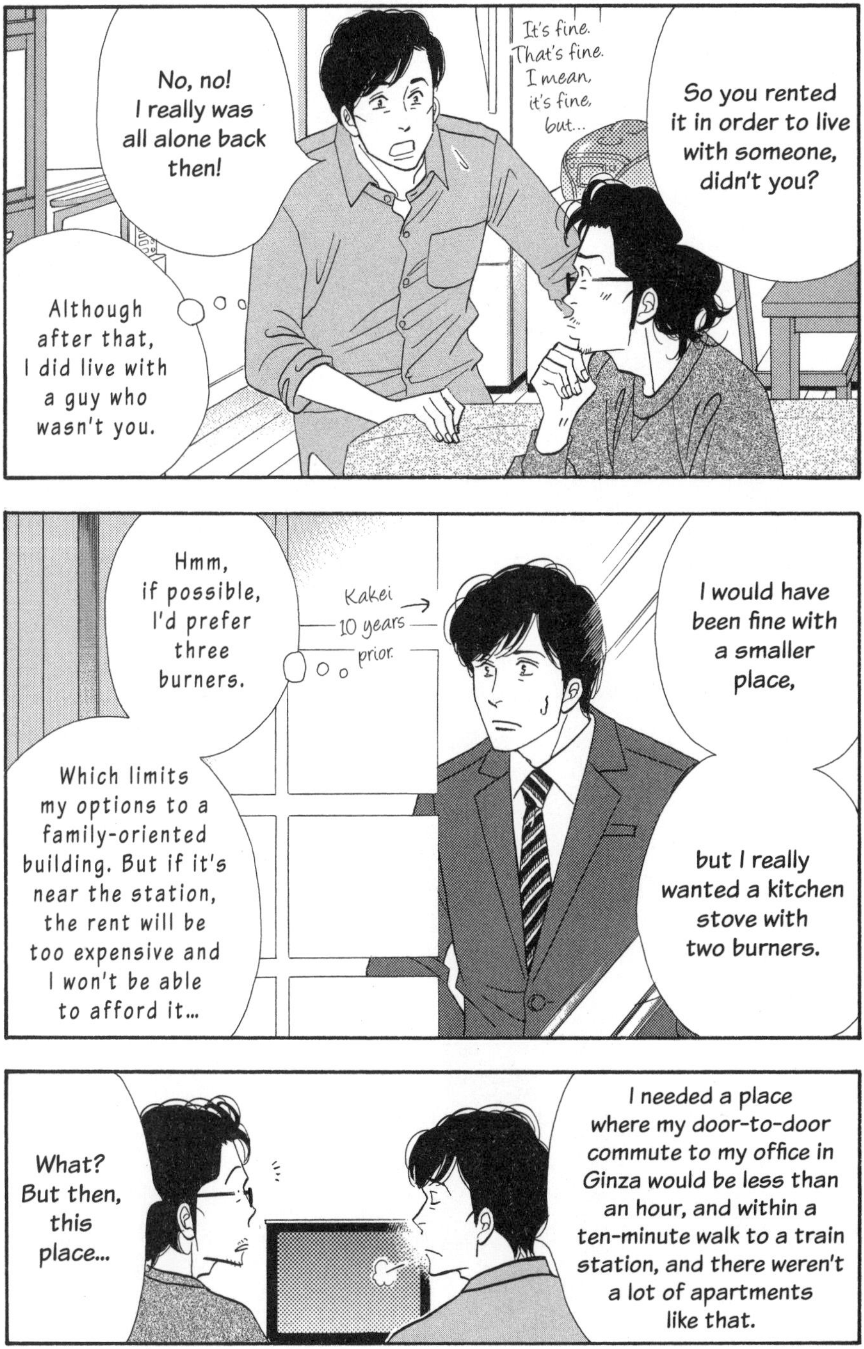
So you rented it in order to live with someone, didn't you?
It's fine. That's fine. I mean, it's fine, but...
No, no! I really was all alone back then!
Although after that, I did live with a guy who wasn't you.
I would have been fine with a smaller place,
but I really wanted a kitchen stove with two burners.
Kakei 10 years prior.
Hmm, if possible, I'd prefer three burners.
Which limits my options to a family-oriented building. But if it's near the station, the rent will be too expensive and I won't be able to afford it...
I needed a place where my door-to-door commute to my office in Ginza would be less than an hour, and within a ten-minute walk to a train station, and there weren't a lot of apartments like that.
What? But then, this place...

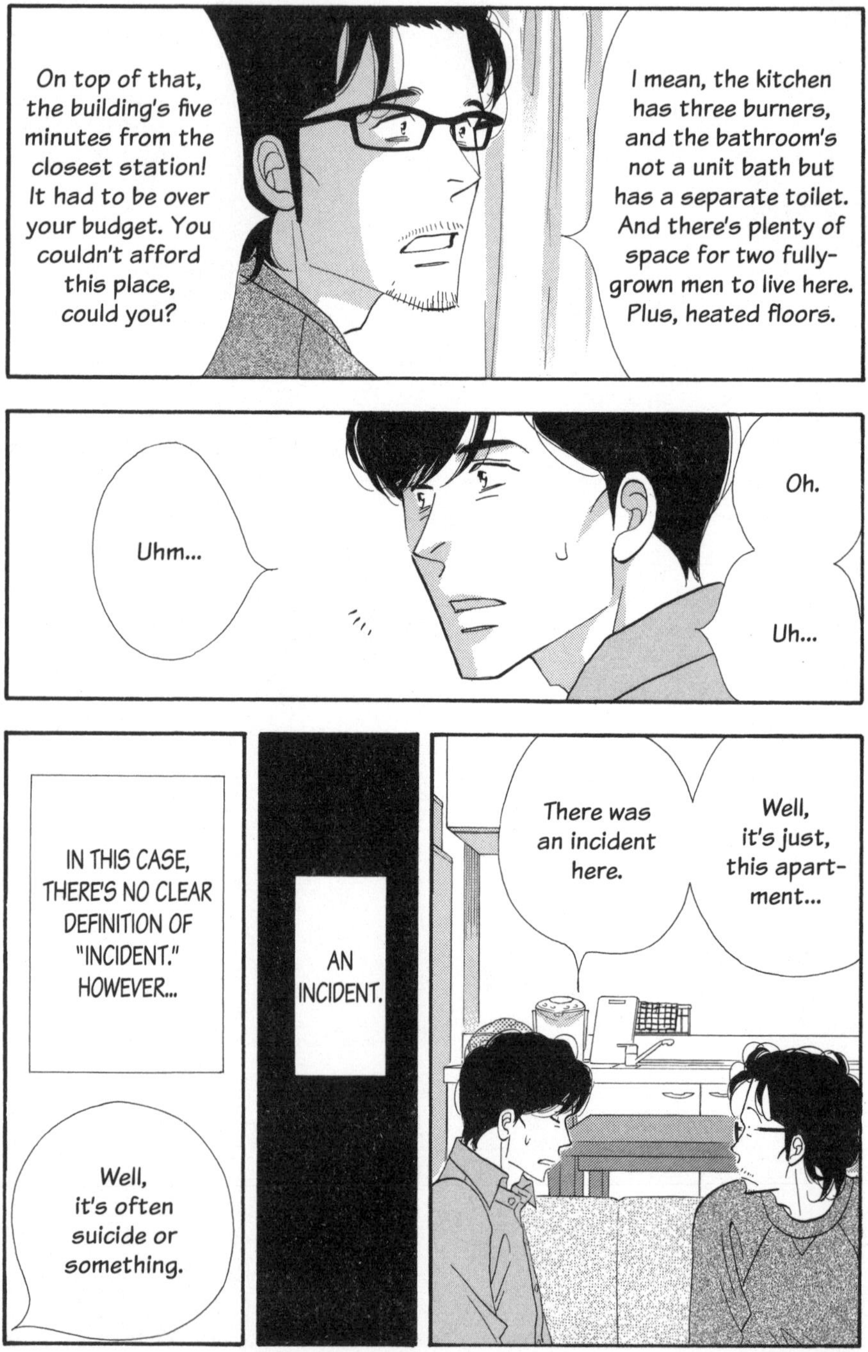
I mean, the kitchen has three burners, and the bathroom's not a unit bath but has a separate toilet. And there's plenty of space for two fully-grown men to live here. Plus, heated floors.
On top of that, the building's five minutes from the closest station! It had to be over your budget. You couldn't afford this place, could you?
Oh.
Uh...
Uhm...
Well, it's just, this apartment...
There was an incident here.
AN INCIDENT.
IN THIS CASE, THERE'S NO CLEAR DEFINITION OF "INCIDENT." HOWEVER...
Well, it's often suicide or something.

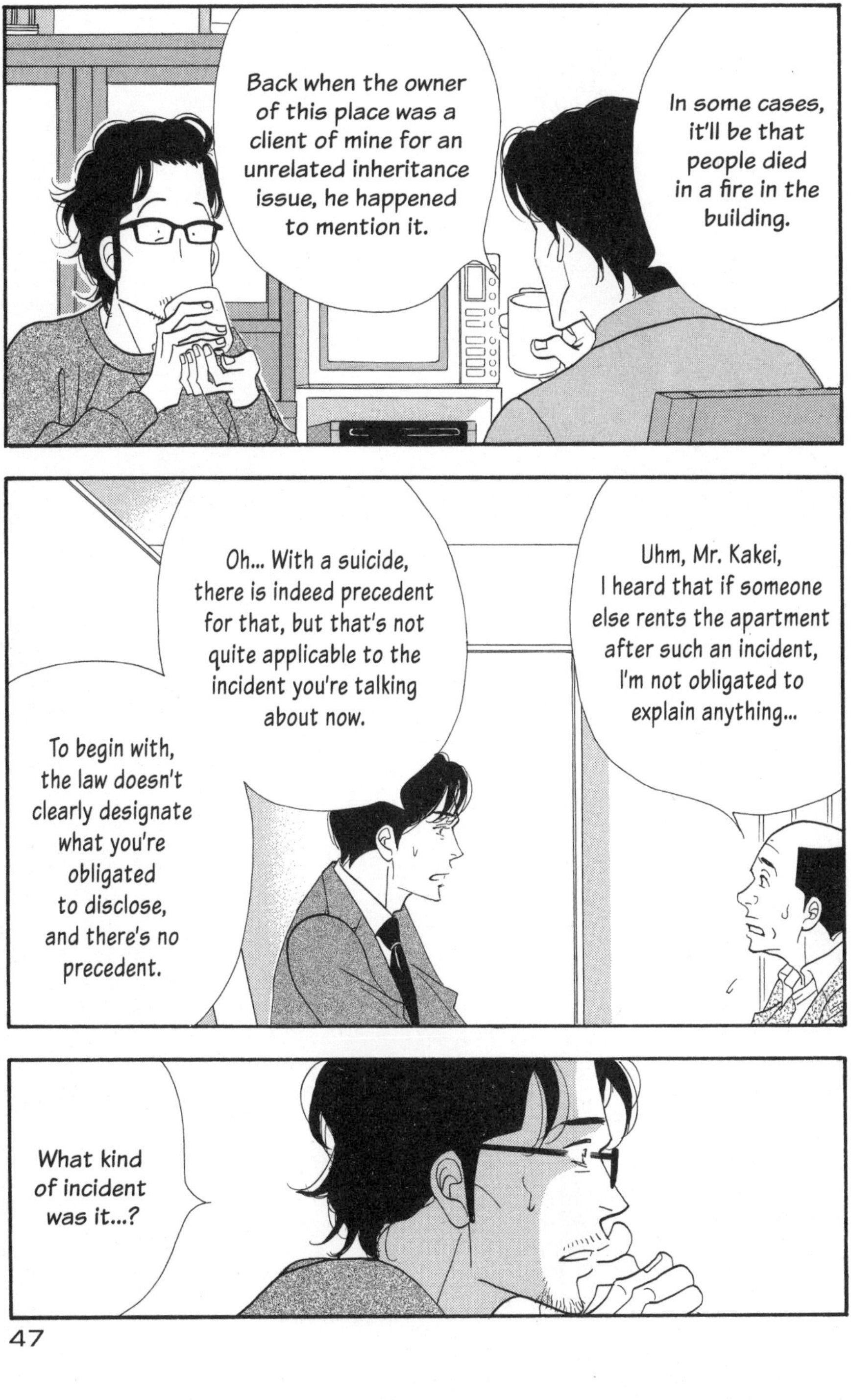
In some cases, it'll be that people died in a fire in the building.
Back when the owner of this place was a client of mine for an unrelated inheritance issue, he happened to mention it.
Uhm, Mr. Kakei, I heard that if someone else rents the apartment after such an incident, I'm not obligated to explain anything...
Oh... With a suicide, there is indeed precedent for that, but that's not quite applicable to the incident you're talking about now.
To begin with, the law doesn't clearly designate what you're obligated to disclose, and there's no precedent.
What kind of incident was it...?

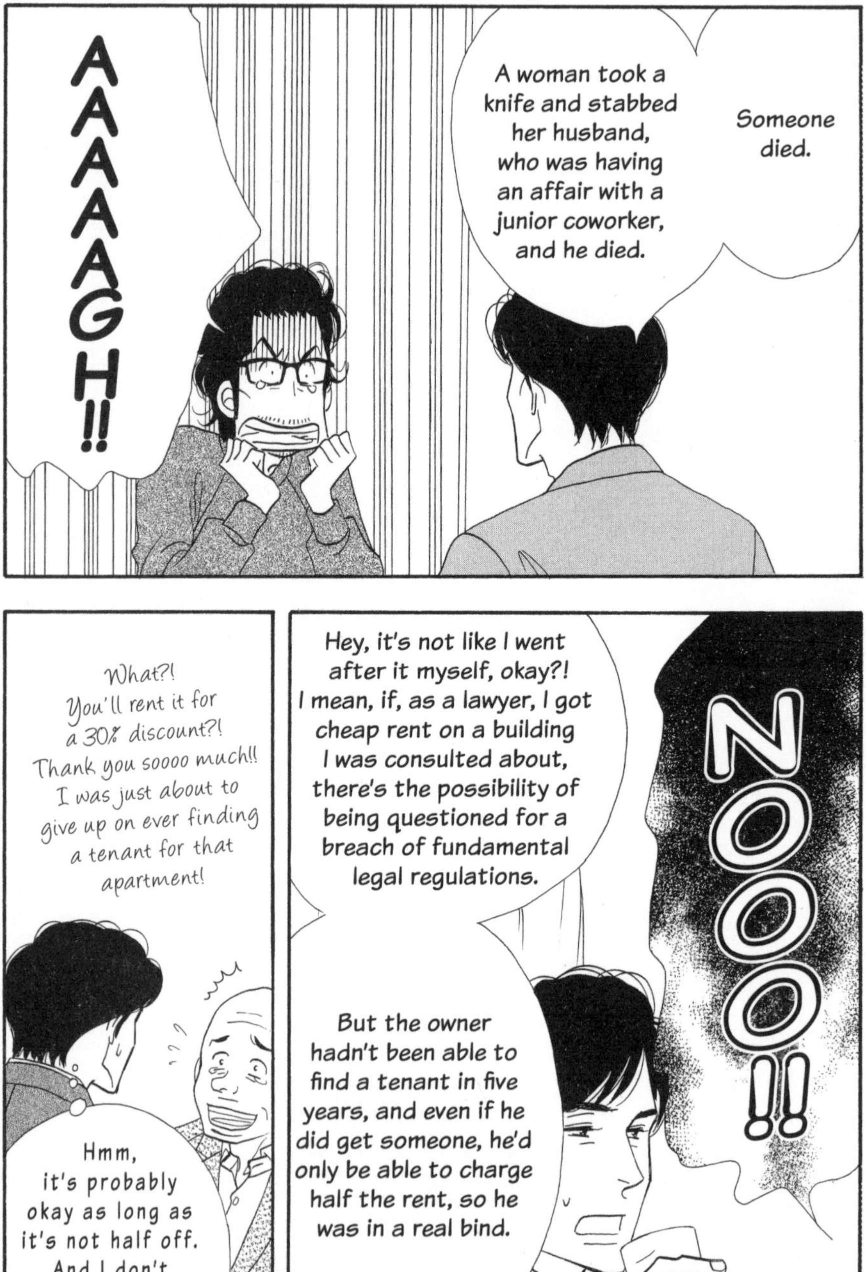
Someone died.
A woman took a knife and stabbed her husband, who was having an affair with a junior coworker, and he died.
AAAAAGH!!
ZOOOO!!
Hey, it's not like I went after it myself, okay?! I mean, if, as a lawyer, I got cheap rent on a building I was consulted about, there's the possibility of being questioned for a breach of fundamental legal regulations.
But the owner hadn't been able to find a tenant in five years, and even if he did get someone, he'd only be able to charge half the rent, so he was in a real bind.
What?! You'll rent it for a 30% discount?! Thank you soooo much!! I was just about to give up on ever finding a tenant for that apartment!
Hmm, it's probably okay as long as it's not half off. And I don't believe in ghosts.

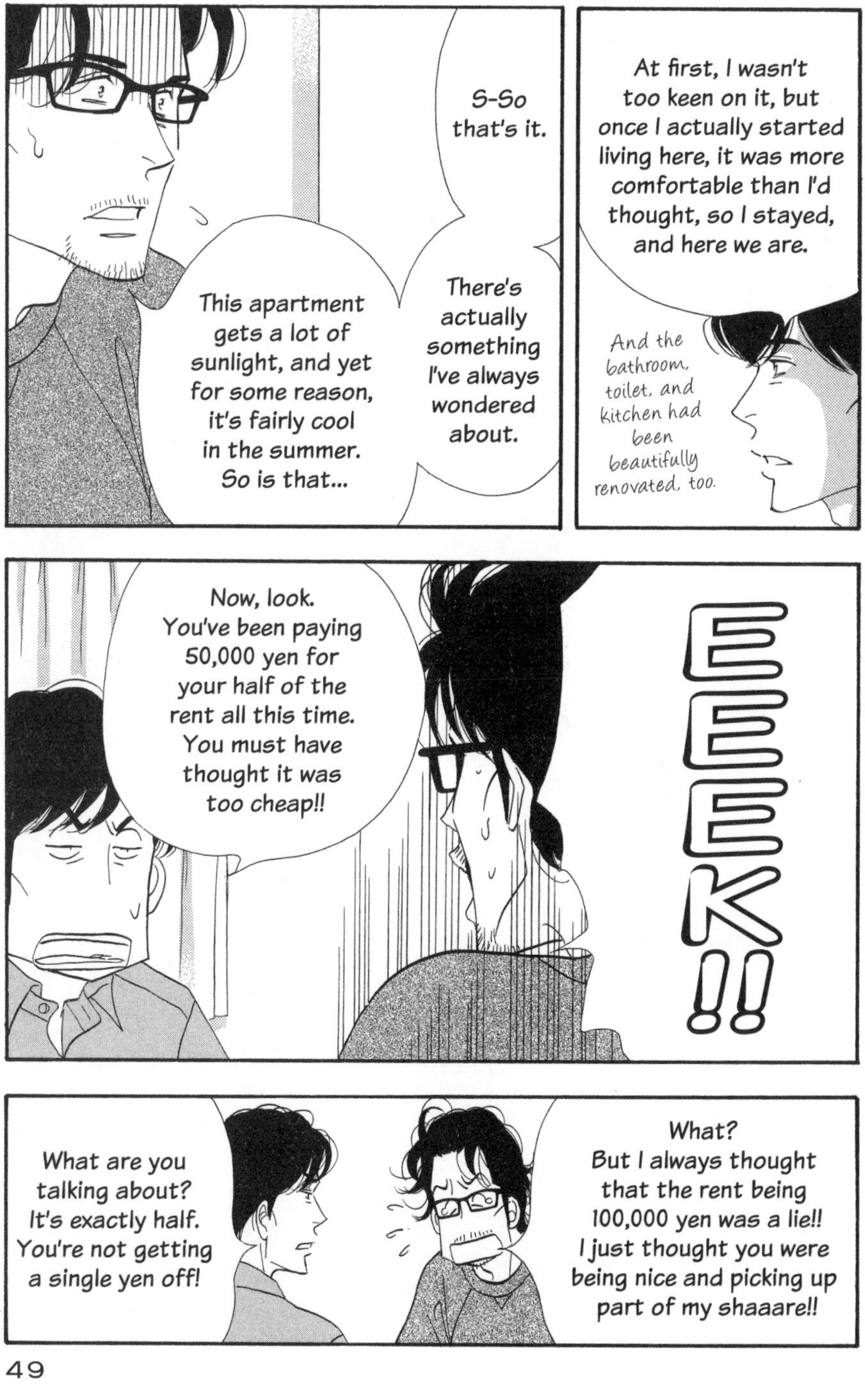
At first, I wasn't too keen on it, but once I actually started living here, it was more comfortable than I'd thought, so I stayed, and here we are.
And the bathroom, toilet, and kitchen had been beautifully renovated, too.
S-So that's it.
There's actually something I've always wondered about.
This apartment gets a lot of sunlight, and yet for some reason, it's fairly cool in the summer. So is that...
Now, look. You've been paying 50,000 yen for your half of the rent all this time. You must have thought it was too cheap!!
EEEK!!
What? But I always thought that the rent being 100,000 yen was a lie!! I just thought you were being nice and picking up part of my shaaare!!
What are you talking about? It's exactly half. You're not getting a single yen off!

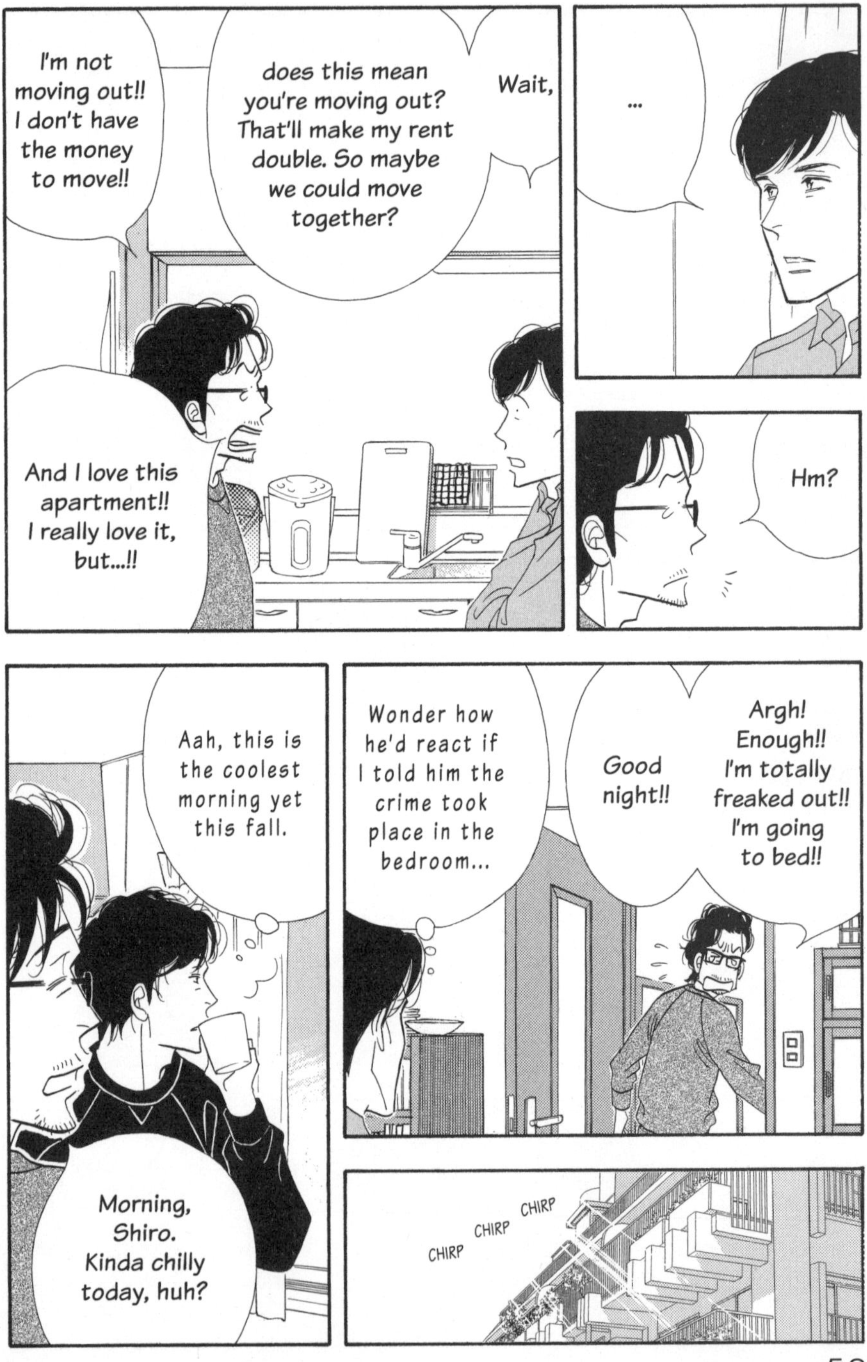
...
Hm?
Wait,
does this mean you're moving out? That'll make my rent double. So maybe we could move together?
I'm not moving out!! I don't have the money to move!!
And I love this apartment!! I really love it, but...!!
Argh! Enough!! I'm totally freaked out!! I'm going to bed!!
Good night!!
Wonder how he'd react if I told him the crime took place in the bedroom...
CHIRP
CHIRP
CHIRP
Aah, this is the coolest morning yet this fall.
Morning, Shiro. Kinda chilly today, huh?

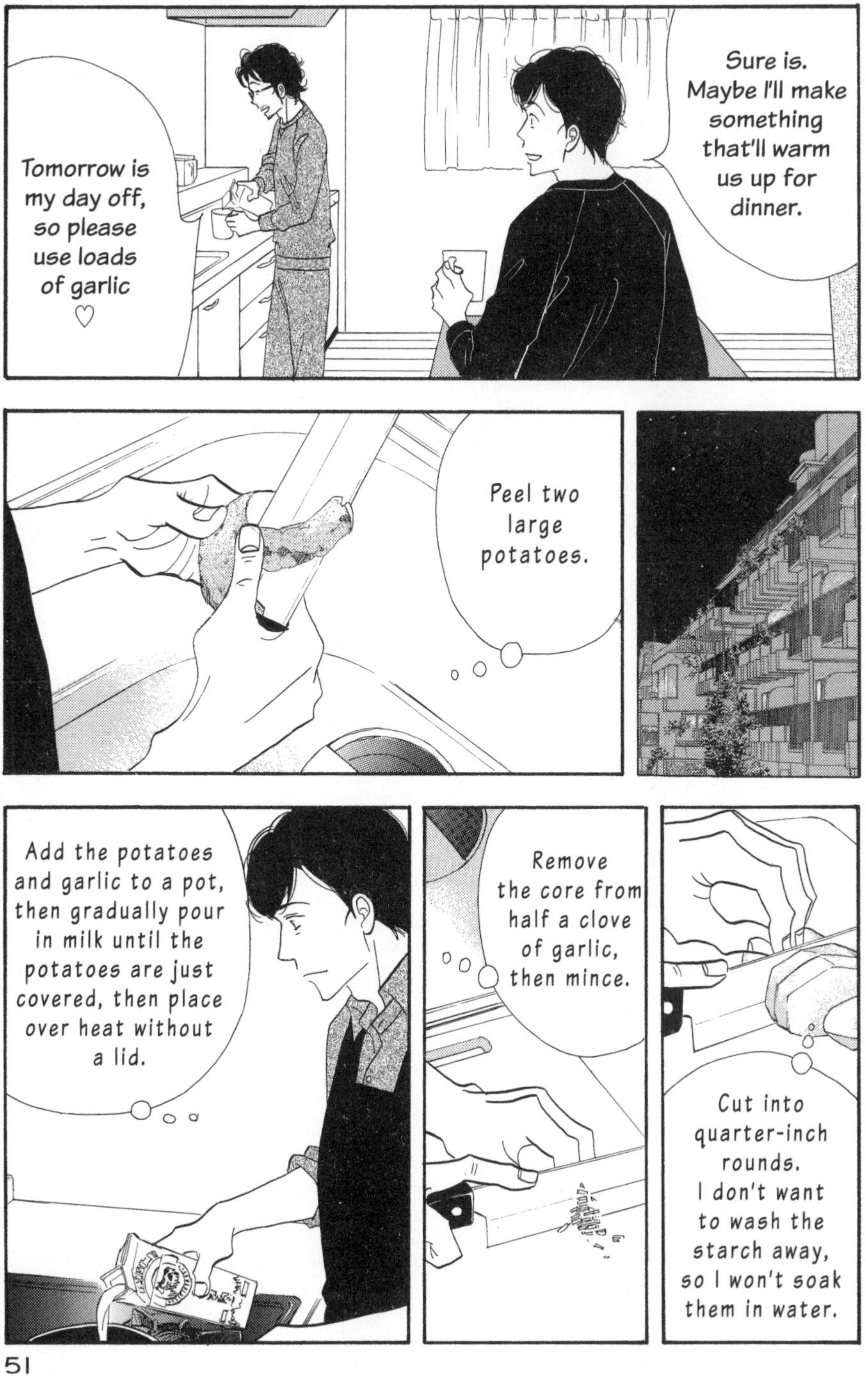
Sure is. Maybe I'll make something that'll warm us up for dinner.
Tomorrow is my day off, so please use loads of garlic ♡
Peel two large potatoes.
Cut into quarter-inch rounds. I don't want to wash the starch away, so I won't soak them in water.
Remove the core from half a clove of garlic, then mince.
Add the potatoes and garlic to a pot, then gradually pour in milk until the potatoes are just covered, then place over heat without a lid.

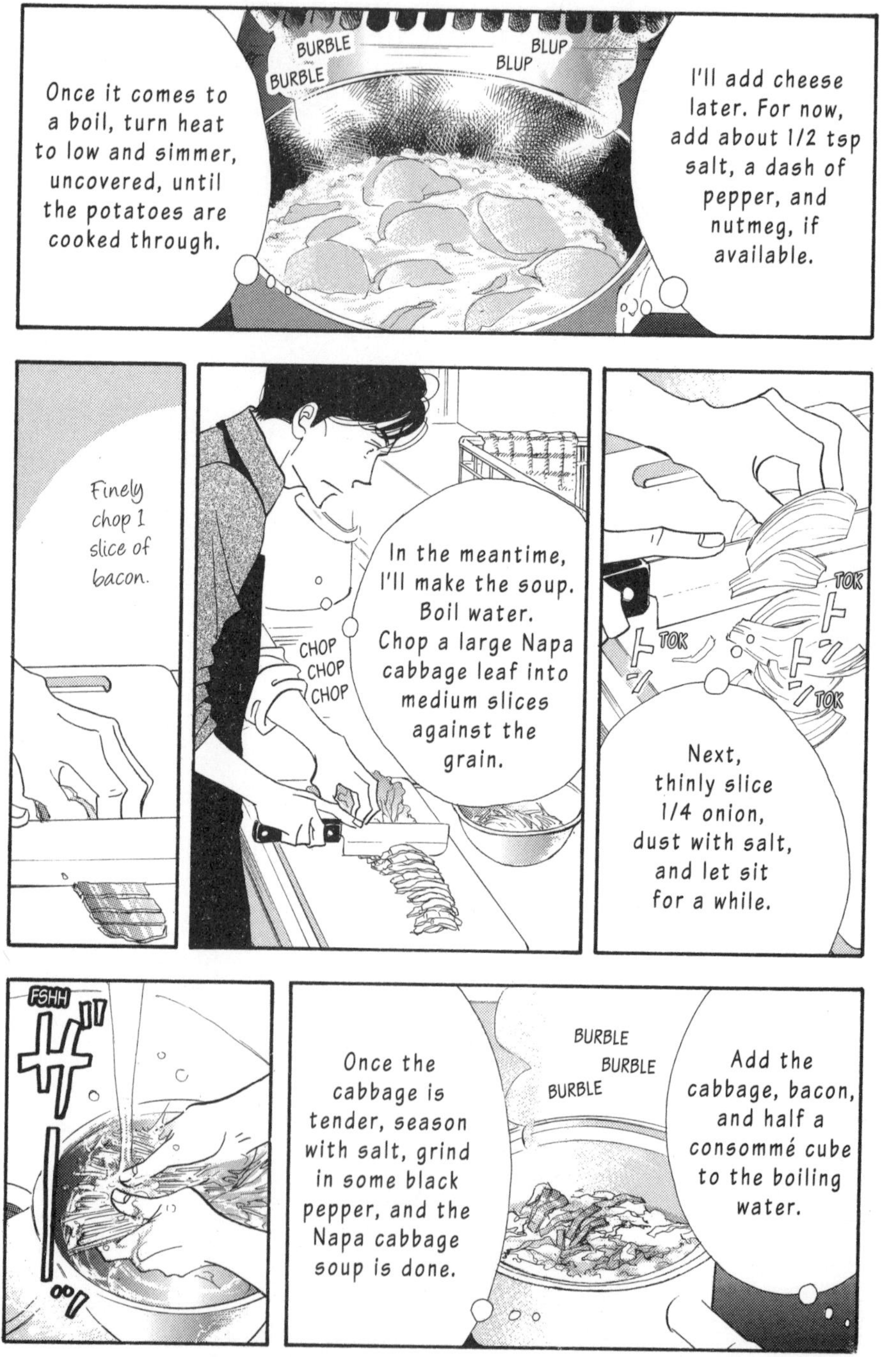
I'll add cheese later. For now, add about 1/2 tsp salt, a dash of pepper, and nutmeg, if available.
BLUP BLUP
BURBLE BURBLE
Once it comes to a boil, turn heat to low and simmer, uncovered, until the potatoes are cooked through.
TOK TOK TOK
Next, thinly slice 1/4 onion, dust with salt, and let sit for a while.
In the meantime, I'll make the soup. Boil water. Chop a large Napa cabbage leaf into medium slices against the grain.
CHOP CHOP CHOP
Finely chop 1 slice of bacon.
Add the cabbage, bacon, and half a consommé cube to the boiling water.
BURBLE BURBLE BURBLE
Once the cabbage is tender, season with salt, grind in some black pepper, and the Napa cabbage soup is done.
FSHH

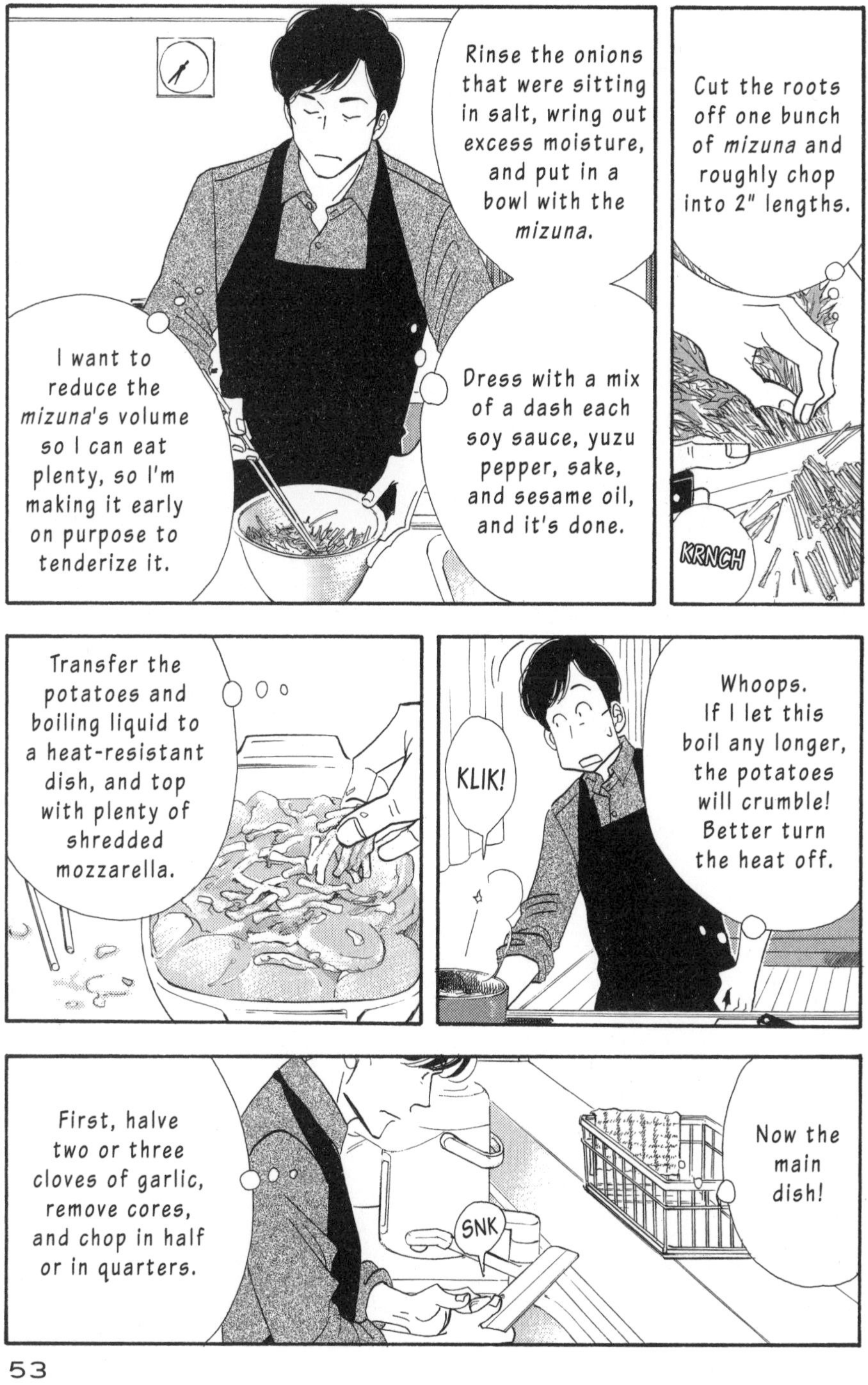
Cut the roots off one bunch of *mizuna* and roughly chop into 2" lengths.
KRNCH
Rinse the onions that were sitting in salt, wring out excess moisture, and put in a bowl with the *mizuna*.
Dress with a mix of a dash each soy sauce, yuzu pepper, sake, and sesame oil, and it's done.
I want to reduce the *mizuna*'s volume so I can eat plenty, so I'm making it early on purpose to tenderize it.
Whoops. If I let this boil any longer, the potatoes will crumble! Better turn the heat off.
KLIK!
Transfer the potatoes and boiling liquid to a heat-resistant dish, and top with plenty of shredded mozzarella.
Now the main dish!
SNK
First, halve two or three cloves of garlic, remove cores, and chop in half or in quarters.

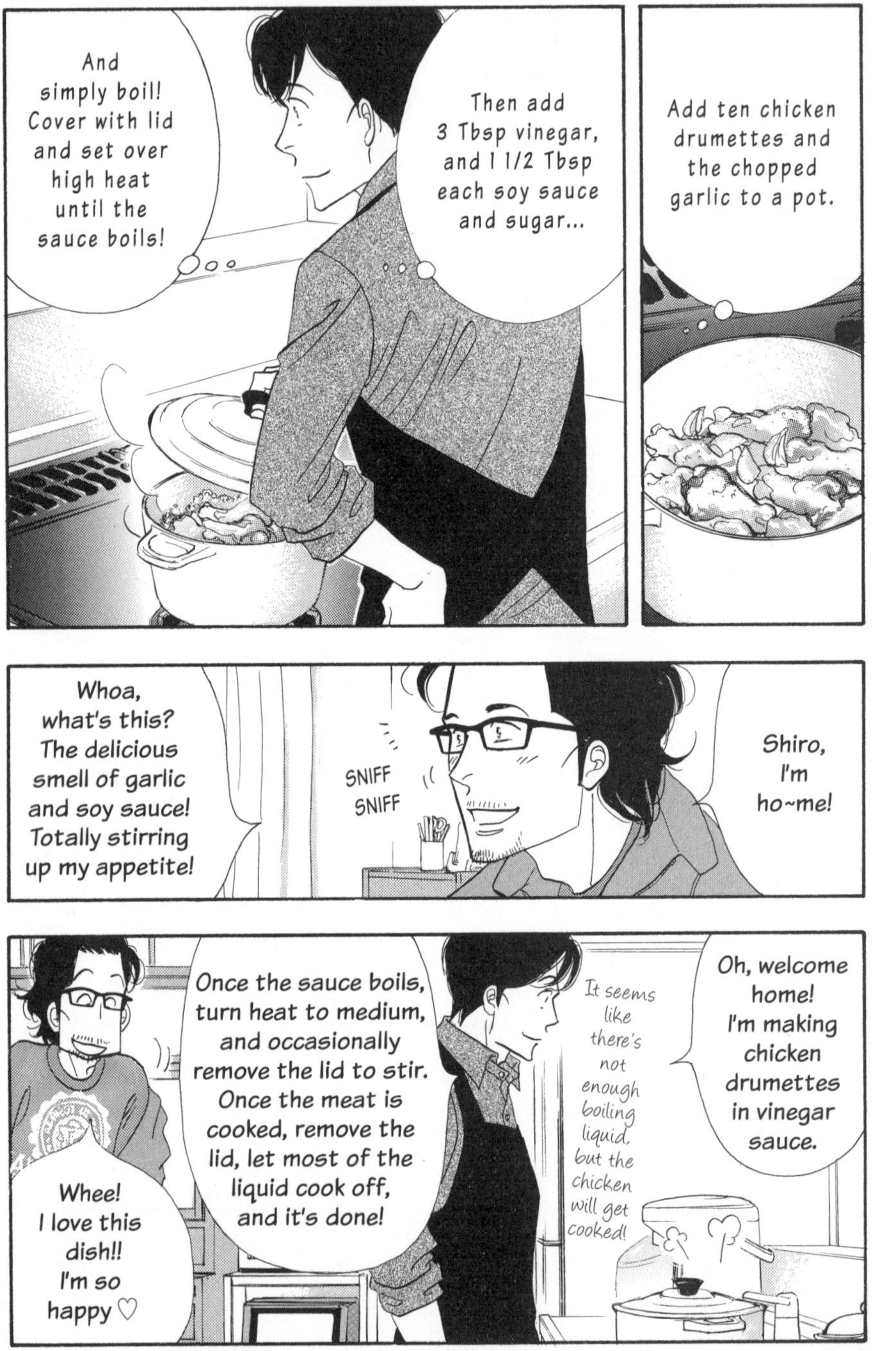
Add ten chicken drumettes and the chopped garlic to a pot.
Then add 3 Tbsp vinegar, and 1 1/2 Tbsp each soy sauce and sugar...
And simply boil! Cover with lid and set over high heat until the sauce boils!
Shiro, I'm ho~me!
SNIFF SNIFF
Whoa, what's this? The delicious smell of garlic and soy sauce! Totally stirring up my appetite!
Oh, welcome home! I'm making chicken drumettes in vinegar sauce.
It seems like there's not enough boiling liquid, but the chicken will get cooked!
Once the sauce boils, turn heat to medium, and occasionally remove the lid to stir. Once the meat is cooked, remove the lid, let most of the liquid cook off, and it's done!
Whee! I love this dish!! I'm so happy ♡

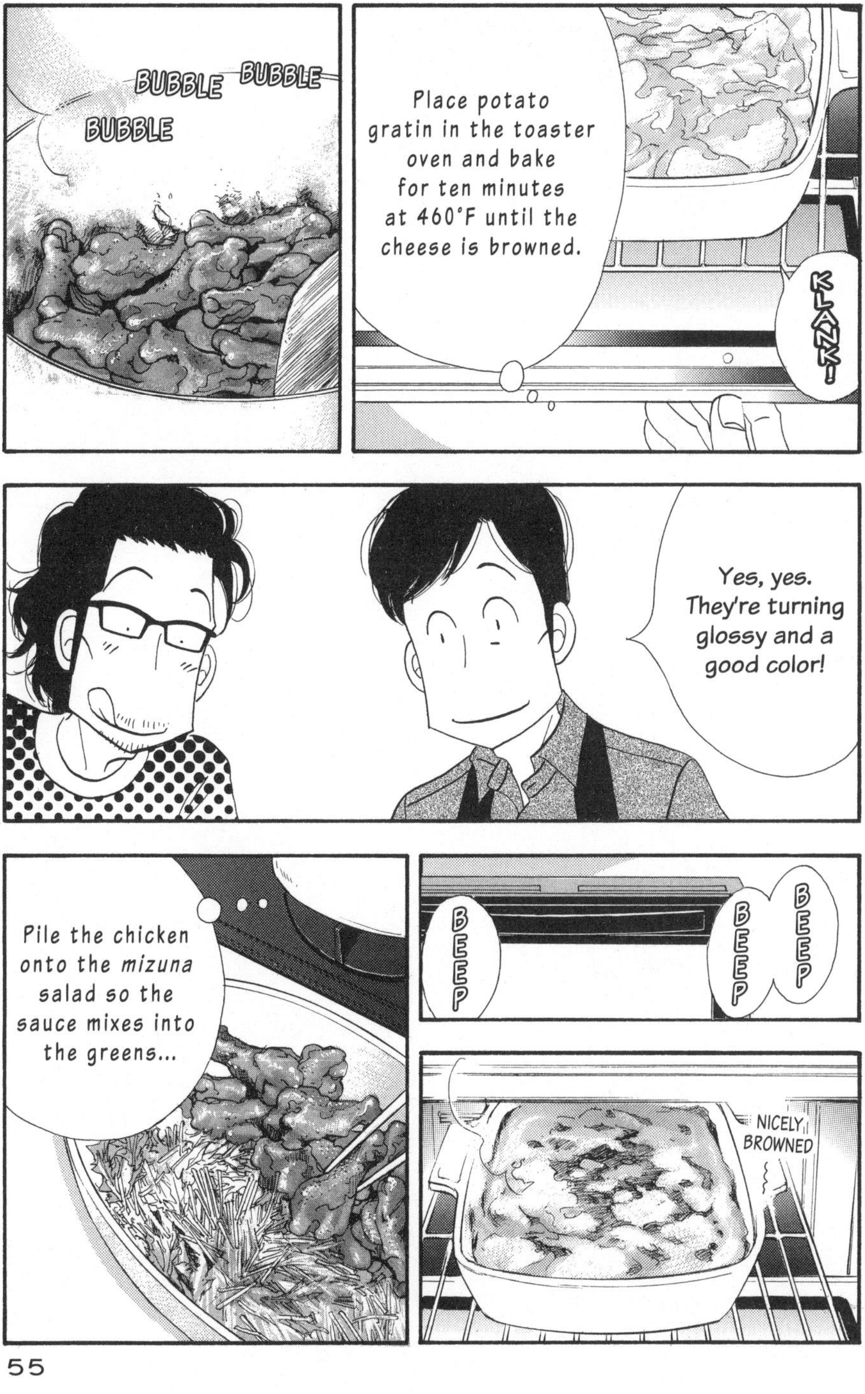
Place potato gratin in the toaster oven and bake for ten minutes at 460°F until the cheese is browned.
KLANK!
BUBBLE BUBBLE
BUBBLE
Yes, yes. They're turning glossy and a good color!
BEEP
BEEP
BEEP
NICELY BROWNED
Pile the chicken onto the *mizuna* salad so the sauce mixes into the greens...

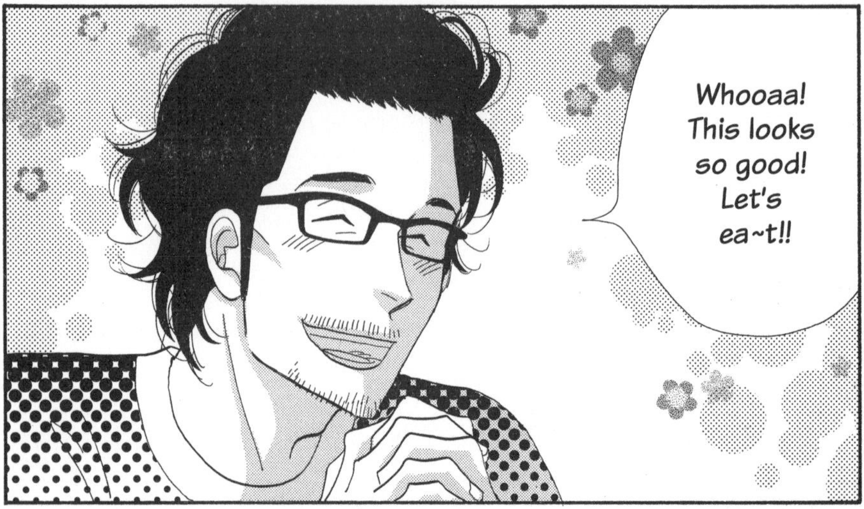
Whooaa! This looks so good! Let's ea~t!!

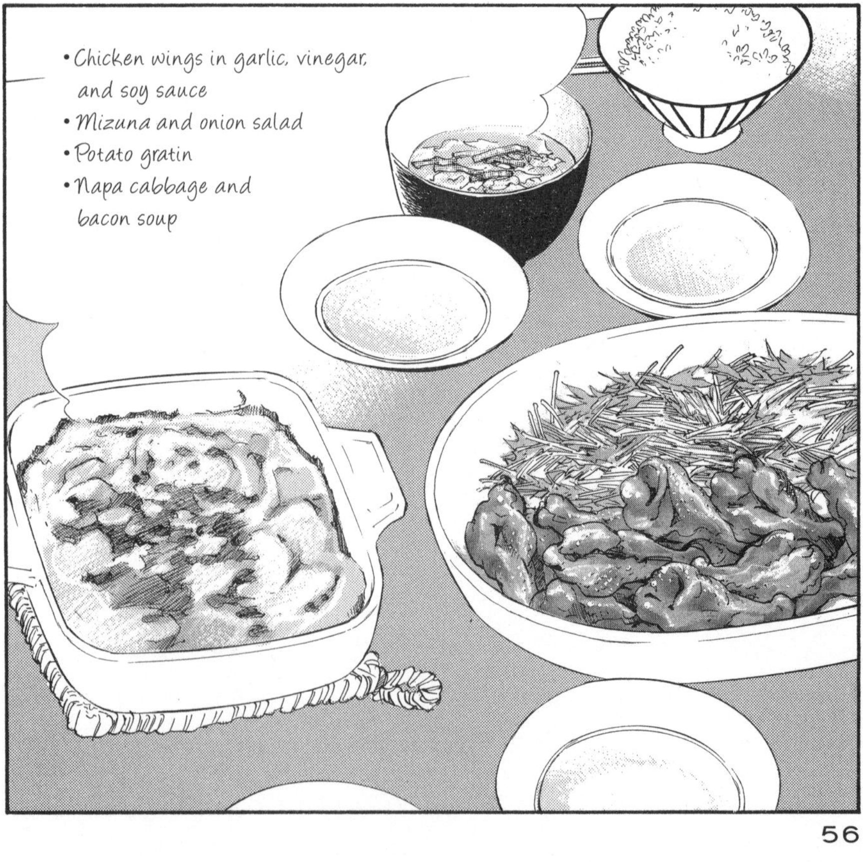
•Chicken wings in garlic, vinegar, and soy sauce
•Mizuna and onion salad
•Potato gratin
•Napa cabbage and bacon soup

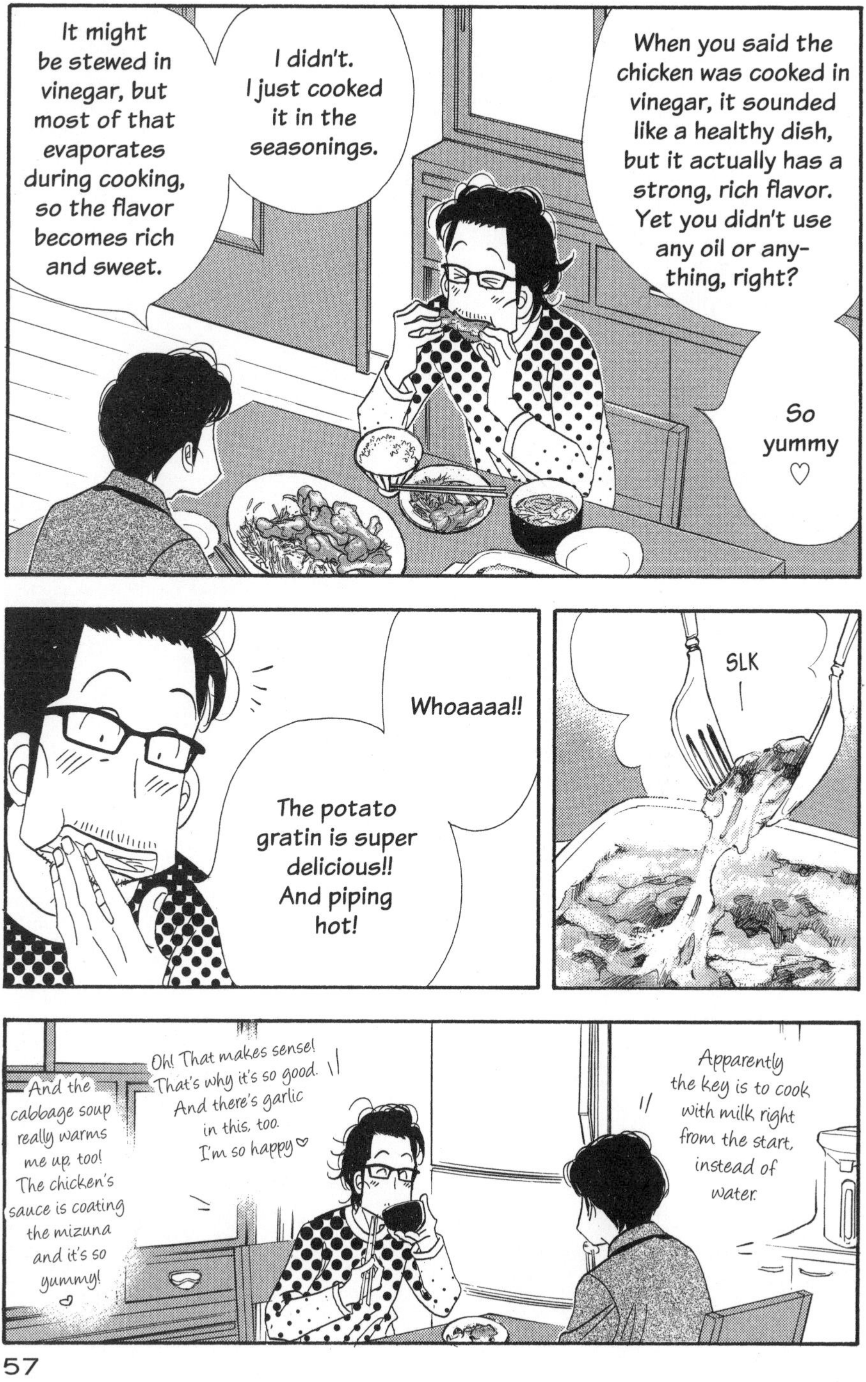
When you said the chicken was cooked in vinegar, it sounded like a healthy dish, but it actually has a strong, rich flavor. Yet you didn't use any oil or any-thing, right?
I didn't. I just cooked it in the seasonings.
It might be stewed in vinegar, but most of that evaporates during cooking, so the flavor becomes rich and sweet.
So yummy ♡
SLK
Whoaaaa!!
The potato gratin is super delicious!! And piping hot!
Apparently the key is to cook with milk right from the start, instead of water.
Oh! That makes sense! That's why it's so good. And there's garlic in this, too. I'm so happy ♡
And the cabbage soup really warms me up, too! The chicken's sauce is coating the mizuna and it's so yummy! ♡

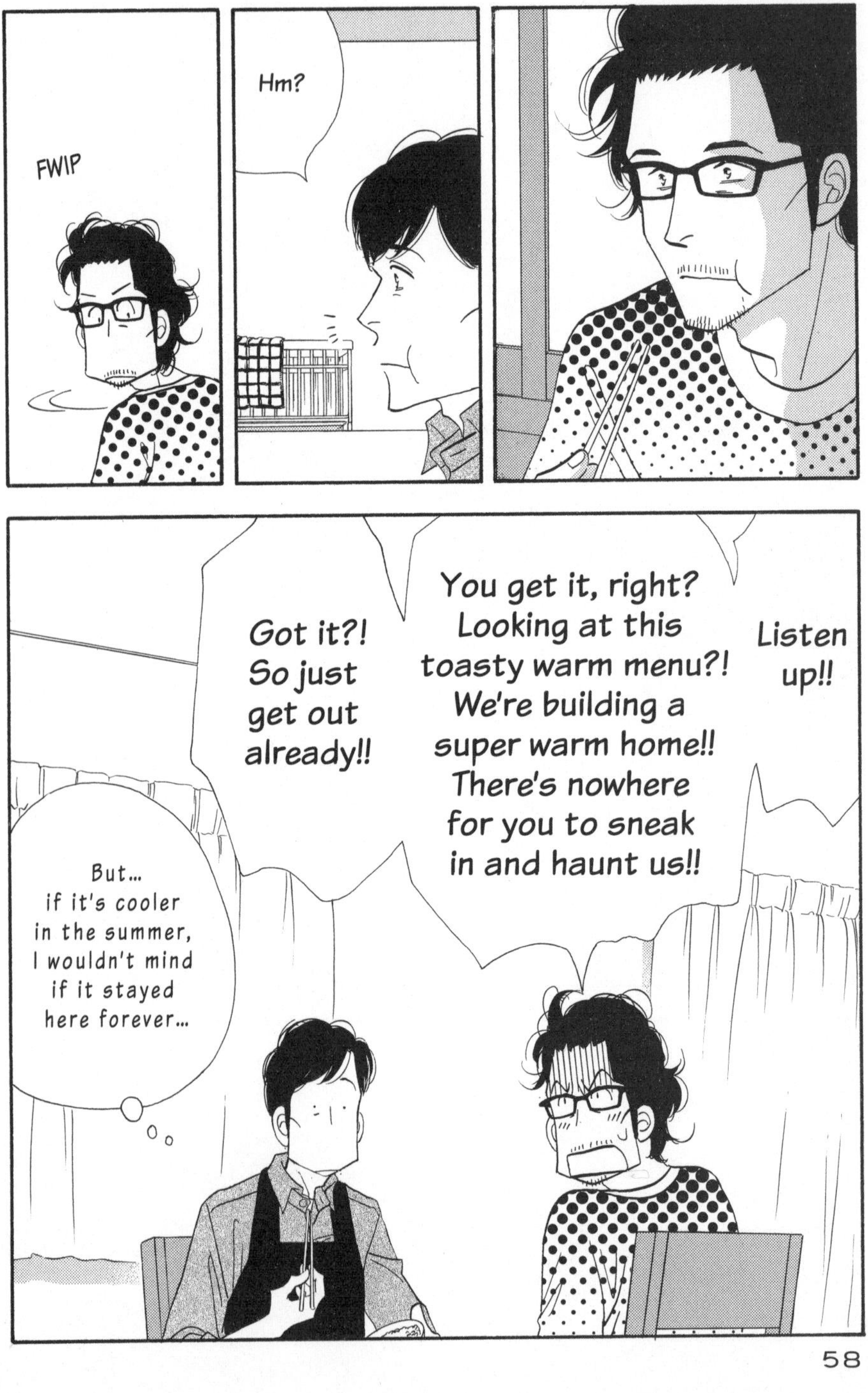
Hm?
FWIP
Listen up!!
You get it, right? Looking at this toasty warm menu?! We're building a super warm home!! There's nowhere for you to sneak in and haunt us!!
Got it?! So just get out already!!
But... if it's cooler in the summer, I wouldn't mind if it stayed here forever...

For the **potato gratin**, if you pour in a light 1/2 C of fresh cream before you add the cheese, the flavor is even richer.

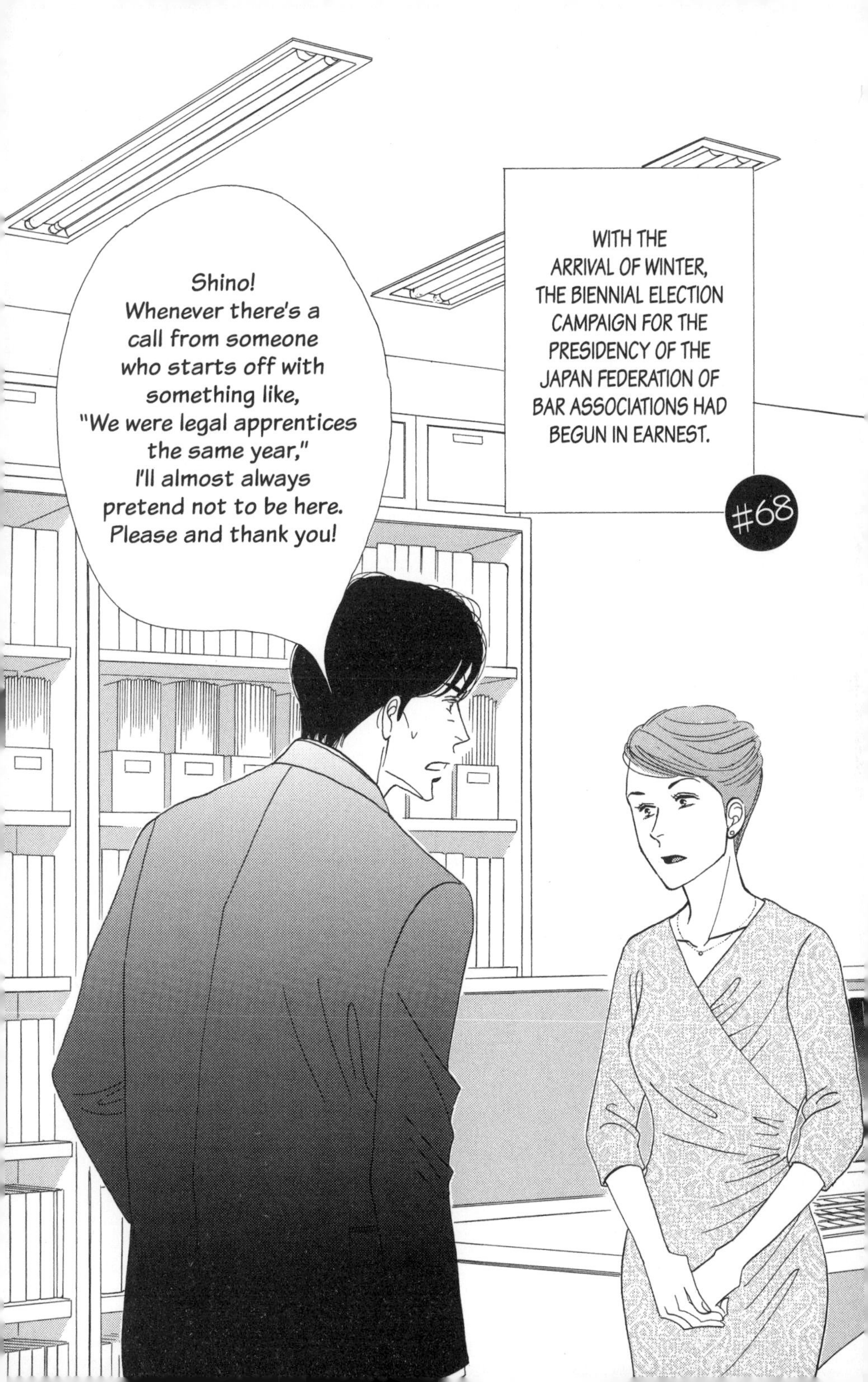
WITH THE ARRIVAL OF WINTER, THE BIENNIAL ELECTION CAMPAIGN FOR THE PRESIDENCY OF THE JAPAN FEDERATION OF BAR ASSOCIATIONS HAD BEGUN IN EARNEST.
#68
Shino! Whenever there's a call from someone who starts off with something like, "We were legal apprentices the same year," I'll almost always pretend not to be here. Please and thank you!

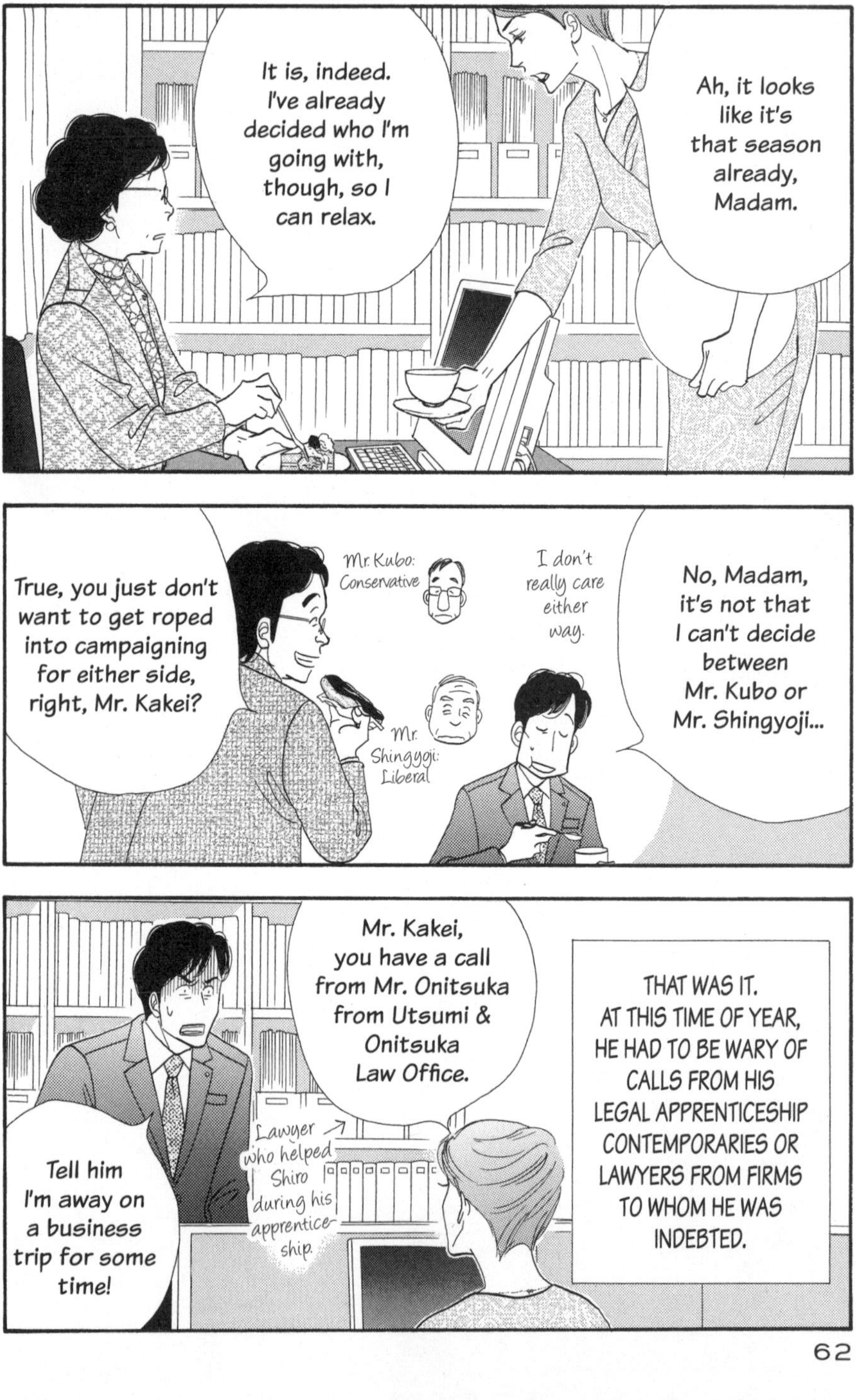
Ah, it looks like it's that season already, Madam.
It is, indeed. I've already decided who I'm going with, though, so I can relax.
No, Madam, it's not that I can't decide between Mr. Kubo or Mr. Shingyoji...
I don't really care either way.
Mr. Kubo: Conservative
Mr. Shingyoji: Liberal
True, you just don't want to get roped into campaigning for either side, right, Mr. Kakei?
THAT WAS IT. AT THIS TIME OF YEAR, HE HAD TO BE WARY OF CALLS FROM HIS LEGAL APPRENTICESHIP CONTEMPORARIES OR LAWYERS FROM FIRMS TO WHOM HE WAS INDEBTED.
Mr. Kakei, you have a call from Mr. Onitsuka from Utsumi & Onitsuka Law Office.
Lawyer who helped Shiro during his apprenticeship.
Tell him I'm away on a business trip for some time!

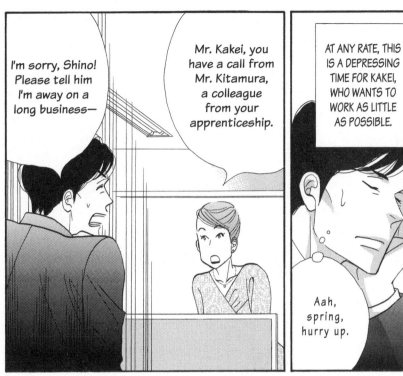

AT ANY RATE, THIS IS A DEPRESSING TIME FOR KAKEI, WHO WANTS TO WORK AS LITTLE AS POSSIBLE.
Aah, spring, hurry up.
Mr. Kakei, you have a call from Mr. Kitamura, a colleague from your apprenticeship.
I'm sorry, Shino! Please tell him I'm away on a long business—
Hm?
Kitamura?
MAKOTO KITAMURA.
HE AIMED FOR THE BAR EXAM WHILE WORKING AT A FOOD COMPANY, FINALLY PASSING AFTER 14 YEARS. HE WAS THE ELDEST AMONGST THAT CLASS OF APPRENTICES.

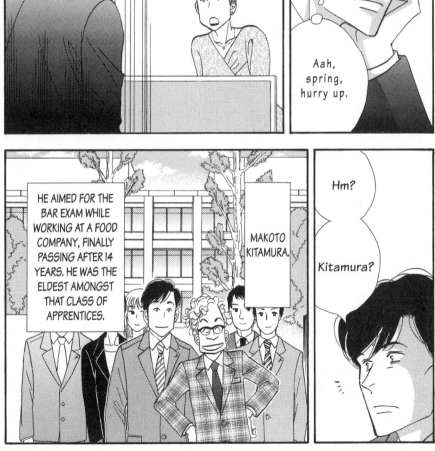

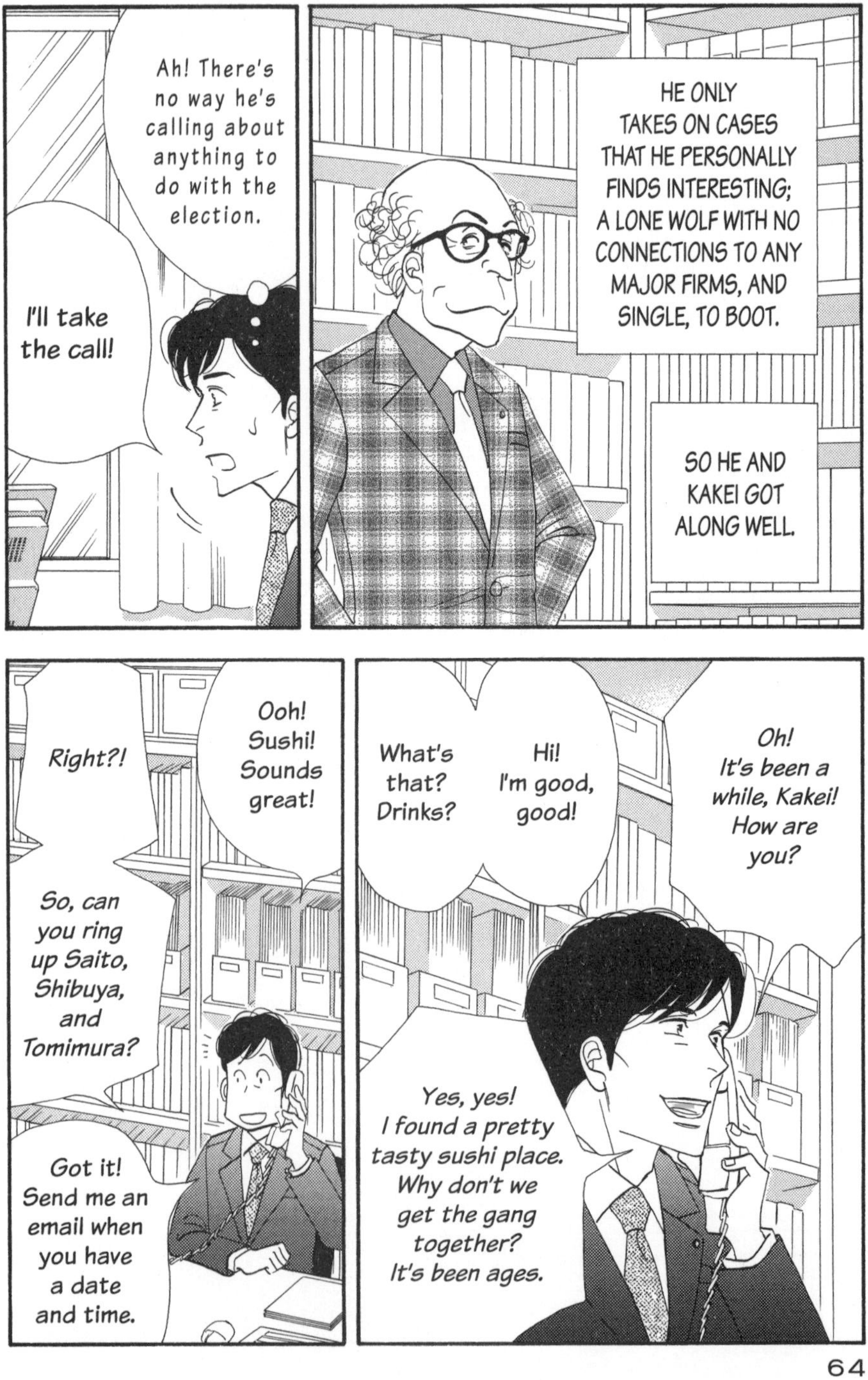
HE ONLY TAKES ON CASES THAT HE PERSONALLY FINDS INTERESTING; A LONE WOLF WITH NO CONNECTIONS TO ANY MAJOR FIRMS, AND SINGLE, TO BOOT.
SO HE AND KAKEI GOT ALONG WELL.
Ah! There's no way he's calling about anything to do with the election.
I'll take the call!
Oh! It's been a while, Kakei! How are you?
Hi! I'm good, good!
What's that? Drinks?
Yes, yes! I found a pretty tasty sushi place. Why don't we get the gang together? It's been ages.
Ooh! Sushi! Sounds great!
Right?!
So, can you ring up Saito, Shibuya, and Tomimura?
Got it! Send me an email when you have a date and time.

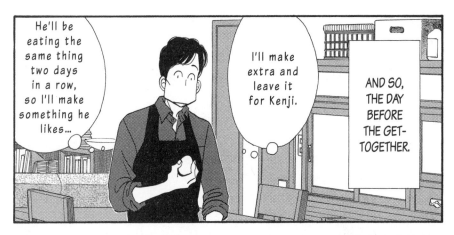

AND SO, THE DAY BEFORE THE GET-TOGETHER.
I'll make extra and leave it for Kenji.
He'll be eating the same thing two days in a row, so I'll make something he likes...
Place an egg in lightly-salted water. Bring water to a boil, boiling egg for twelve minutes or until hard-boiled.
BOMF
Thinly slice half an onion along the grain, sprinkle with salt, and stir.
WHUK!
WHUK!
WHUK!
Roughly chop a quarter of a *kabocha*, place in a heat-resistant bowl with a little water and salt, cover with plastic wrap, and microwave for six to seven minutes.

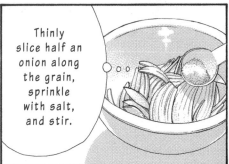

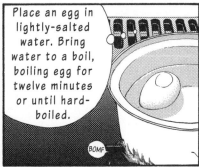

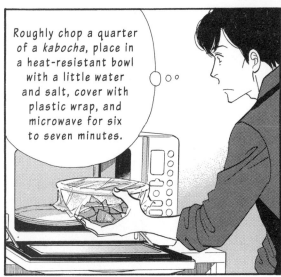

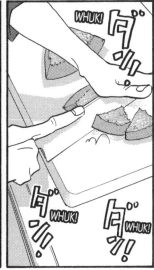

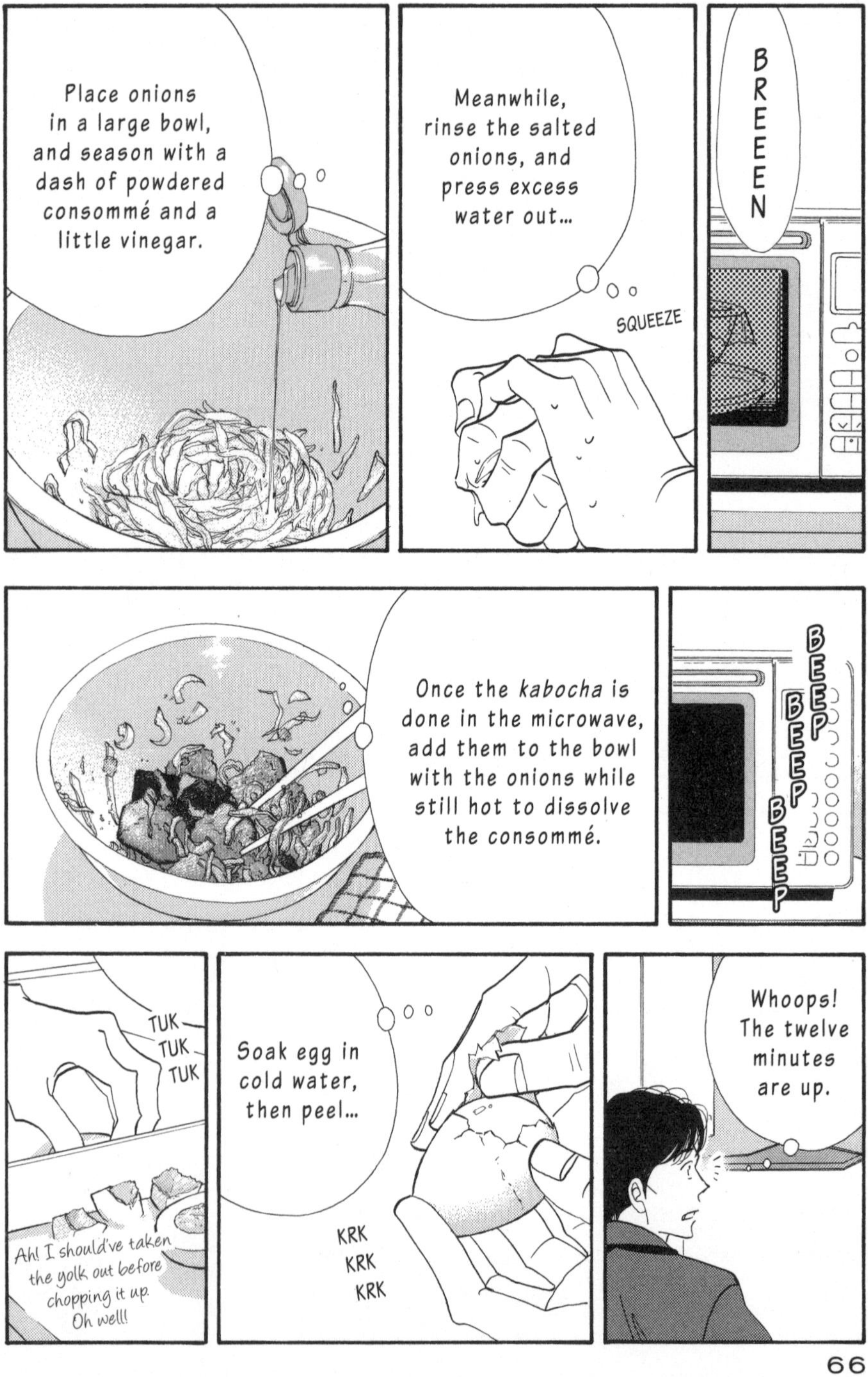
BREEEN
Meanwhile, rinse the salted onions, and press excess water out...
SQUEEZE
Place onions in a large bowl, and season with a dash of powdered consommé and a little vinegar.
BEEP BEEP BEEP
Once the *kabocha* is done in the microwave, add them to the bowl with the onions while still hot to dissolve the consommé.
Whoops! The twelve minutes are up.
Soak egg in cold water, then peel...
KRK KRK KRK
TUK TUK TUK
Ah! I should've taken the yolk out before chopping it up. Oh well!

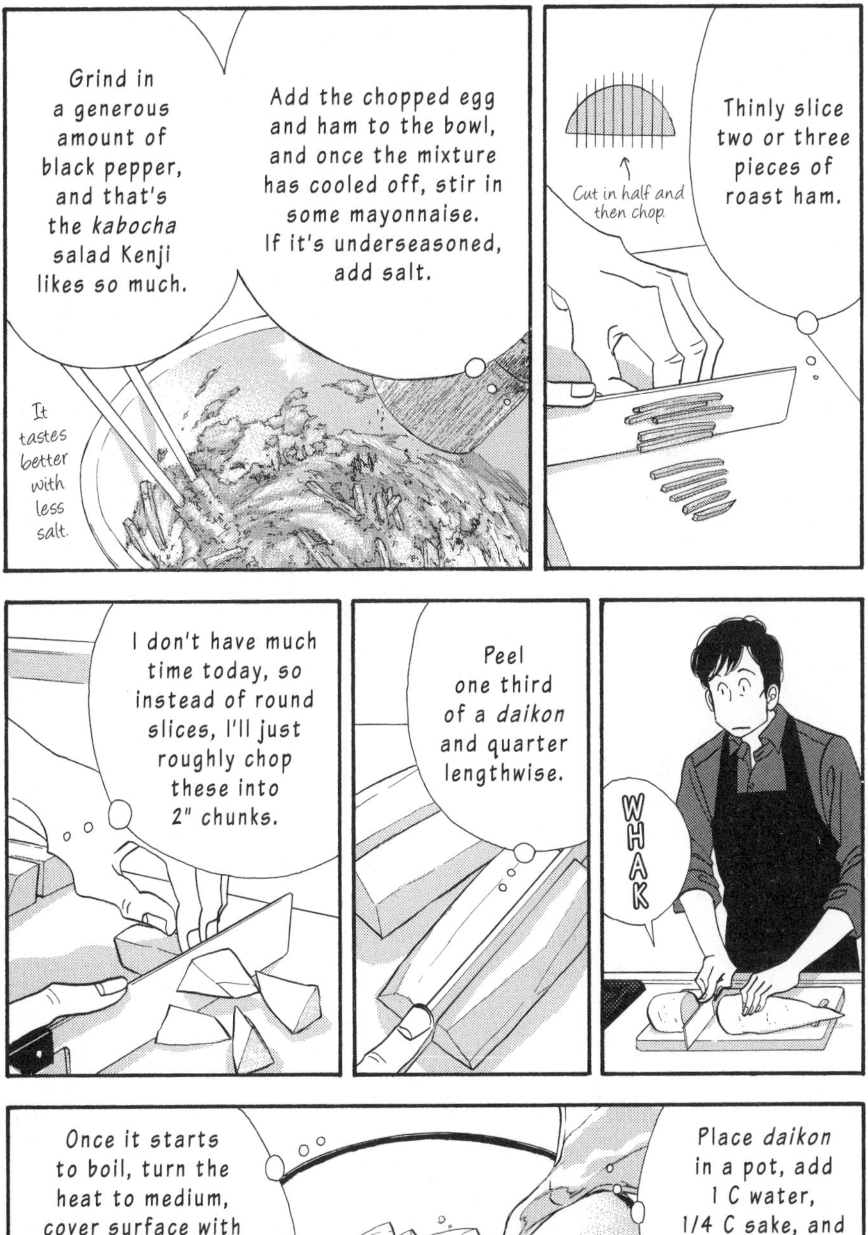

Thinly slice two or three pieces of roast ham.
Cut in half and then chop.
Add the chopped egg and ham to the bowl, and once the mixture has cooled off, stir in some mayonnaise. If it's underseasoned, add salt.
Grind in a generous amount of black pepper, and that's the *kabocha* salad Kenji likes so much.
It tastes better with less salt.
WHAK
Peel one third of a *daikon* and quarter lengthwise.
I don't have much time today, so instead of round slices, I'll just roughly chop these into 2" chunks.
Place *daikon* in a pot, add 1 C water, 1/4 C sake, and 1 Tbsp sugar, and place over heat.
Once it starts to boil, turn the heat to medium, cover surface with aluminum foil or a drop lid, and simmer for ten minutes.

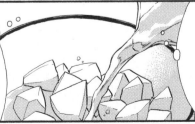

While that cooks, I'll make the miso soup.
Roughly chop 1 large bunch of komatsuna spinach.
Bring water to a boil, add komatsuna with half a sheet of thin fried tofu that's been finely sliced.
BURBLE BURBLE
Briefly boil, add some dashi, dissolve miso paste into the broth, and it's done.
SPLK
For two squid, grasp the base of the tentacles with your fingers, and pull out, taking care to avoid rupturing the intestines...
YANK
Cut below the eyes, remove the beak in the center, then strip off the suckers.
Remove the cartilage and cut the body into 1" rings, then cut the tentacles into groups of two or three.
Then place squid into the pot with the daikon.

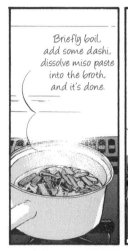

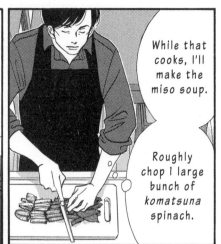

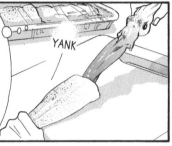

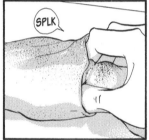

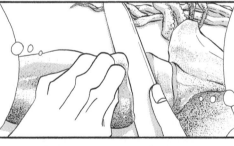

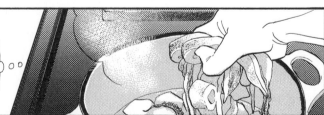

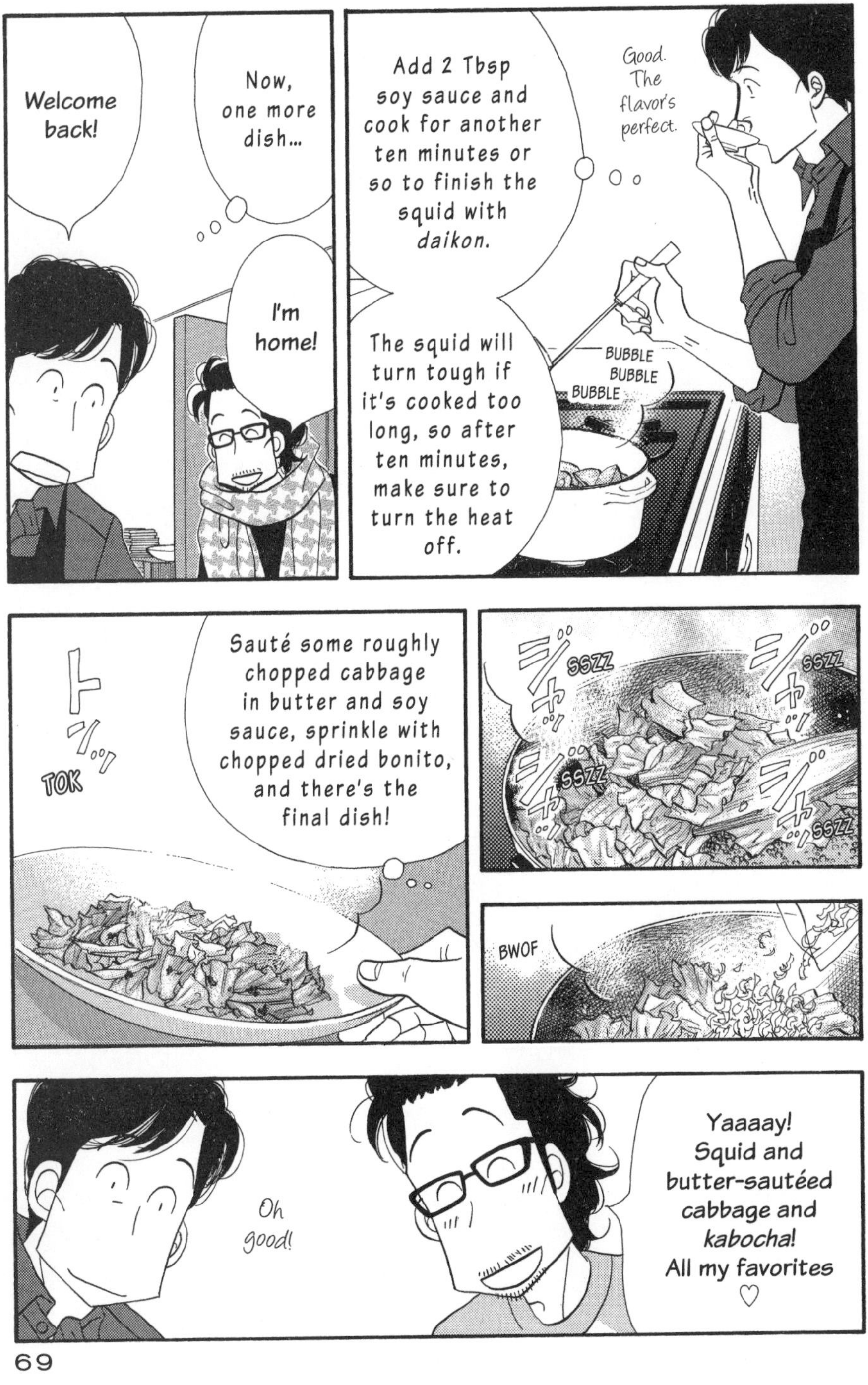
Good. The flavor's perfect.
Add 2 Tbsp soy sauce and cook for another ten minutes or so to finish the squid with *daikon*.
The squid will turn tough if it's cooked too long, so after ten minutes, make sure to turn the heat off.
BUBBLE BUBBLE BUBBLE
Now, one more dish...
Welcome back!
I'm home!
SSZZ
SSZZ
SSZZ
SSZZ
BWOF
Sauté some roughly chopped cabbage in butter and soy sauce, sprinkle with chopped dried bonito, and there's the final dish!
TOK
Yaaaay! Squid and butter-sautéed cabbage and *kabocha*! All my favorites ♡
Oh good!

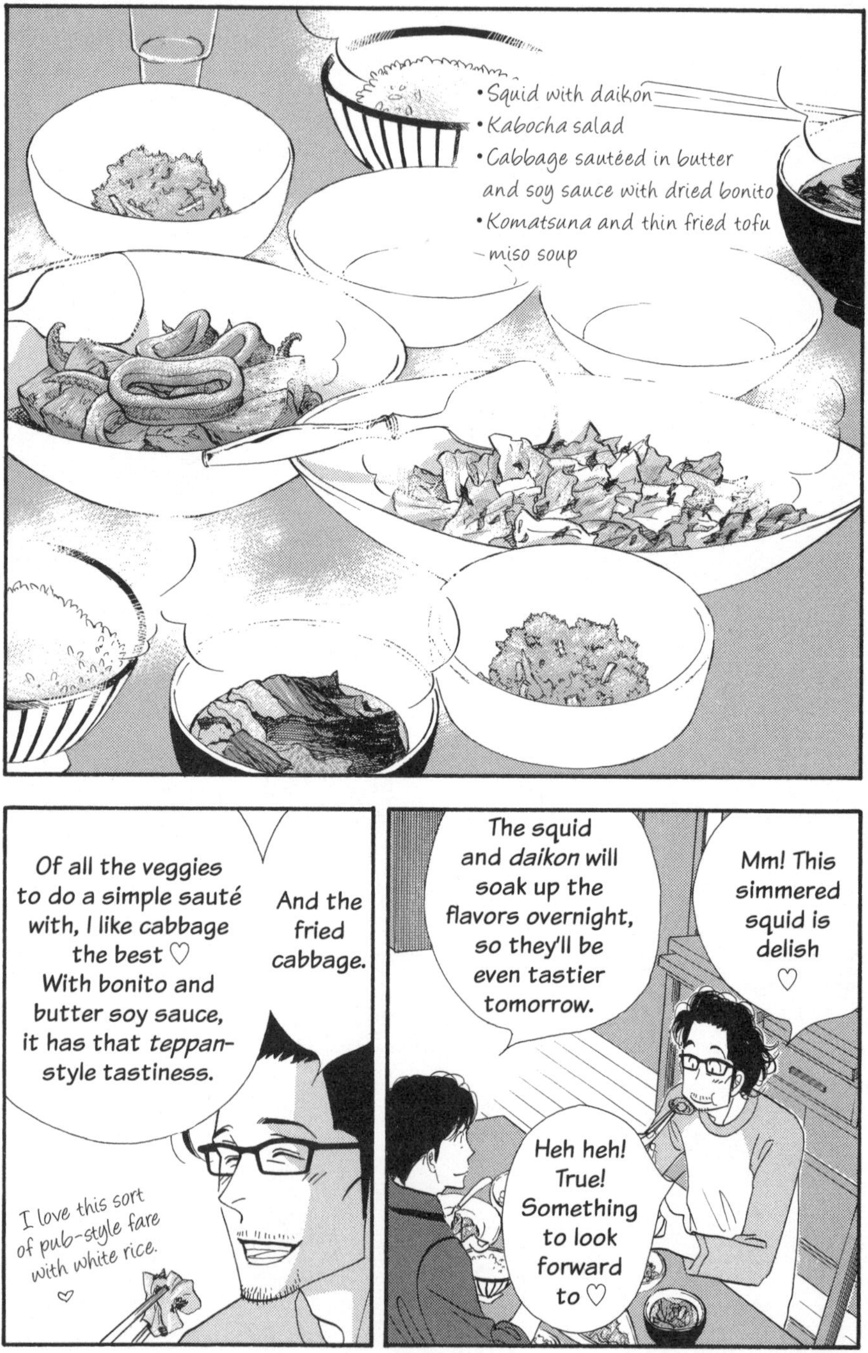
•Squid with daikon
•Kabocha salad
•Cabbage sautéed in butter and soy sauce with dried bonito
•Komatsuna and thin fried tofu miso soup
Mm! This simmered squid is delish ♡
The squid and daikon will soak up the flavors overnight, so they'll be even tastier tomorrow.
Heh heh! True! Something to look forward to ♡
And the fried cabbage.
Of all the veggies to do a simple sauté with, I like cabbage the best ♡ With bonito and butter soy sauce, it has that teppan-style tastiness.
I love this sort of pub-style fare with white rice. ♡

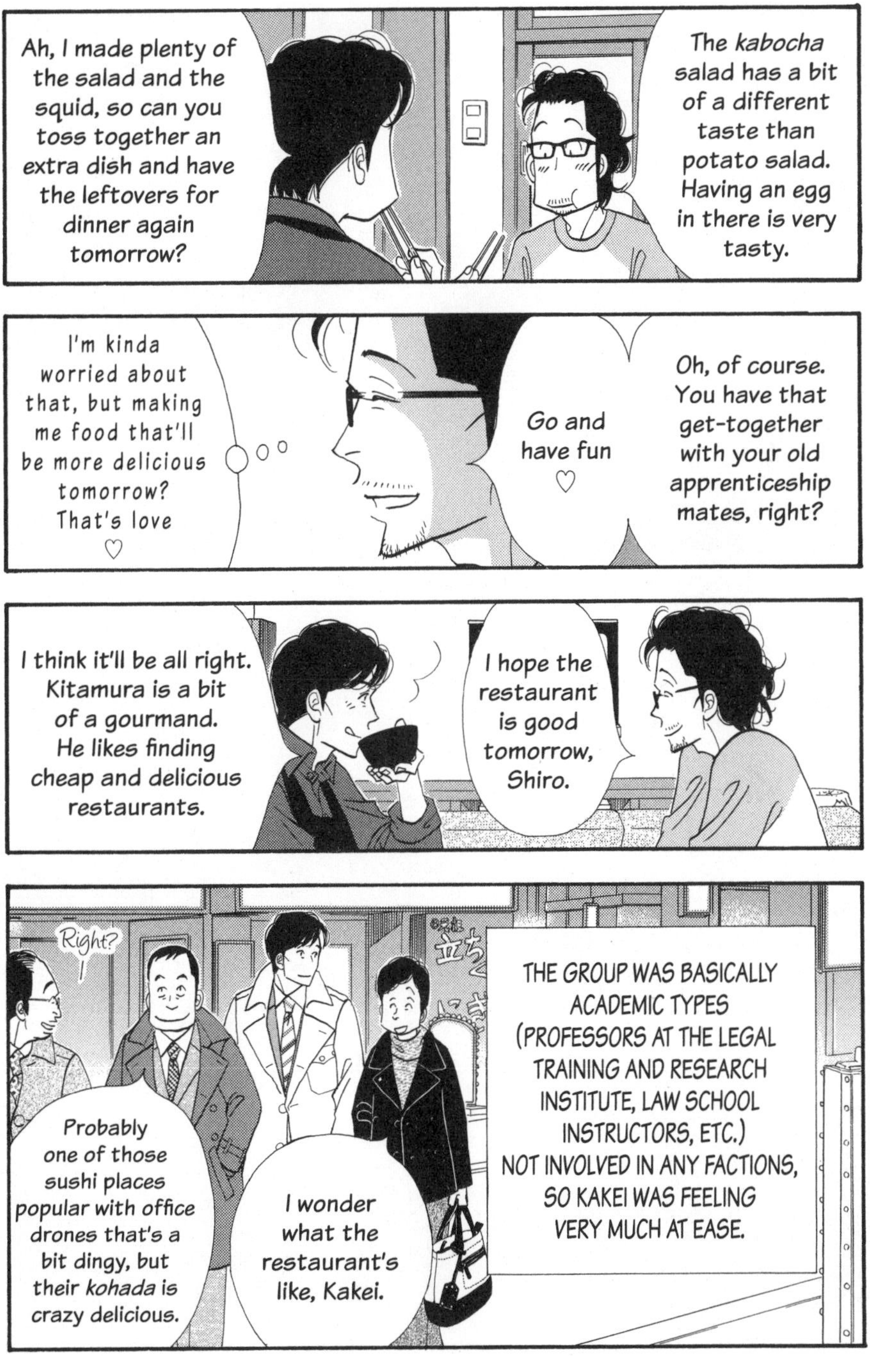
The *kabocha* salad has a bit of a different taste than potato salad. Having an egg in there is very tasty.
Ah, I made plenty of the salad and the squid, so can you toss together an extra dish and have the leftovers for dinner again tomorrow?
Oh, of course. You have that get-together with your old apprenticeship mates, right?
Go and have fun ♡
I'm kinda worried about that, but making me food that'll be more delicious tomorrow? That's love ♡
I hope the restaurant is good tomorrow, Shiro.
I think it'll be all right. Kitamura is a bit of a gourmand. He likes finding cheap and delicious restaurants.
THE GROUP WAS BASICALLY ACADEMIC TYPES (PROFESSORS AT THE LEGAL TRAINING AND RESEARCH INSTITUTE, LAW SCHOOL INSTRUCTORS, ETC.) NOT INVOLVED IN ANY FACTIONS, SO KAKEI WAS FEELING VERY MUCH AT EASE.
I wonder what the restaurant's like, Kakei.
Probably one of those sushi places popular with office drones that's a bit dingy, but their *kohada* is crazy delicious.
Right?!

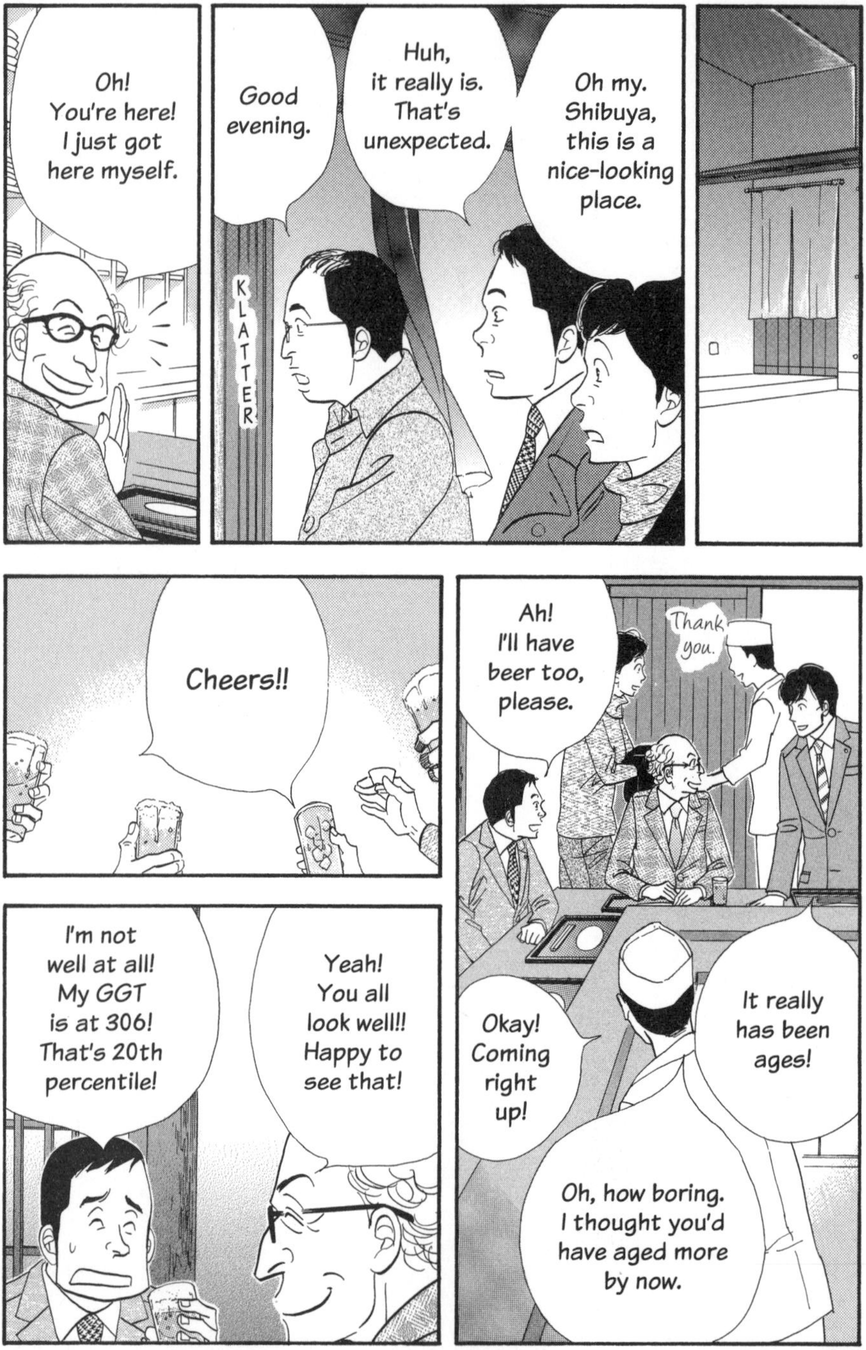
Oh my. Shibuya, this is a nice-looking place.
Huh, it really is. That's unexpected.
Good evening.
KLATTER
Oh! You're here! I just got here myself.
Thank you.
Ah! I'll have beer too, please.
It really has been ages!
Okay! Coming right up!
Oh, how boring. I thought you'd have aged more by now.
Cheers!!
Yeah! You all look well!! Happy to see that!
I'm not well at all! My GGT is at 306! That's 20th percentile!

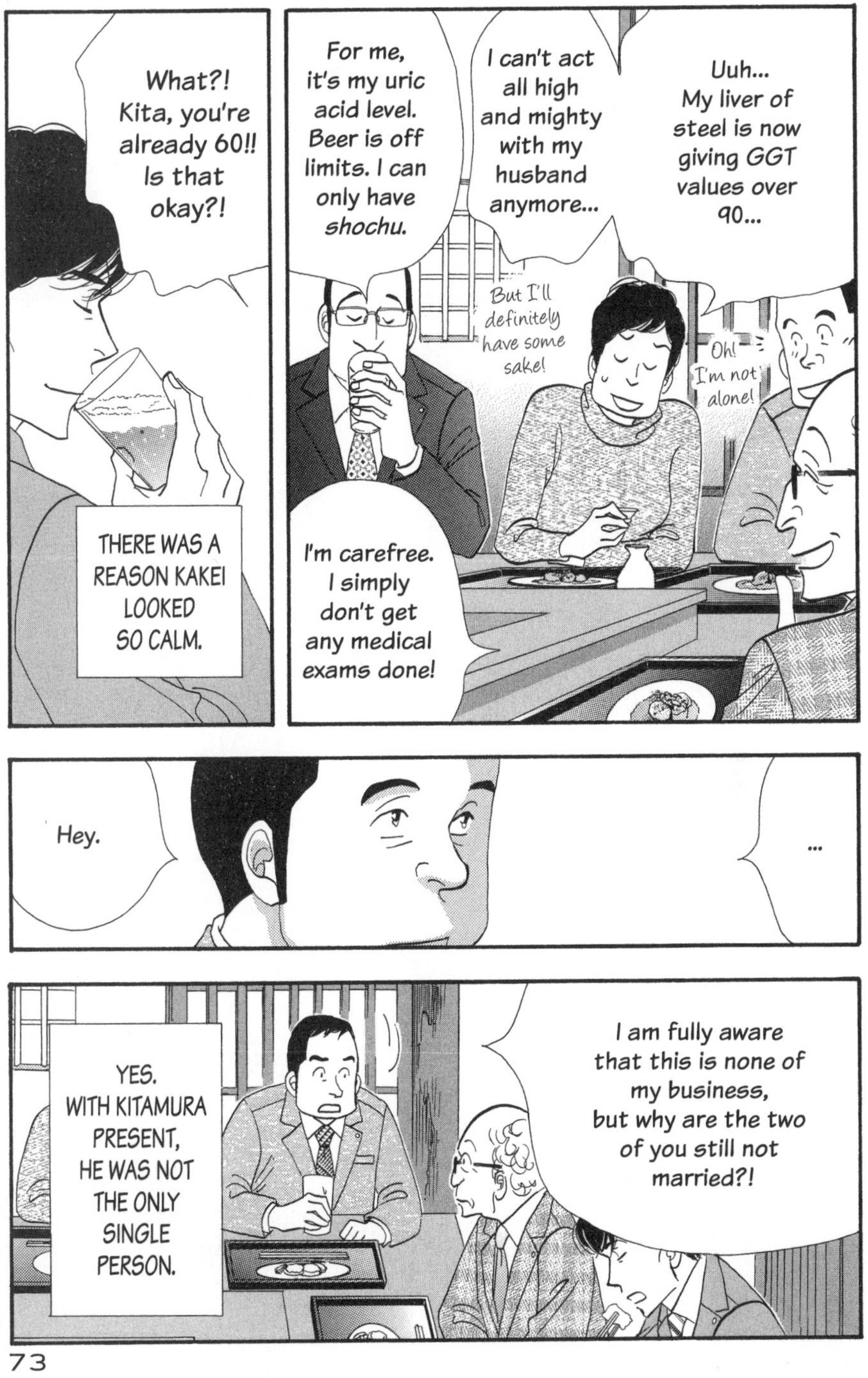
Uuh... My liver of steel is now giving GGT values over 90...
Oh! I'm not alone!
I can't act all high and mighty with my husband anymore...
But I'll definitely have some sake!
For me, it's my uric acid level. Beer is off limits. I can only have shochu.
I'm carefree. I simply don't get any medical exams done!
What?! Kita, you're already 60!! Is that okay?!
THERE WAS A REASON KAKEI LOOKED SO CALM.
...
Hey.
I am fully aware that this is none of my business, but why are the two of you still not married?!
YES. WITH KITAMURA PRESENT, HE WAS NOT THE ONLY SINGLE PERSON.

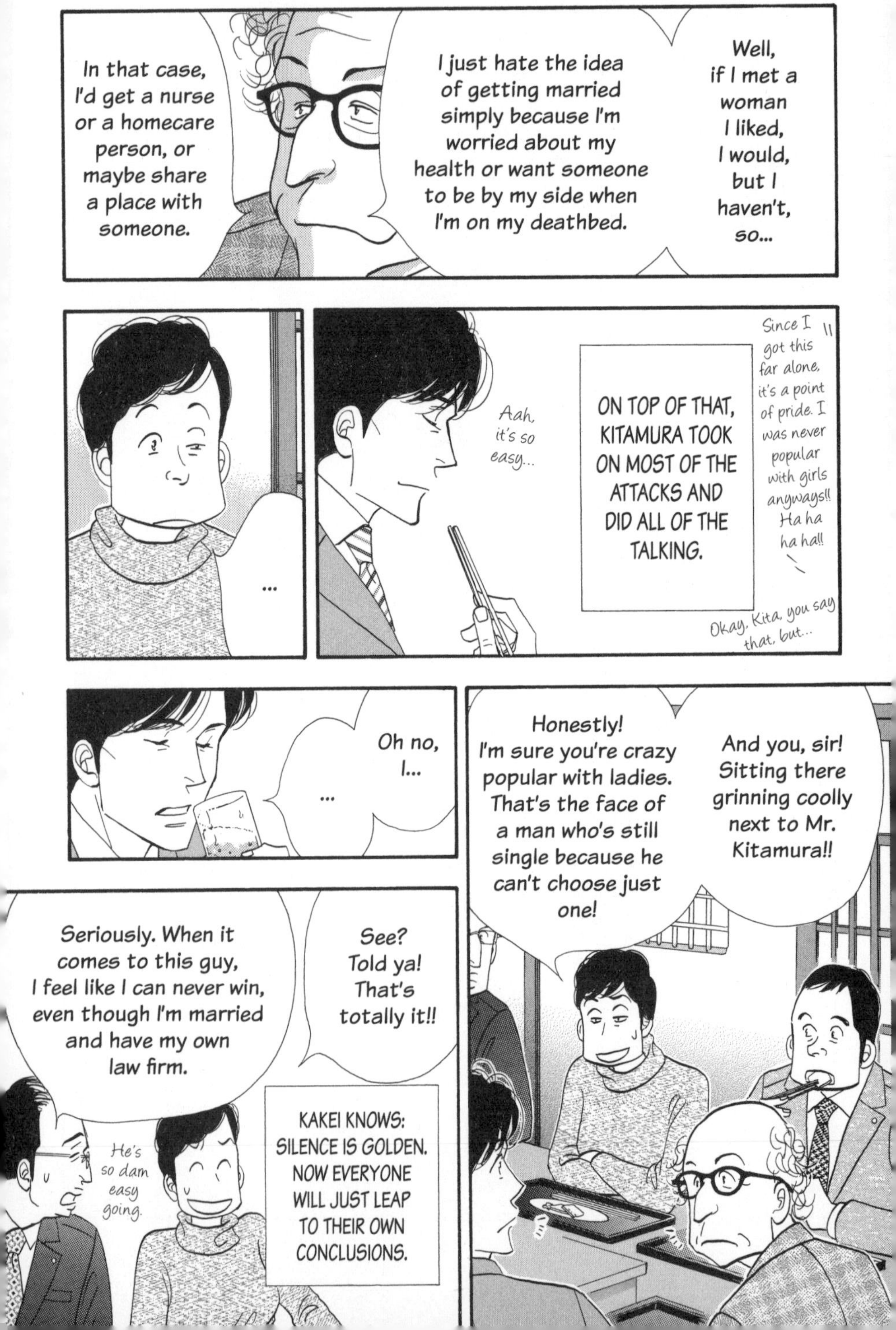
Well, if I met a woman I liked, I would, but I haven't, so...
I just hate the idea of getting married simply because I'm worried about my health or want someone to be by my side when I'm on my deathbed.
In that case, I'd get a nurse or a homecare person, or maybe share a place with someone.
Since I got this far alone, it's a point of pride. I was never popular with girls anyways!! Ha ha ha ha!!
ON TOP OF THAT, KITAMURA TOOK ON MOST OF THE ATTACKS AND DID ALL OF THE TALKING.
Aah, it's so easy...
Okay, Kita, you say that, but...
...
And you, sir! Sitting there grinning coolly next to Mr. Kitamura!!
Honestly! I'm sure you're crazy popular with ladies. That's the face of a man who's still single because he can't choose just one!
Oh no, I...
...
See? Told ya! That's totally it!!
Seriously. When it comes to this guy, I feel like I can never win, even though I'm married and have my own law firm.
KAKEI KNOWS: SILENCE IS GOLDEN. NOW EVERYONE WILL JUST LEAP TO THEIR OWN CONCLUSIONS.
He's so dam easy going.

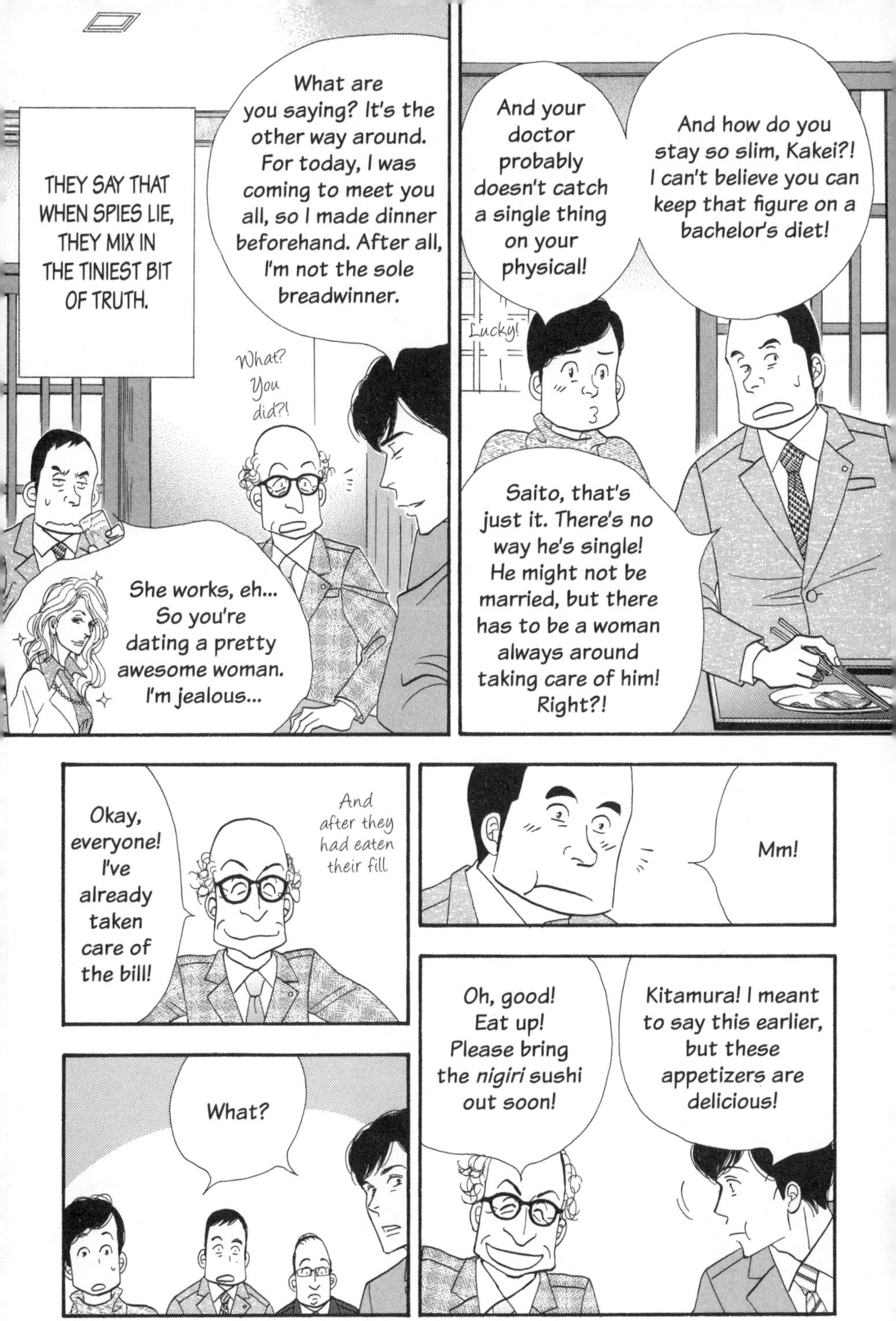
And how do you stay so slim, Kakei?! I can't believe you can keep that figure on a bachelor's diet!
And your doctor probably doesn't catch a single thing on your physical!
Lucky!
Saito, that's just it. There's no way he's single! He might not be married, but there has to be a woman always around taking care of him! Right?!
What are you saying? It's the other way around. For today, I was coming to meet you all, so I made dinner beforehand. After all, I'm not the sole breadwinner.
THEY SAY THAT WHEN SPIES LIE, THEY MIX IN THE TINIEST BIT OF TRUTH.
What? You did?!
She works, eh... So you're dating a pretty awesome woman. I'm jealous...
Mm!
And after they had eaten their fill
Okay, everyone! I've already taken care of the bill!
Kitamura! I meant to say this earlier, but these appetizers are delicious!
Oh, good! Eat up! Please bring the *nigiri* sushi out soon!
What?

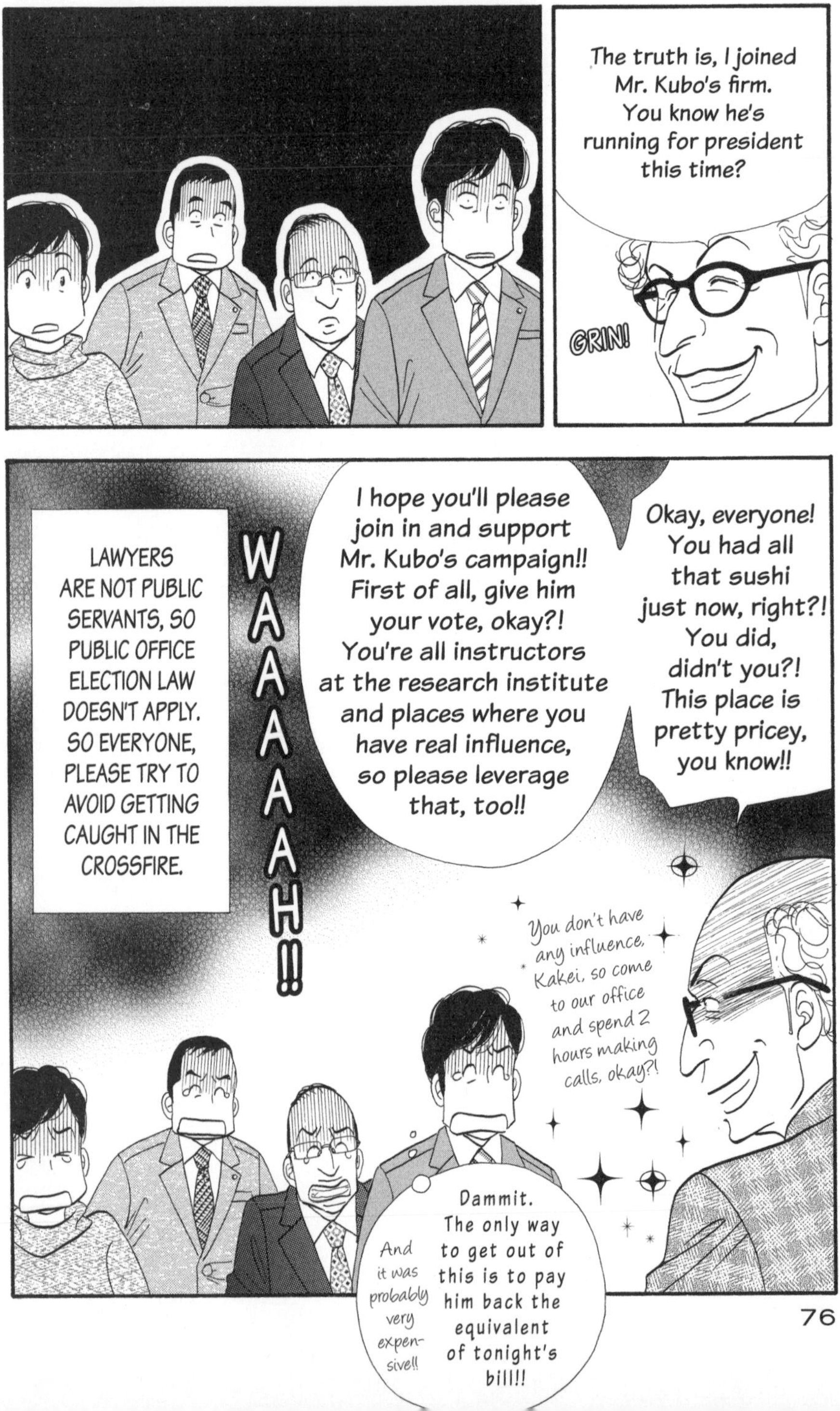
The truth is, I joined Mr. Kubo's firm. You know he's running for president this time?
GRIN!
Okay, everyone! You had all that sushi just now, right?! You did, didn't you?! This place is pretty pricey, you know!!
I hope you'll please join in and support Mr. Kubo's campaign!! First of all, give him your vote, okay?! You're all instructors at the research institute and places where you have real influence, so please leverage that, too!!
WAAAAAAH!!
LAWYERS ARE NOT PUBLIC SERVANTS, SO PUBLIC OFFICE ELECTION LAW DOESN'T APPLY. SO EVERYONE, PLEASE TRY TO AVOID GETTING CAUGHT IN THE CROSSFIRE.
You don't have any influence, Kakei, so come to our office and spend 2 hours making calls, okay?!
Dammit. The only way to get out of this is to pay him back the equivalent of tonight's bill!!
And it was probably very expen-sive!!

Everything is tasty with **fried cabbage**:
salt, pepper, and butter flavor;
consommé powder and pepper flavor;
bonito sauce with butter...

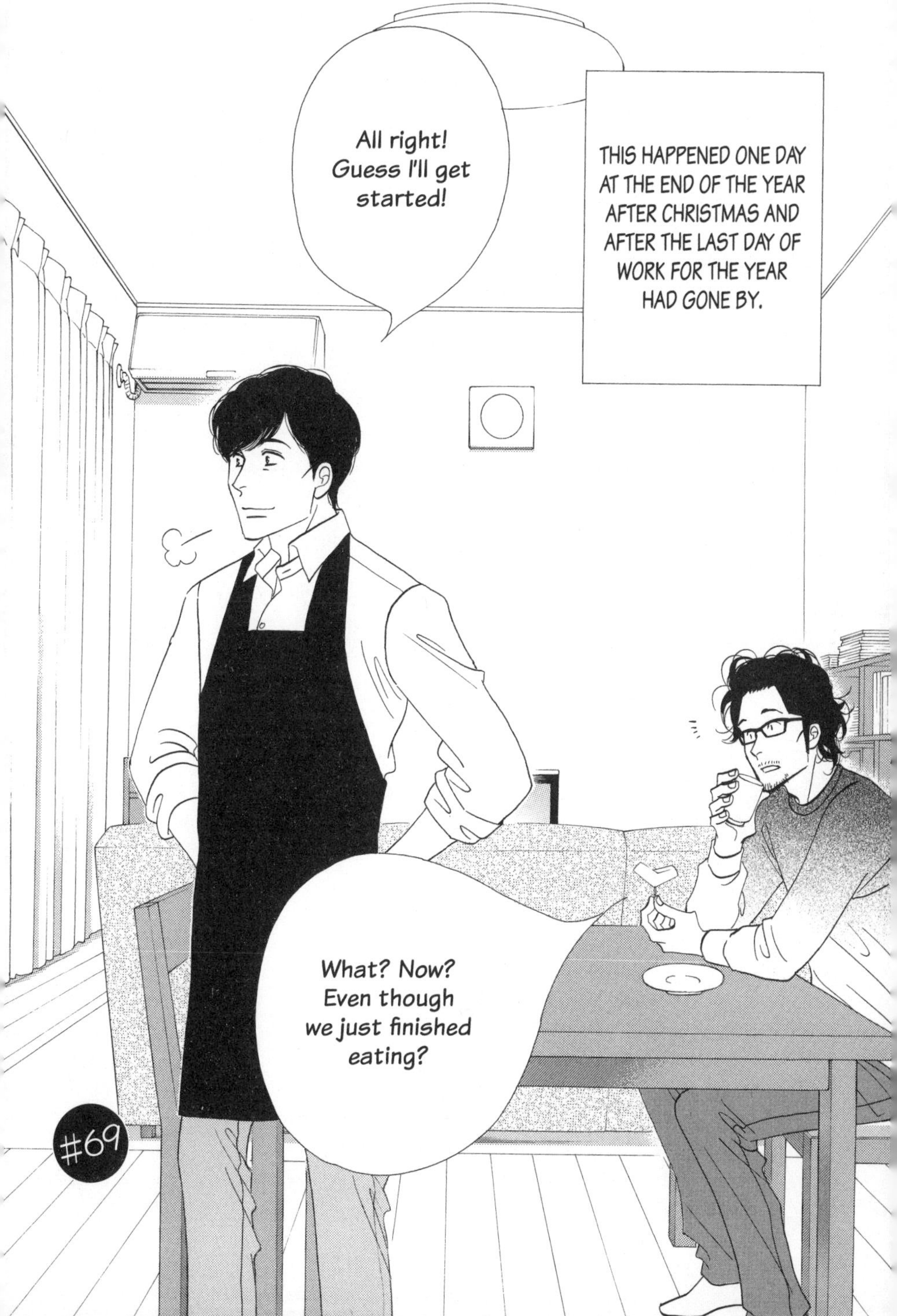
THIS HAPPENED ONE DAY AT THE END OF THE YEAR AFTER CHRISTMAS AND AFTER THE LAST DAY OF WORK FOR THE YEAR HAD GONE BY.
All right! Guess I'll get started!
What? Now? Even though we just finished eating?
#69

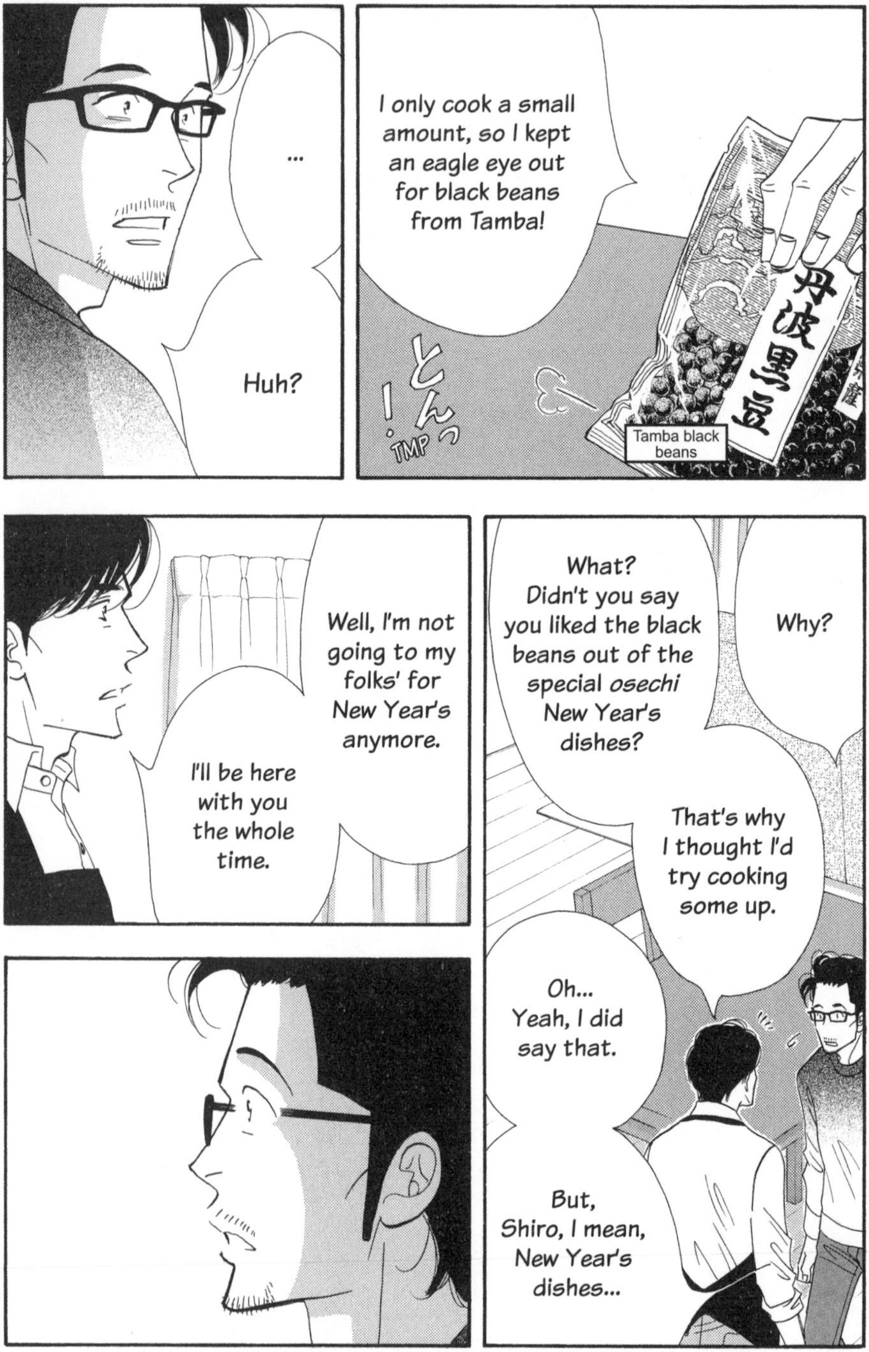
I only cook a small amount, so I kept an eagle eye out for black beans from Tamba!
とんっ
TMP
丹波黒豆
Tamba black beans
...
Huh?
Why?
What? Didn't you say you liked the black beans out of the special *osechi* New Year's dishes?
That's why I thought I'd try cooking some up.
Oh... Yeah, I did say that.
But, Shiro, I mean, New Year's dishes...
Well, I'm not going to my folks' for New Year's anymore.
I'll be here with you the whole time.

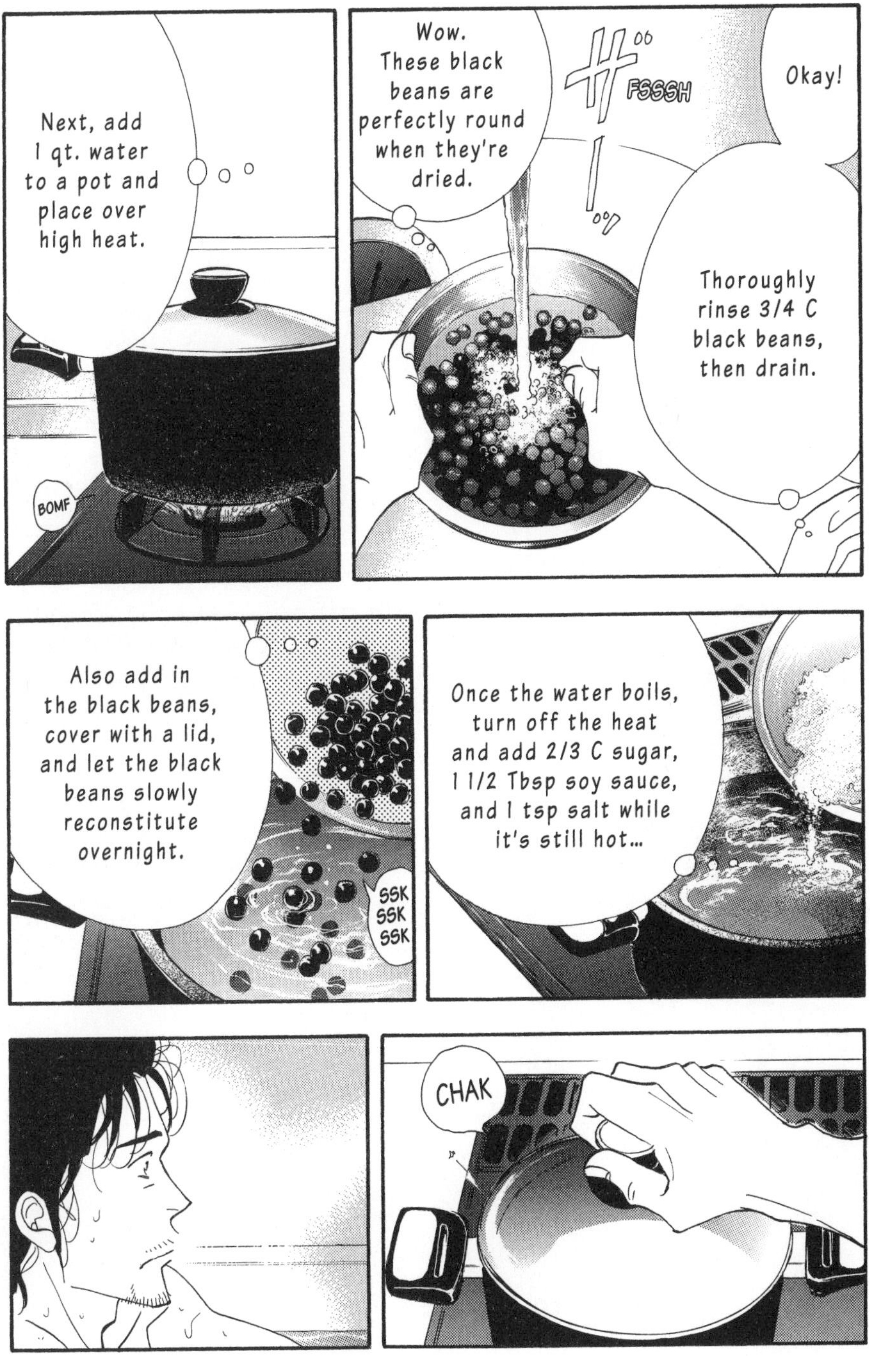
Okay!
Thoroughly rinse 3/4 C black beans, then drain.
FSSSH
Wow. These black beans are perfectly round when they're dried.
Next, add 1 qt. water to a pot and place over high heat.
BOMF
Once the water boils, turn off the heat and add 2/3 C sugar, 1 1/2 Tbsp soy sauce, and 1 tsp salt while it's still hot...
Also add in the black beans, cover with a lid, and let the black beans slowly reconstitute overnight.
SSK SSK SSK
CHAK

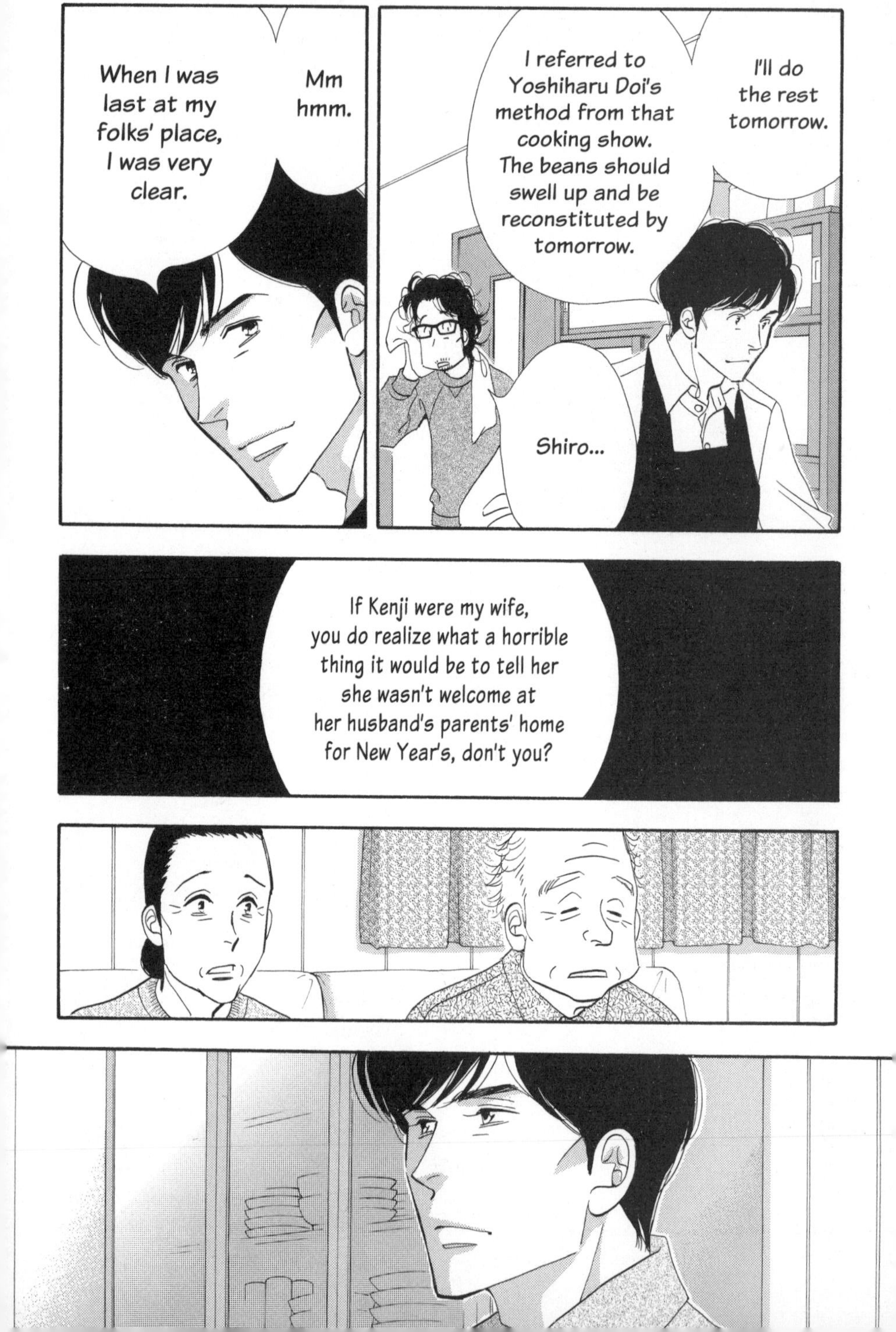
I'll do the rest tomorrow.
I referred to Yoshiharu Doi's method from that cooking show. The beans should swell up and be reconstituted by tomorrow.
Shiro...
Mm hmm.
When I was last at my folks' place, I was very clear.
If Kenji were my wife, you do realize what a horrible thing it would be to tell her she wasn't welcome at her husband's parents' home for New Year's, don't you?

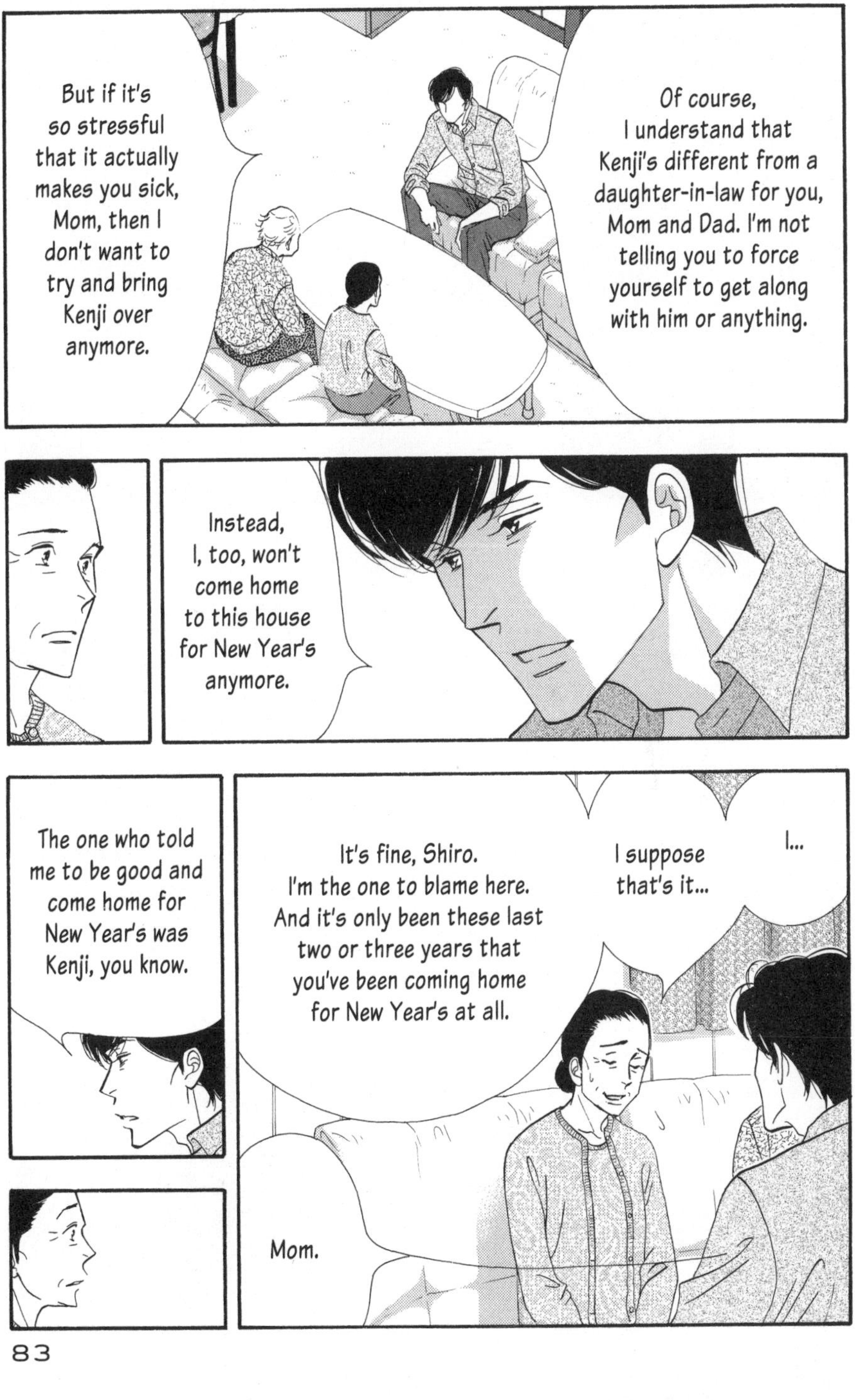

Of course, I understand that Kenji's different from a daughter-in-law for you, Mom and Dad. I'm not telling you to force yourself to get along with him or anything.
But if it's so stressful that it actually makes you sick, Mom, then I don't want to try and bring Kenji over anymore.
Instead, I, too, won't come home to this house for New Year's anymore.
I...
I suppose that's it...
It's fine, Shiro. I'm the one to blame here. And it's only been these last two or three years that you've been coming home for New Year's at all.
Mom.
The one who told me to be good and come home for New Year's was Kenji, you know.

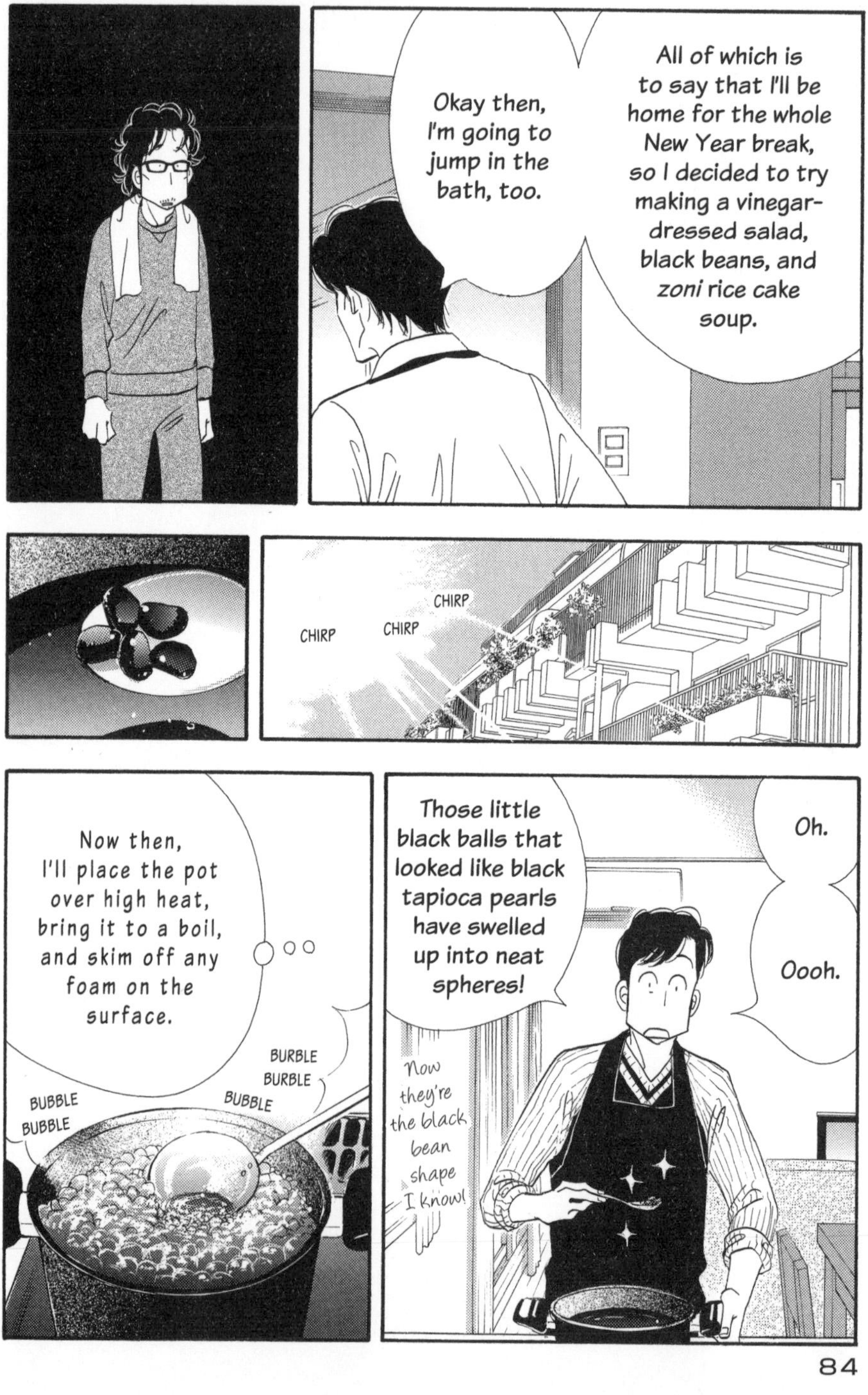
All of which is to say that I'll be home for the whole New Year break, so I decided to try making a vinegar-dressed salad, black beans, and *zoni* rice cake soup.
Okay then, I'm going to jump in the bath, too.
CHIRP
CHIRP
CHIRP
Oh.
Oooh.
Those little black balls that looked like black tapioca pearls have swelled up into neat spheres!
Now they're the black bean shape I know!
Now then, I'll place the pot over high heat, bring it to a boil, and skim off any foam on the surface.
BURBLE BURBLE
BUBBLE
BUBBLE BUBBLE

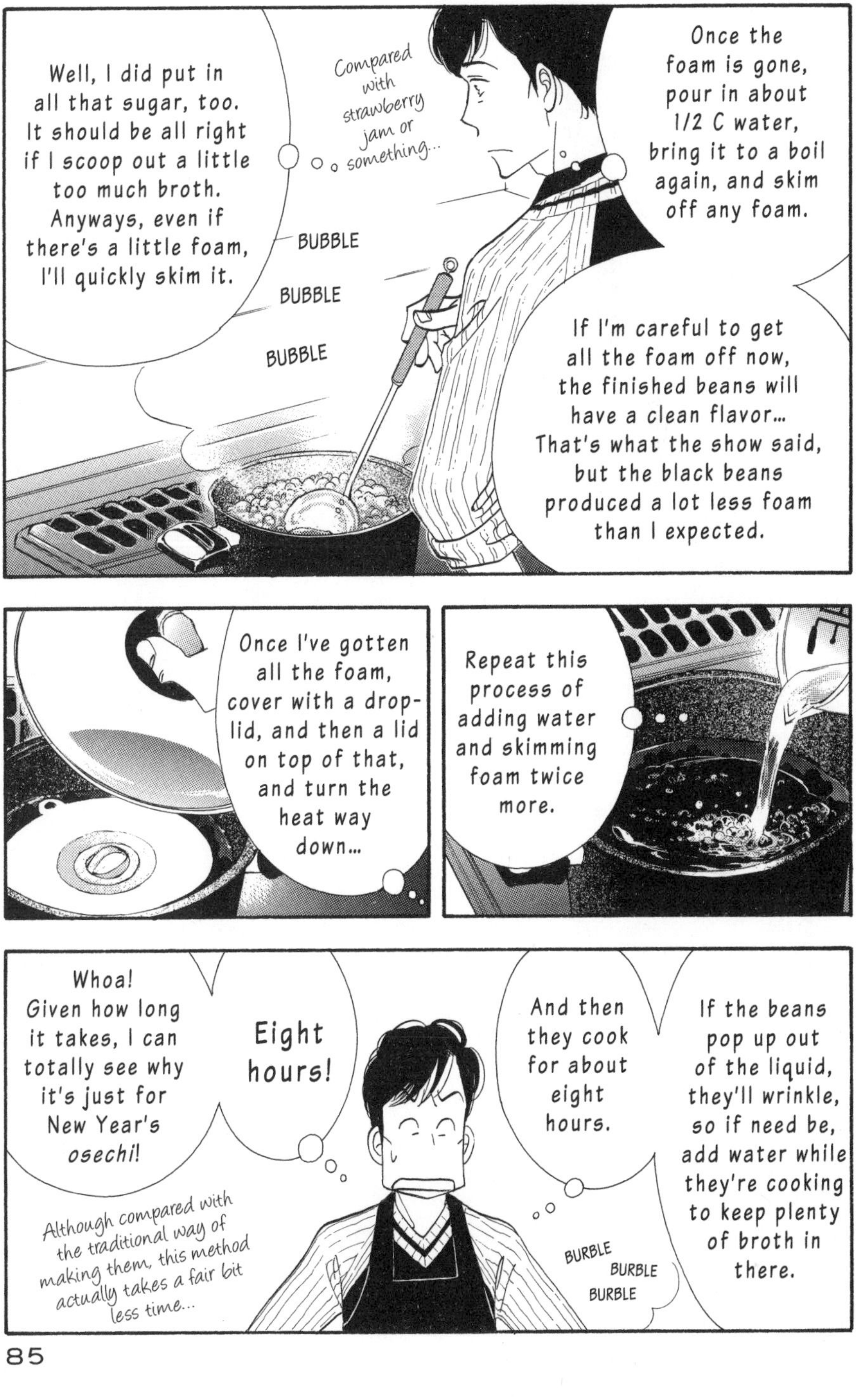
Once the foam is gone, pour in about 1/2 C water, bring it to a boil again, and skim off any foam.
If I'm careful to get all the foam off now, the finished beans will have a clean flavor... That's what the show said, but the black beans produced a lot less foam than I expected.
Compared with strawberry jam or something...
Well, I did put in all that sugar, too. It should be all right if I scoop out a little too much broth. Anyways, even if there's a little foam, I'll quickly skim it.
BUBBLE
BUBBLE
BUBBLE
Repeat this process of adding water and skimming foam twice more.
Once I've gotten all the foam, cover with a drop-lid, and then a lid on top of that, and turn the heat way down...
If the beans pop up out of the liquid, they'll wrinkle, so if need be, add water while they're cooking to keep plenty of broth in there.
And then they cook for about eight hours.
BURBLE
BURBLE
BURBLE
Eight hours!
Whoa! Given how long it takes, I can totally see why it's just for New Year's *osechi*!
Although compared with the traditional way of making them, this method actually takes a fair bit less time...

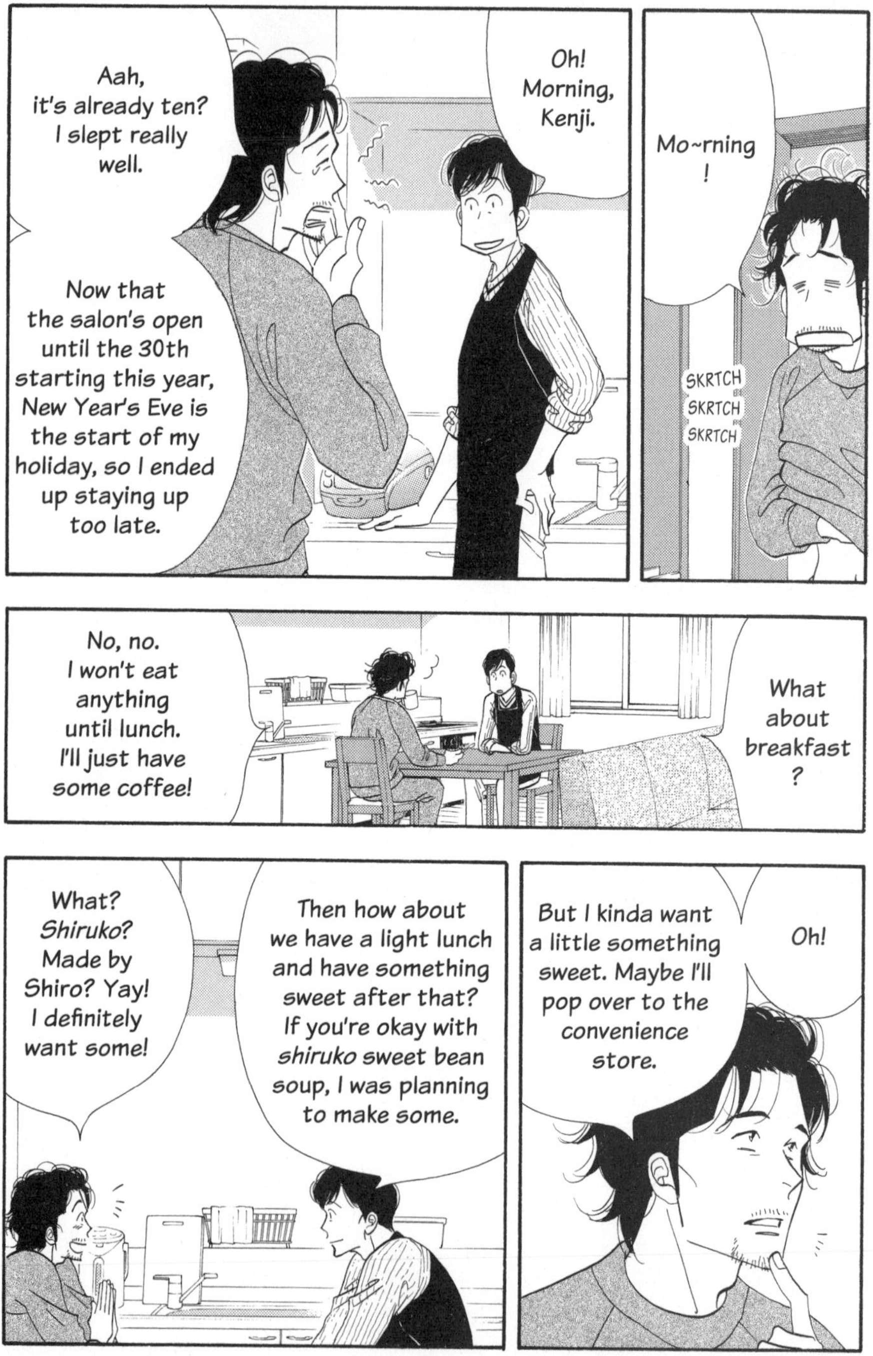
Mo~rning!
SKRTCH SKRTCH SKRTCH
Oh! Morning, Kenji.
Aah, it's already ten? I slept really well.
Now that the salon's open until the 30th starting this year, New Year's Eve is the start of my holiday, so I ended up staying up too late.
What about breakfast?
No, no. I won't eat anything until lunch. I'll just have some coffee!
Oh!
But I kinda want a little something sweet. Maybe I'll pop over to the convenience store.
Then how about we have a light lunch and have something sweet after that? If you're okay with *shiruko* sweet bean soup, I was planning to make some.
What? *Shiruko*? Made by Shiro? Yay! I definitely want some!

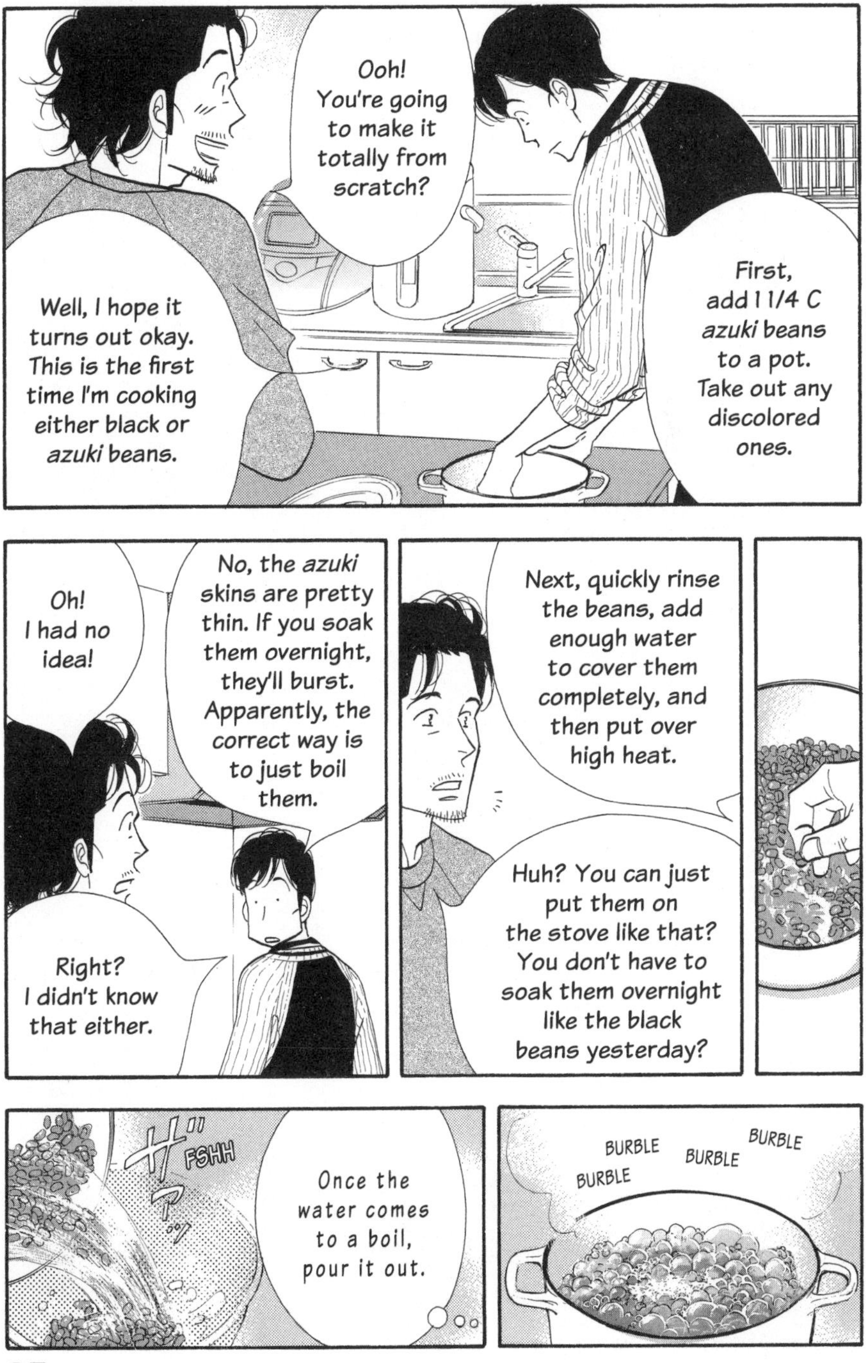
Ooh! You're going to make it totally from scratch?
First, add 1 1/4 C *azuki* beans to a pot. Take out any discolored ones.
Well, I hope it turns out okay. This is the first time I'm cooking either black or *azuki* beans.
Next, quickly rinse the beans, add enough water to cover them completely, and then put over high heat.
Huh? You can just put them on the stove like that? You don't have to soak them overnight like the black beans yesterday?
No, the *azuki* skins are pretty thin. If you soak them overnight, they'll burst. Apparently, the correct way is to just boil them.
Oh! I had no idea!
Right? I didn't know that either.
BURBLE
BURBLE
BURBLE
BURBLE
FSHH
Once the water comes to a boil, pour it out.

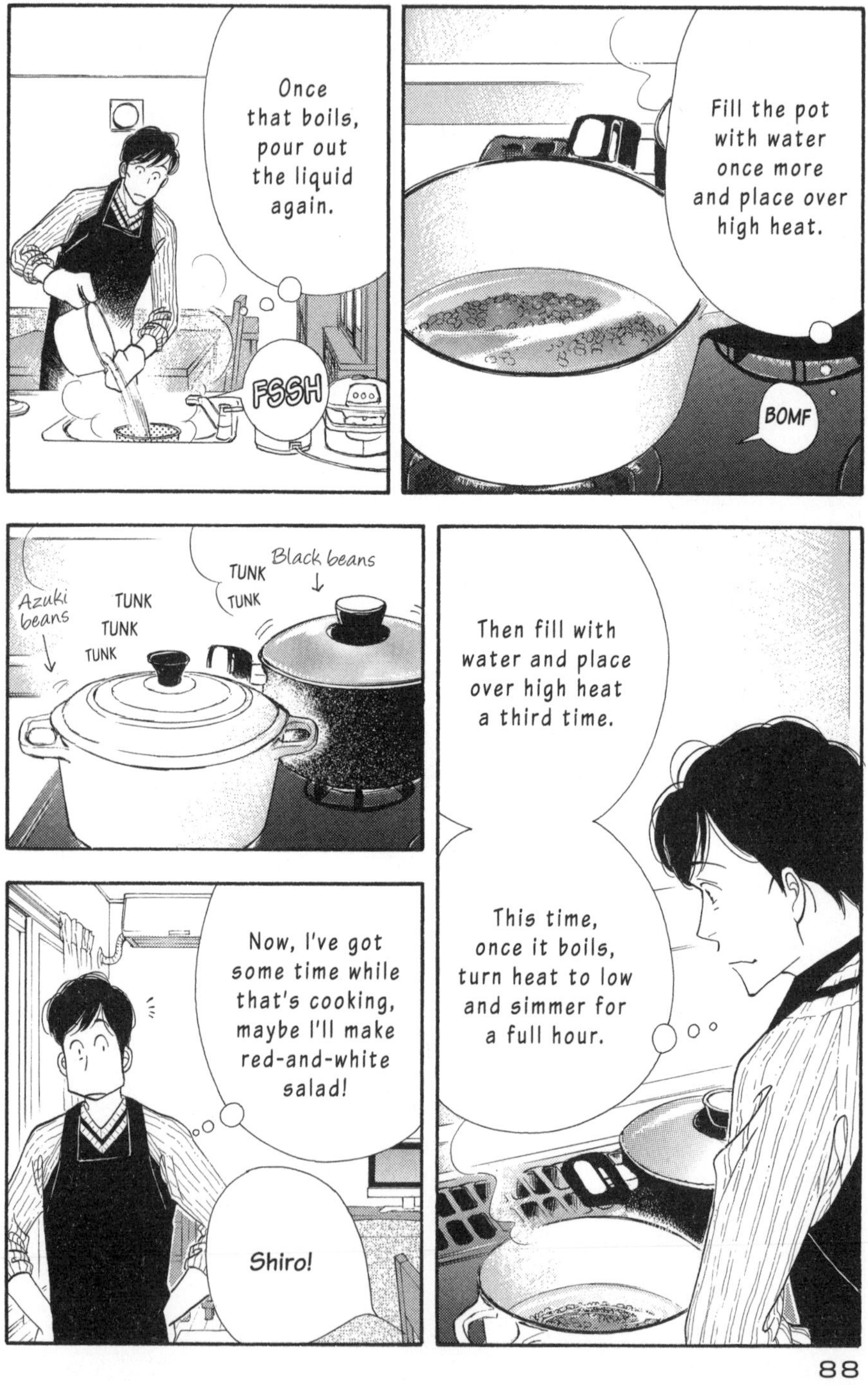
Fill the pot with water once more and place over high heat.
BOMF
Once that boils, pour out the liquid again.
FSSH
Then fill with water and place over high heat a third time.
This time, once it boils, turn heat to low and simmer for a full hour.
Black beans
TUNK
TUNK
TUNK
TUNK
TUNK
Azuki beans
Now, I've got some time while that's cooking, maybe I'll make red-and-white salad!
Shiro!

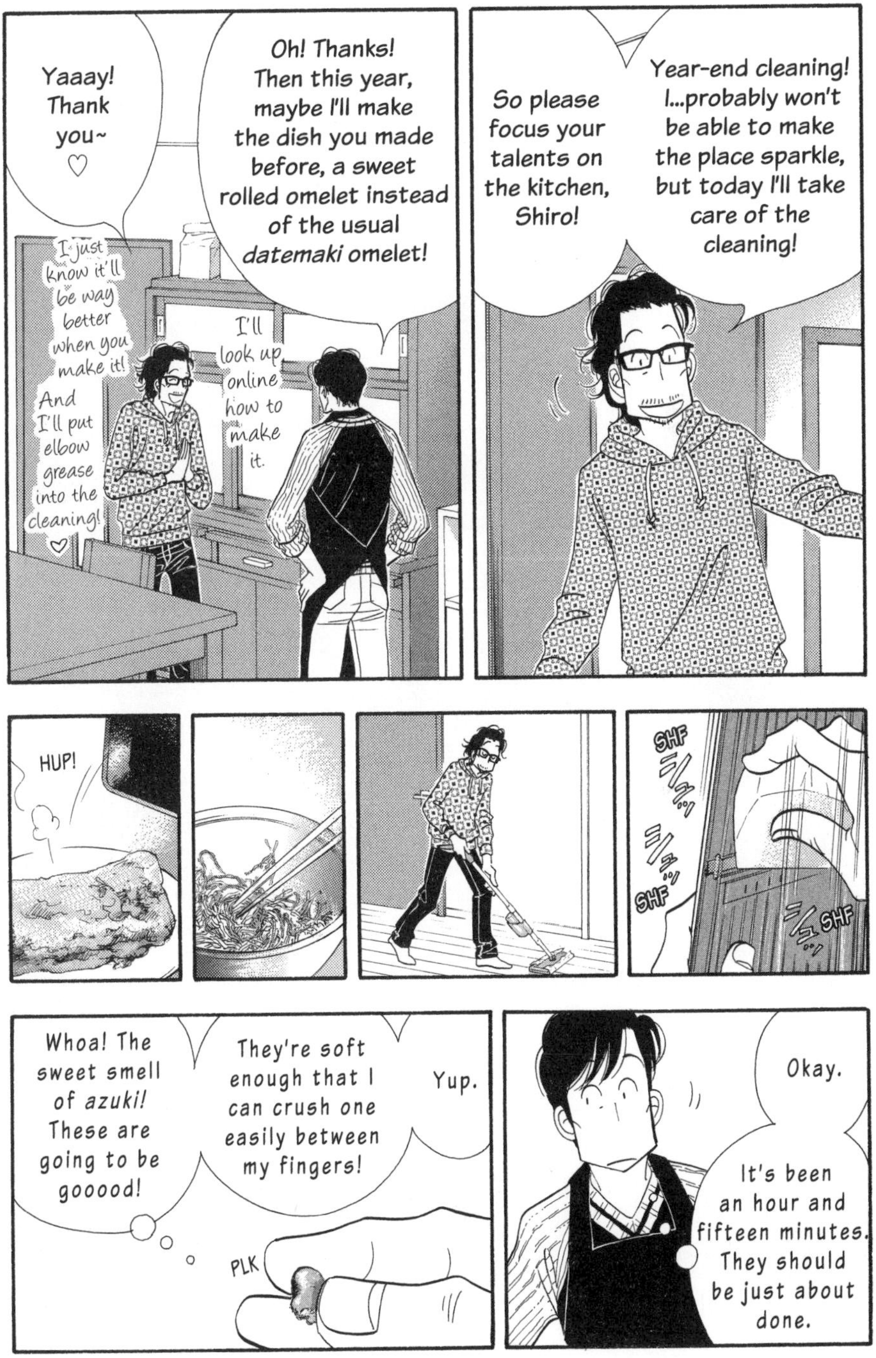
Year-end cleaning! I...probably won't be able to make the place sparkle, but today I'll take care of the cleaning!
So please focus your talents on the kitchen, Shiro!
Oh! Thanks! Then this year, maybe I'll make the dish you made before, a sweet rolled omelet instead of the usual *datemaki* omelet!
Yaaay! Thank you~ ♡
I'll look up online how to make it.
I just know it'll be way better when you make it!
And I'll put elbow grease into the cleaning! ♡
SHF
SHF
SHF
HUP!
Okay.
It's been an hour and fifteen minutes. They should be just about done.
Yup.
They're soft enough that I can crush one easily between my fingers!
Whoa! The sweet smell of *azuki*! These are going to be gooood!
PLK

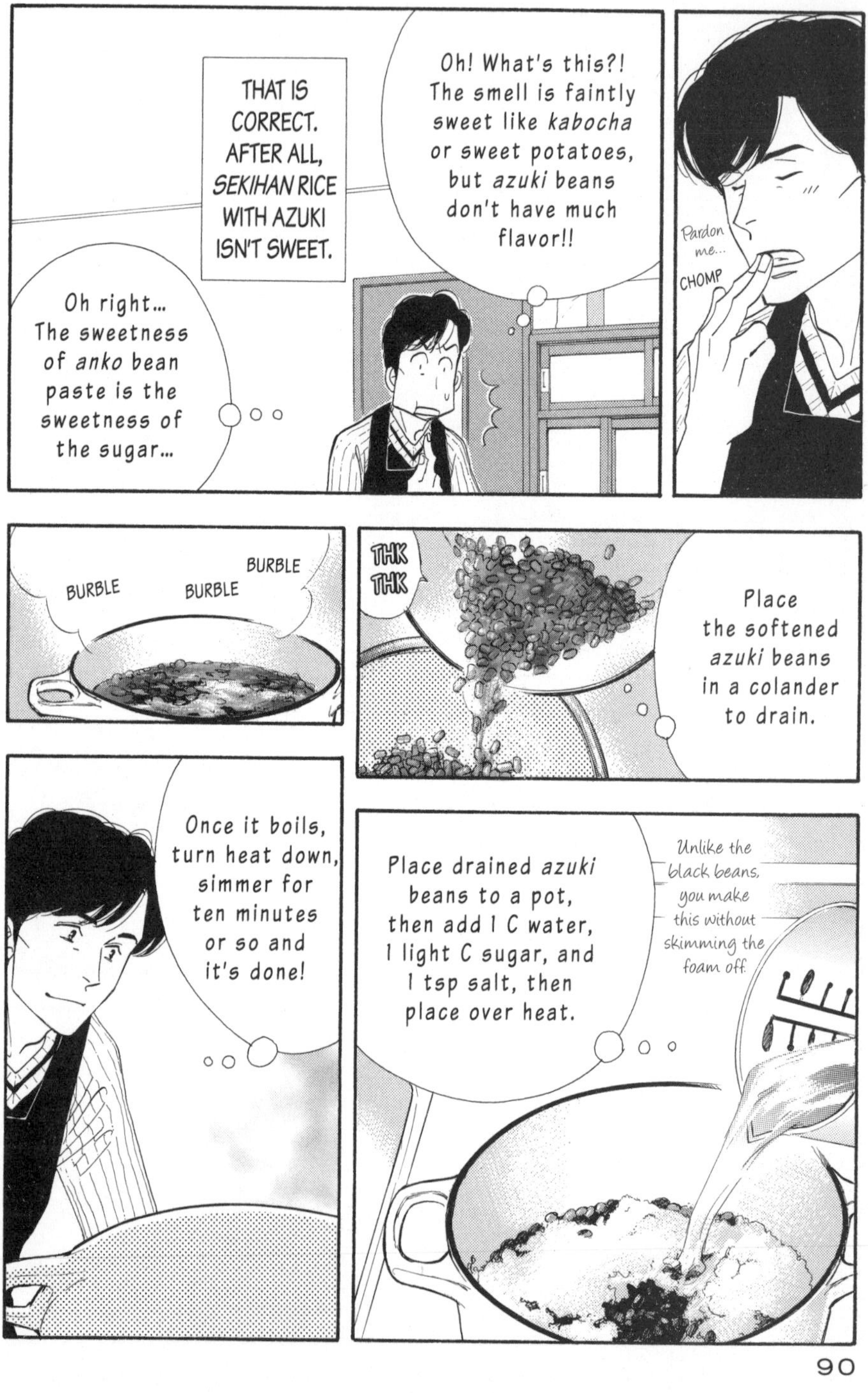
Pardon me...
CHOMP
Oh! What's this?! The smell is faintly sweet like *kabocha* or sweet potatoes, but *azuki* beans don't have much flavor!!
THAT IS CORRECT. AFTER ALL, *SEKIHAN* RICE WITH AZUKI ISN'T SWEET.
Oh right... The sweetness of *anko* bean paste is the sweetness of the sugar...
THK THK
Place the softened *azuki* beans in a colander to drain.
BURBLE
BURBLE
BURBLE
Unlike the black beans, you make this without skimming the foam off.
Place drained *azuki* beans to a pot, then add 1 C water, 1 light C sugar, and 1 tsp salt, then place over heat.
Once it boils, turn heat down, simmer for ten minutes or so and it's done!

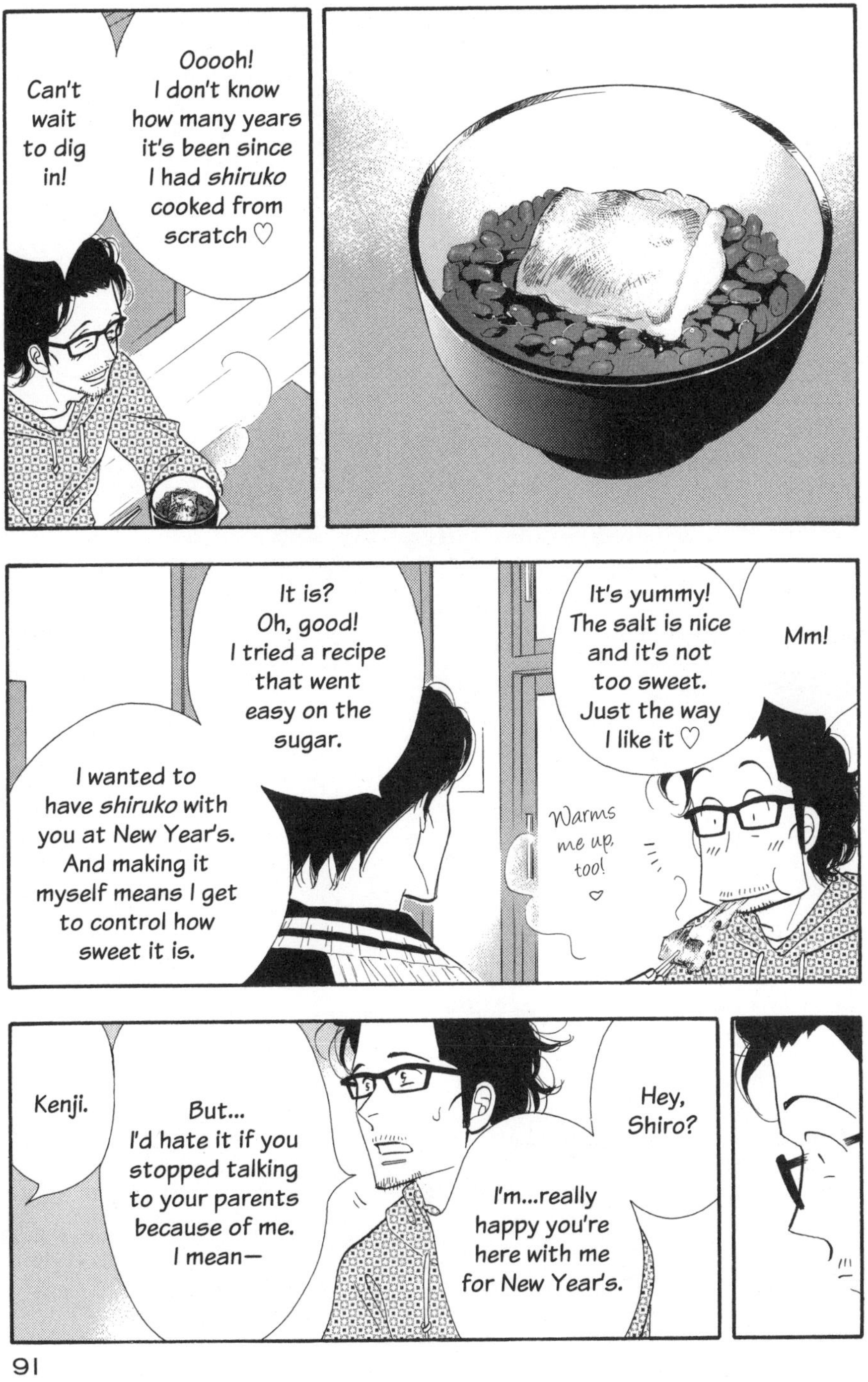
Ooooh! I don't know how many years it's been since I had *shiruko* cooked from scratch ♡
Can't wait to dig in!
Mm!
It's yummy! The salt is nice and it's not too sweet. Just the way I like it ♡
Warms me up, too! ♡
It is? Oh, good! I tried a recipe that went easy on the sugar.
I wanted to have *shiruko* with you at New Year's. And making it myself means I get to control how sweet it is.
Hey, Shiro?
I'm...really happy you're here with me for New Year's.
But... I'd hate it if you stopped talking to your parents because of me. I mean—
Kenji.

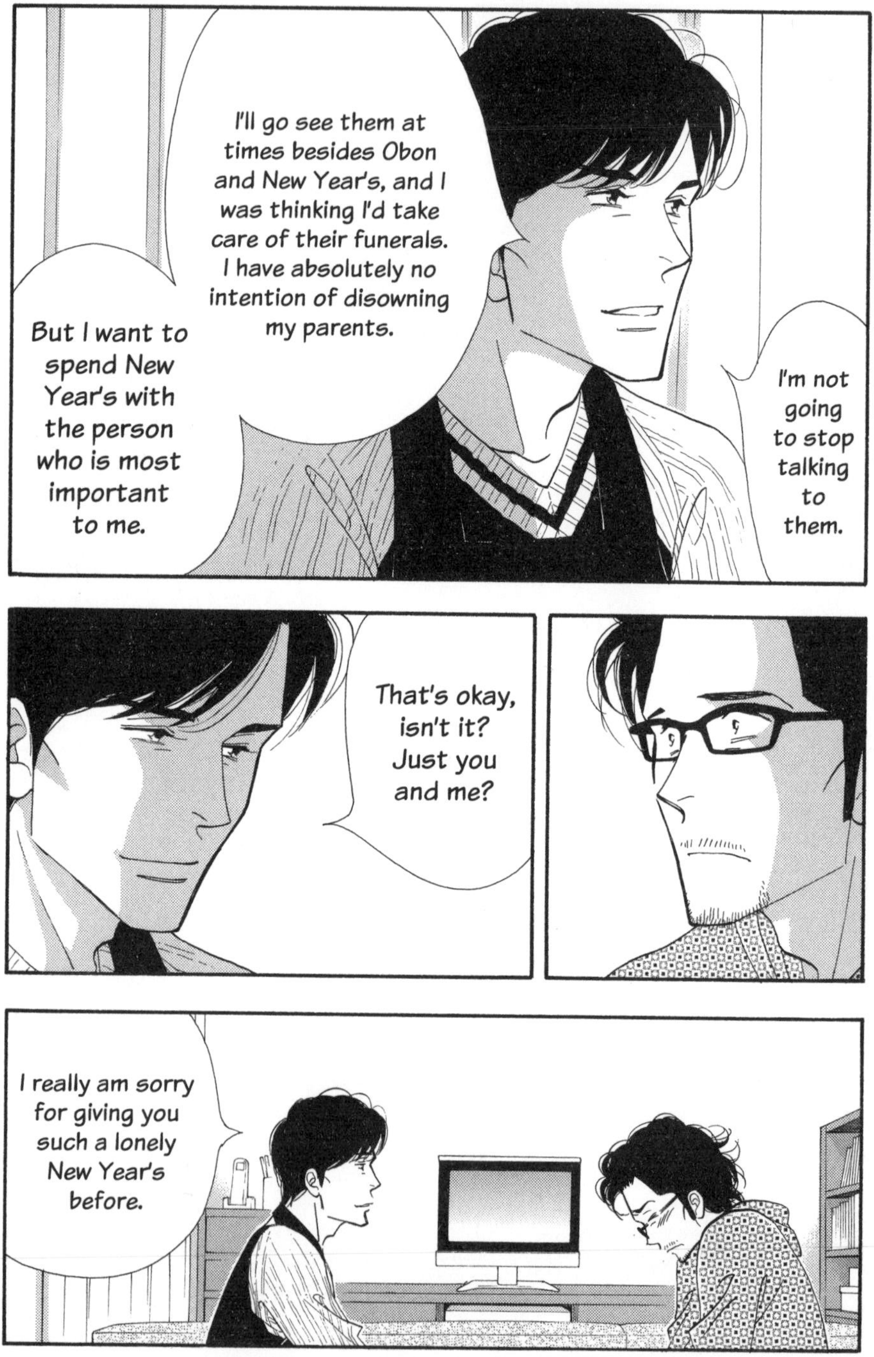
I'm not going to stop talking to them.
I'll go see them at times besides Obon and New Year's, and I was thinking I'd take care of their funerals. I have absolutely no intention of disowning my parents.
But I want to spend New Year's with the person who is most important to me.
That's okay, isn't it? Just you and me?
I really am sorry for giving you such a lonely New Year's before.

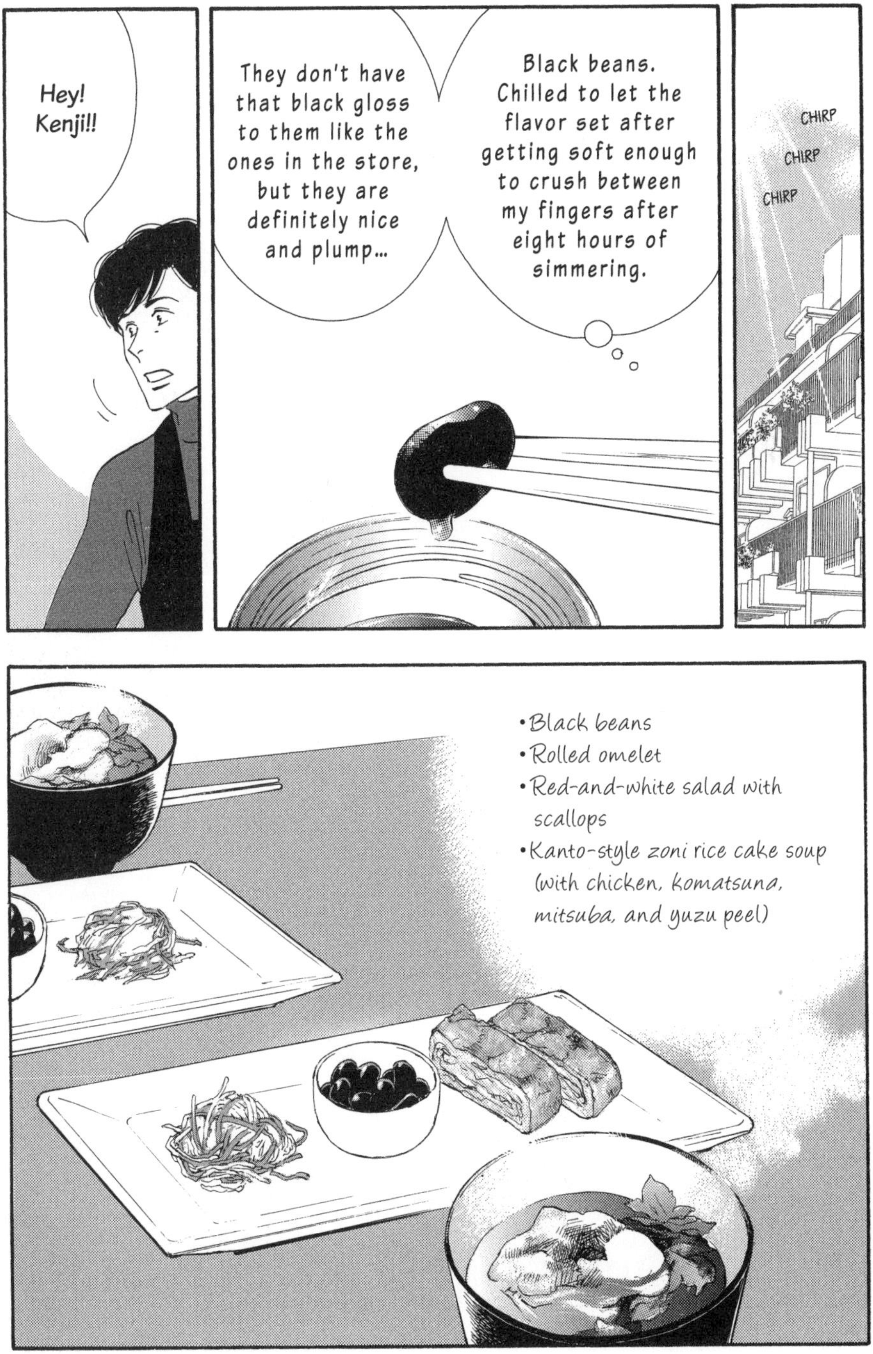
CHIRP
CHIRP
CHIRP
Black beans. Chilled to let the flavor set after getting soft enough to crush between my fingers after eight hours of simmering.
They don't have that black gloss to them like the ones in the store, but they are definitely nice and plump...
Hey! Kenji!!
•Black beans
•Rolled omelet
•Red-and-white salad with scallops
•Kanto-style zoni rice cake soup (with chicken, komatsuna, mitsuba, and yuzu peel)

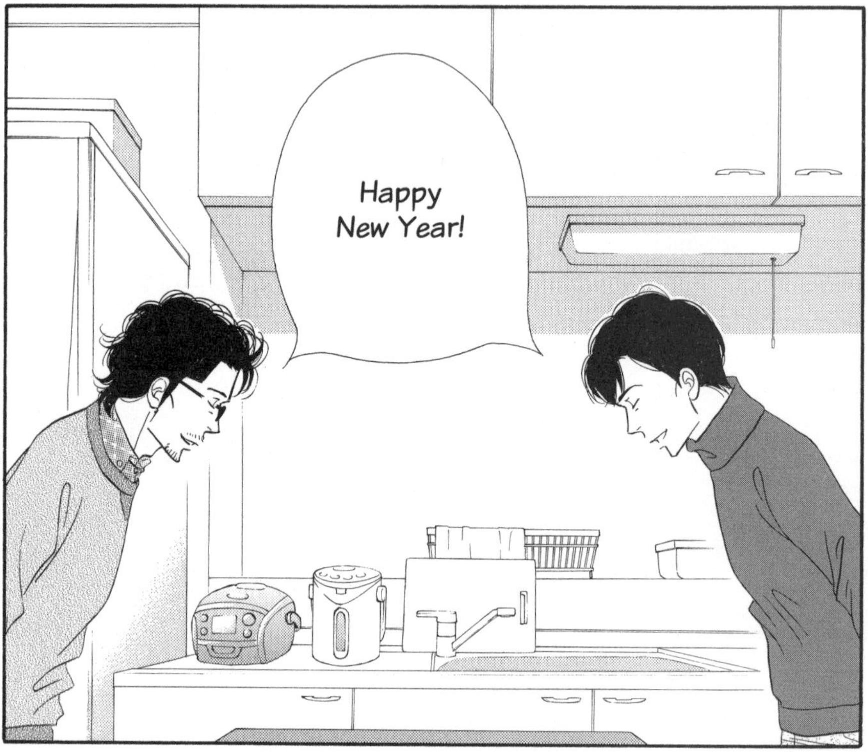
Happy New Year!

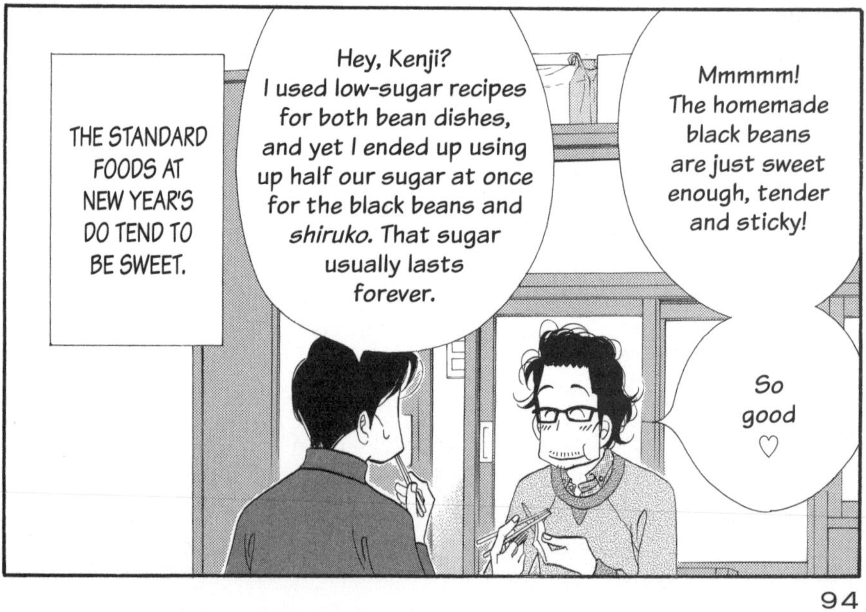
Mmmmm! The homemade black beans are just sweet enough, tender and sticky!
So good ♡
Hey, Kenji? I used low-sugar recipes for both bean dishes, and yet I ended up using up half our sugar at once for the black beans and *shiruko.* That sugar usually lasts forever.
THE STANDARD FOODS AT NEW YEAR'S DO TEND TO BE SWEET.

It isn't used in this **black bean** recipe,
but apparently, they come out very black
if you simmer them with a rusted nail.
They're actually more delicious two days
after cooking, rather than the day after.
You can also freeze the *azuki*-based **anko**.

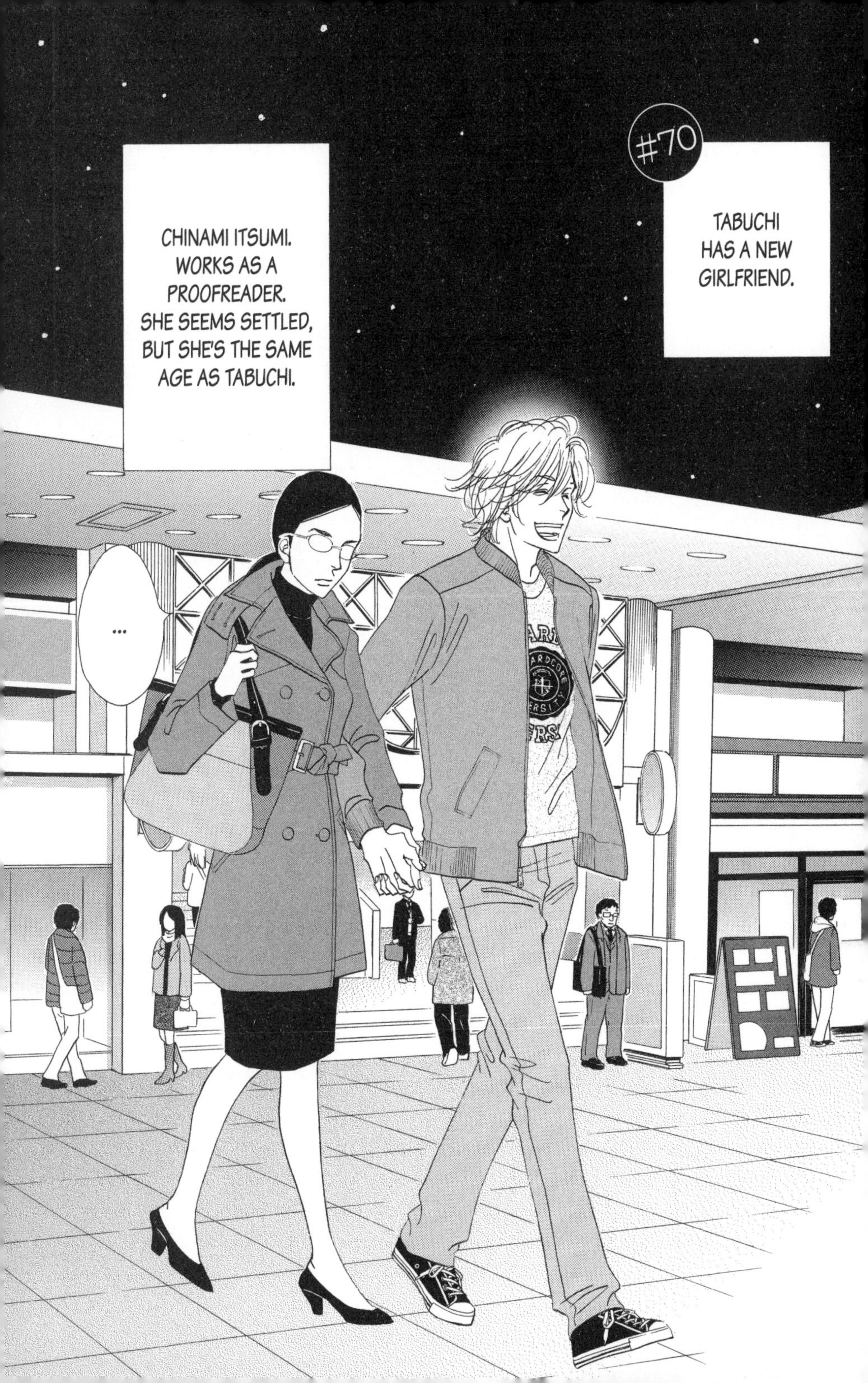
#70
TABUCHI HAS A NEW GIRLFRIEND.
CHINAMI ITSUMI. WORKS AS A PROOFREADER. SHE SEEMS SETTLED, BUT SHE'S THE SAME AGE AS TABUCHI.
...

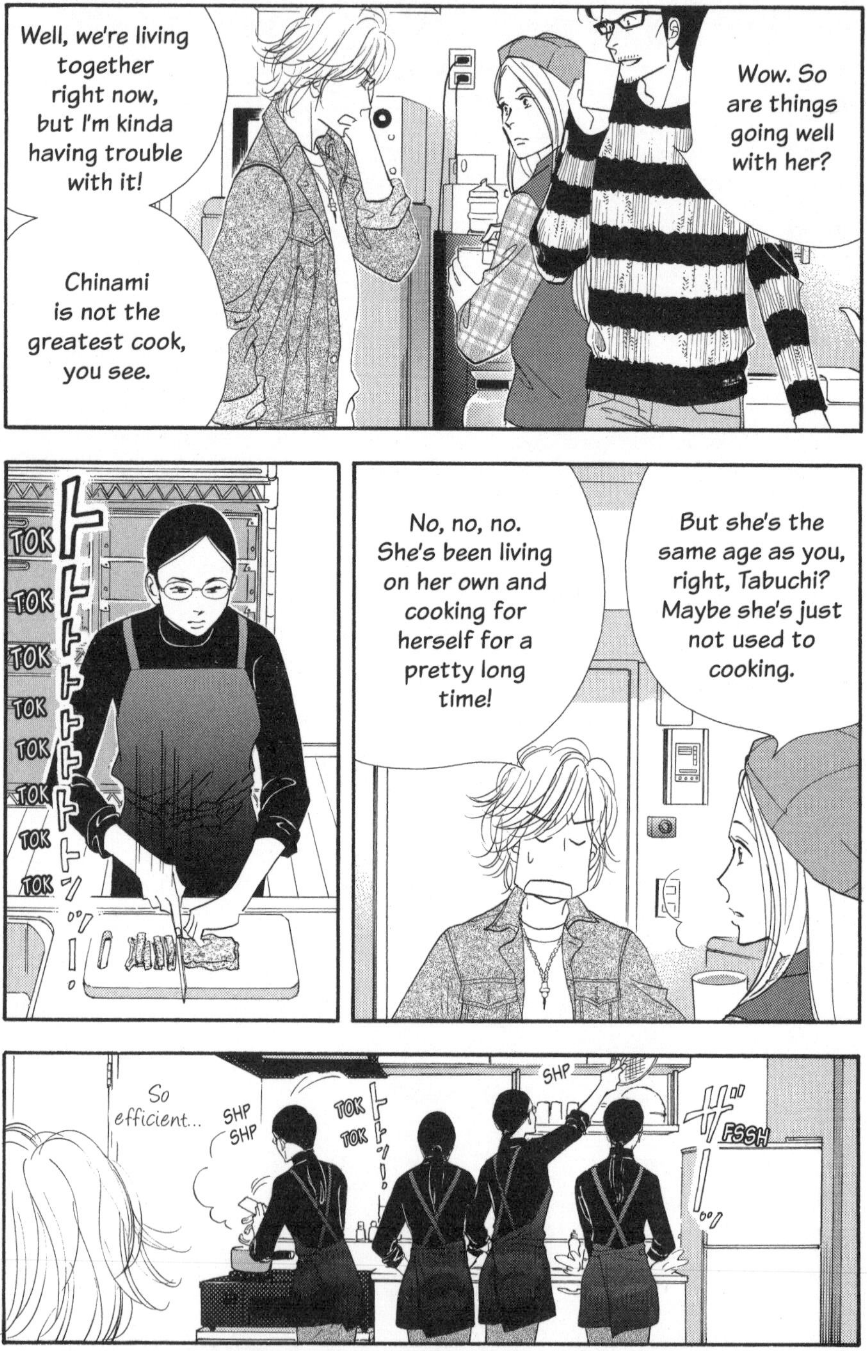
Wow. So are things going well with her?
Well, we're living together right now, but I'm kinda having trouble with it!
Chinami is not the greatest cook, you see.
But she's the same age as you, right, Tabuchi? Maybe she's just not used to cooking.
No, no, no. She's been living on her own and cooking for herself for a pretty long time!
TOK TOK TOK TOK TOK TOK TOK TOK
FSSH
SHP
TOK TOK
SHP SHP
So efficient...

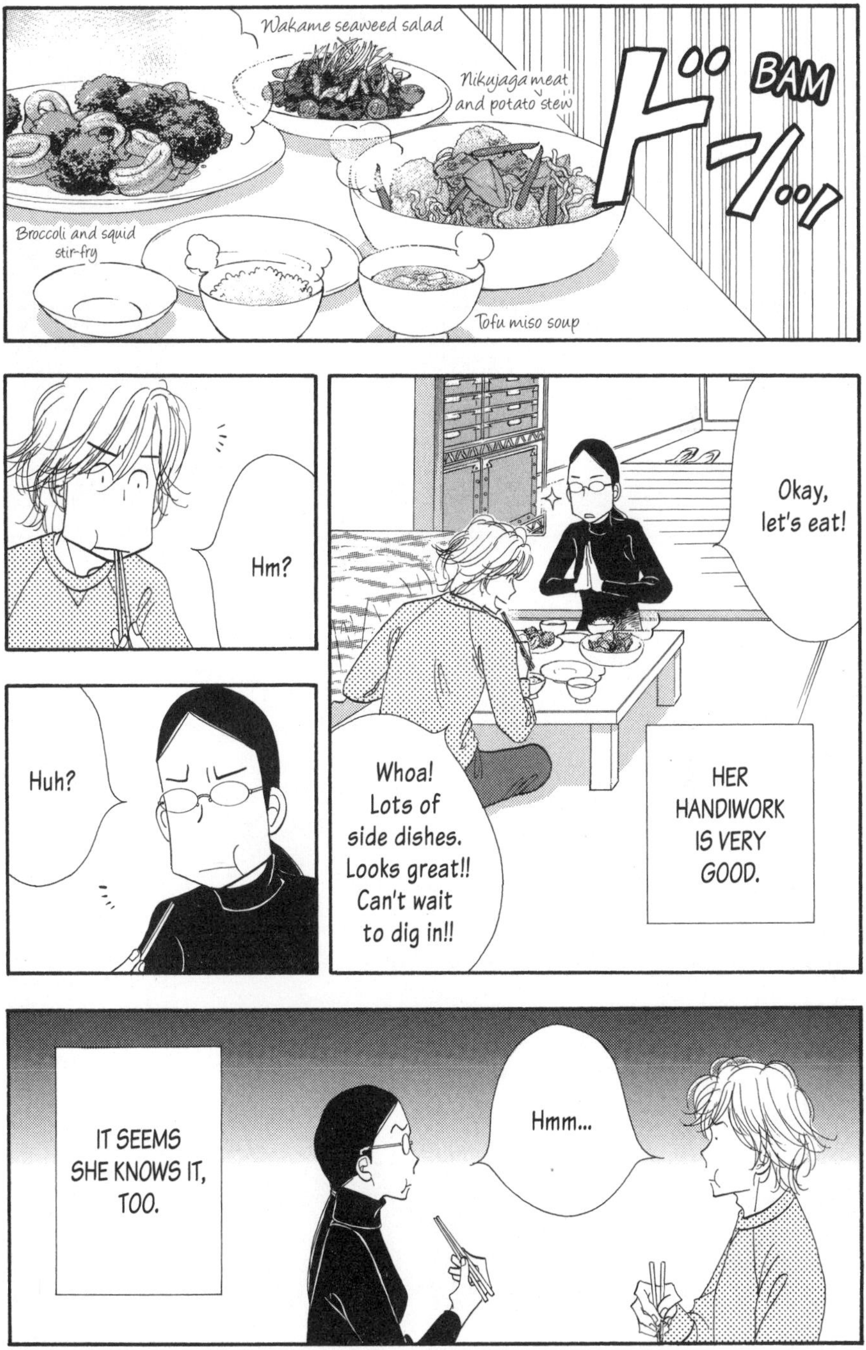
BAM
Nikujaga meat and potato stew
Wakame seaweed salad
Broccoli and squid stir-fry
Tofu miso soup
Okay, let's eat!
HER HANDIWORK IS VERY GOOD.
Whoa! Lots of side dishes. Looks great!! Can't wait to dig in!!
Hm?
Huh?
Hmm...
IT SEEMS SHE KNOWS IT, TOO.

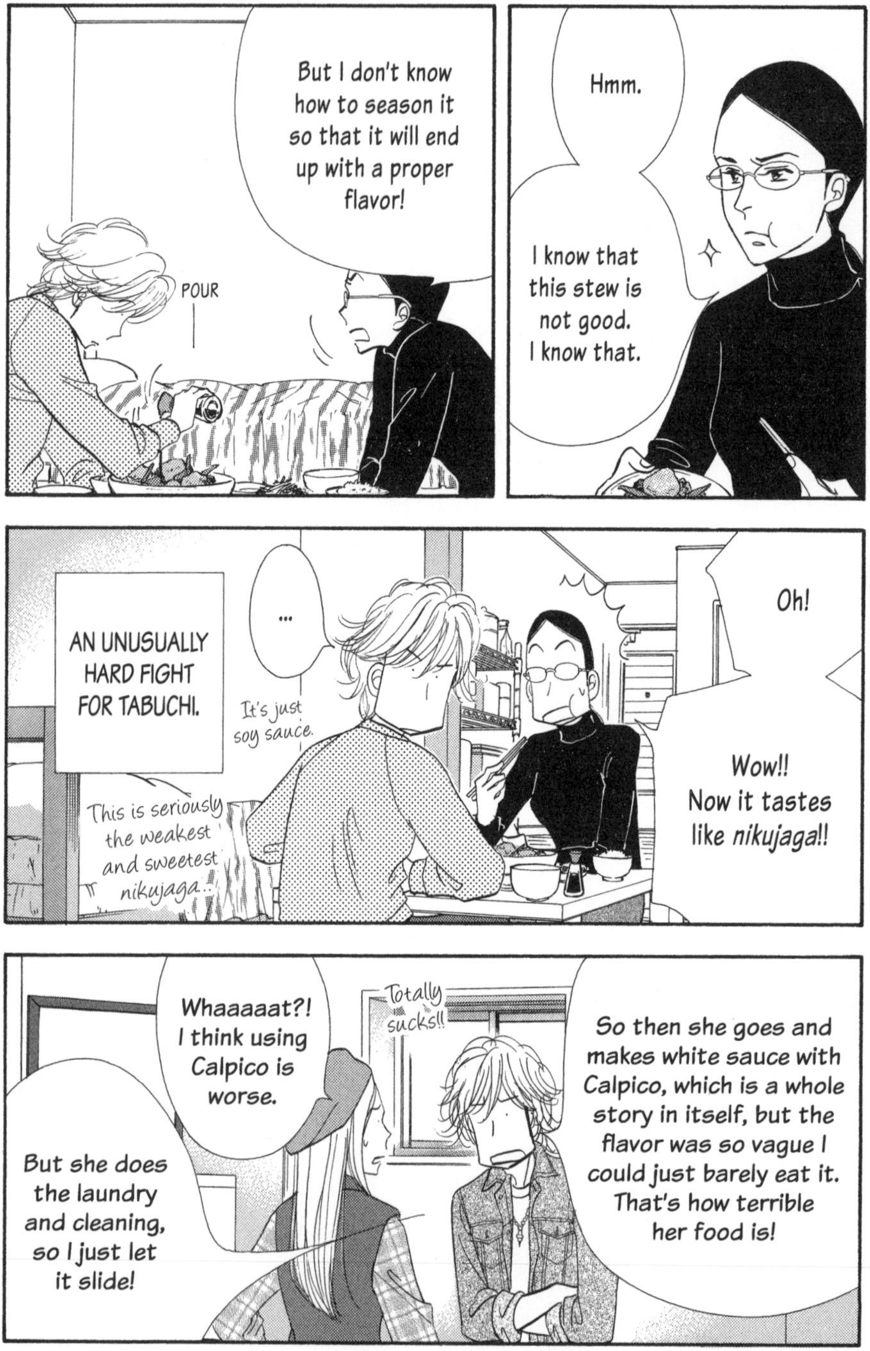
Hmm.
I know that this stew is not good. I know that.
But I don't know how to season it so that it will end up with a proper flavor!
POUR
Oh!
Wow!! Now it tastes like *nikujaga*!!
...
It's just soy sauce.
AN UNUSUALLY HARD FIGHT FOR TABUCHI.
This is seriously the weakest and sweetest nikujaga...
So then she goes and makes white sauce with Calpico, which is a whole story in itself, but the flavor was so vague I could just barely eat it. That's how terrible her food is!
Totally sucks!!
Whaaaaat?! I think using Calpico is worse.
But she does the laundry and cleaning, so I just let it slide!

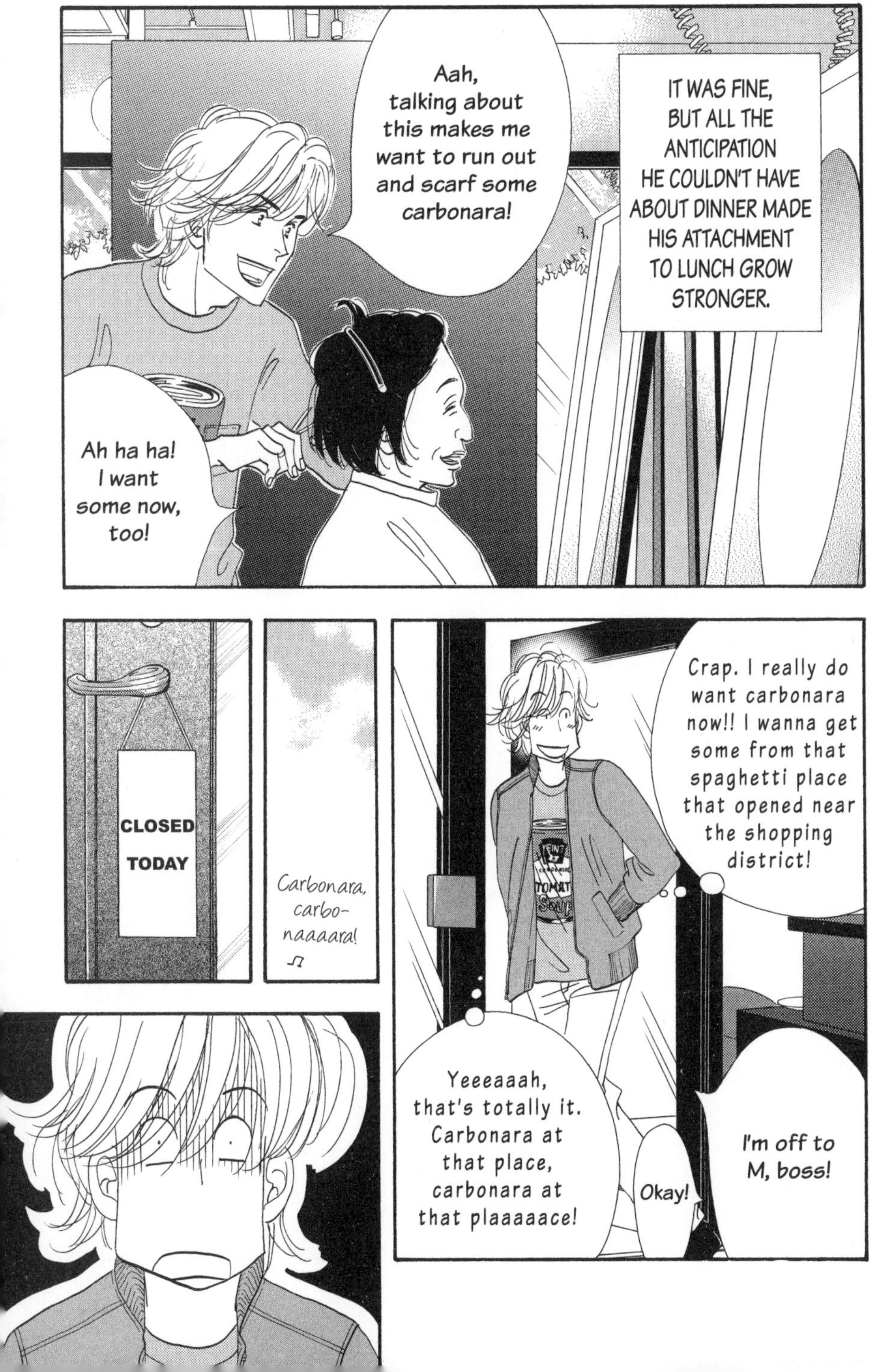
IT WAS FINE, BUT ALL THE ANTICIPATION HE COULDN'T HAVE ABOUT DINNER MADE HIS ATTACHMENT TO LUNCH GROW STRONGER.
Aah, talking about this makes me want to run out and scarf some carbonara!
Ah ha ha! I want some now, too!
Crap. I really do want carbonara now!! I wanna get some from that spaghetti place that opened near the shopping district!
I'm off to M, boss!
Okay!
Yeeeaaah, that's totally it. Carbonara at that place, carbonara at that plaaaaace!
Carbonara, carbo-naaaaara! ♫
CLOSED TODAY

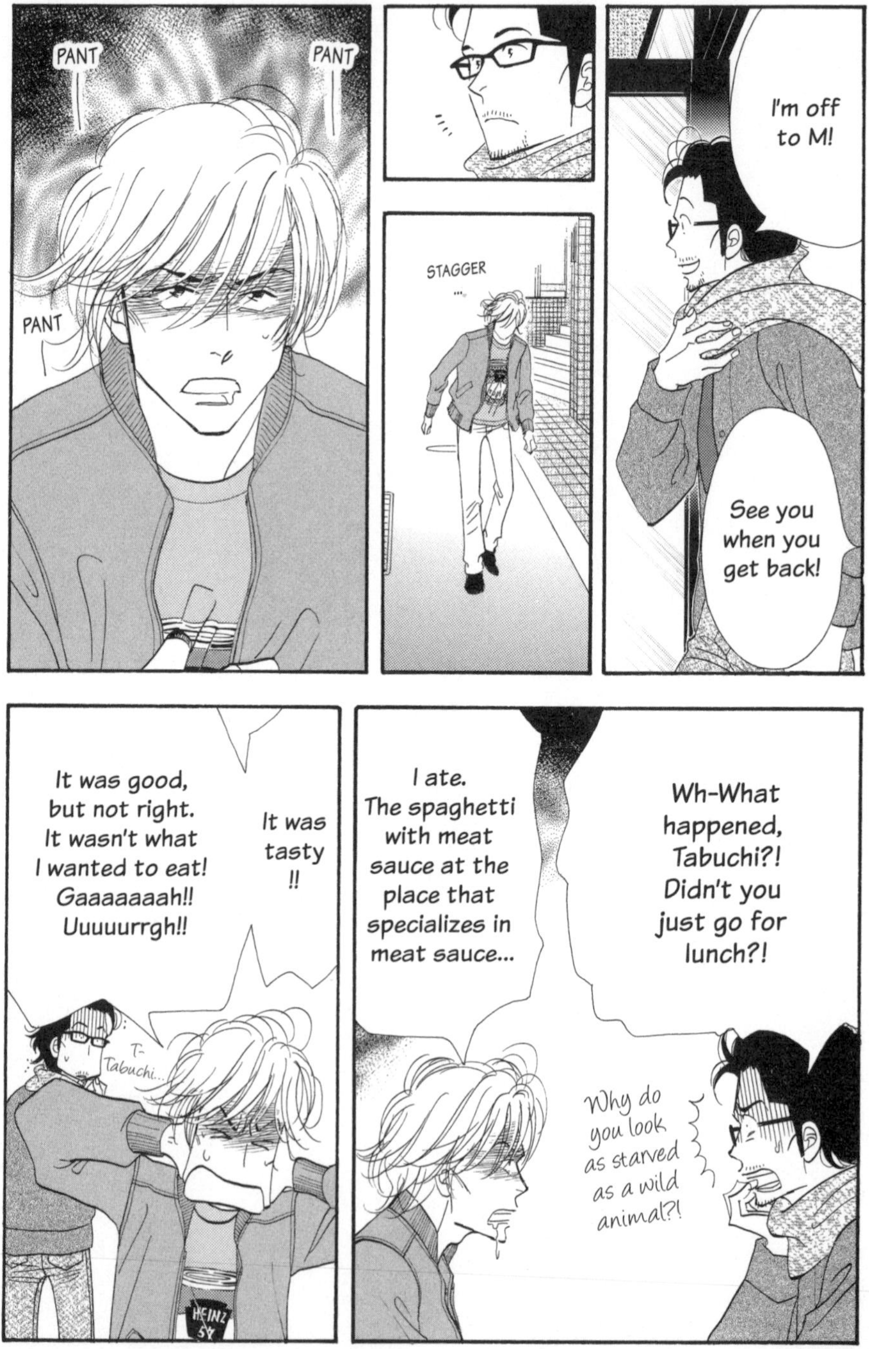
I'm off to M!
See you when you get back!
STAGGER
PANT
PANT
PANT
Wh-What happened, Tabuchi?! Didn't you just go for lunch?!
Why do you look as starved as a wild animal?!
I ate. The spaghetti with meat sauce at the place that specializes in meat sauce...
It was tasty !!
It was good, but not right. It wasn't what I wanted to eat! Gaaaaaaah!! Uuuuurrgh!!
T-Tabuchi...
HEINZ 57

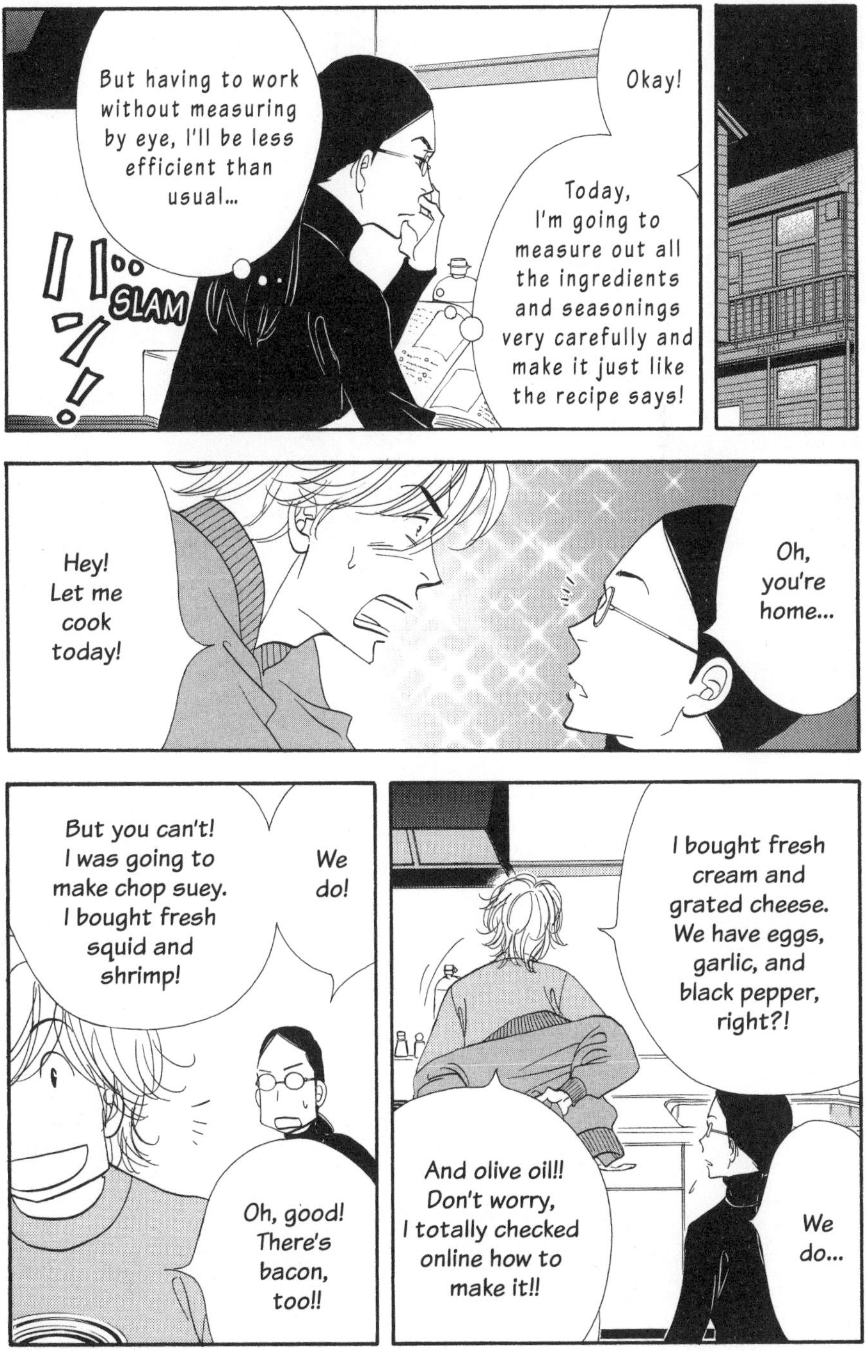
Okay!
Today, I'm going to measure out all the ingredients and seasonings very carefully and make it just like the recipe says!
But having to work without measuring by eye, I'll be less efficient than usual...
SLAM
Oh, you're home...
Hey! Let me cook today!
I bought fresh cream and grated cheese. We have eggs, garlic, and black pepper, right?!
We do...
And olive oil!! Don't worry, I totally checked online how to make it!!
We do!
But you can't! I was going to make chop suey. I bought fresh squid and shrimp!
Oh, good! There's bacon, too!!

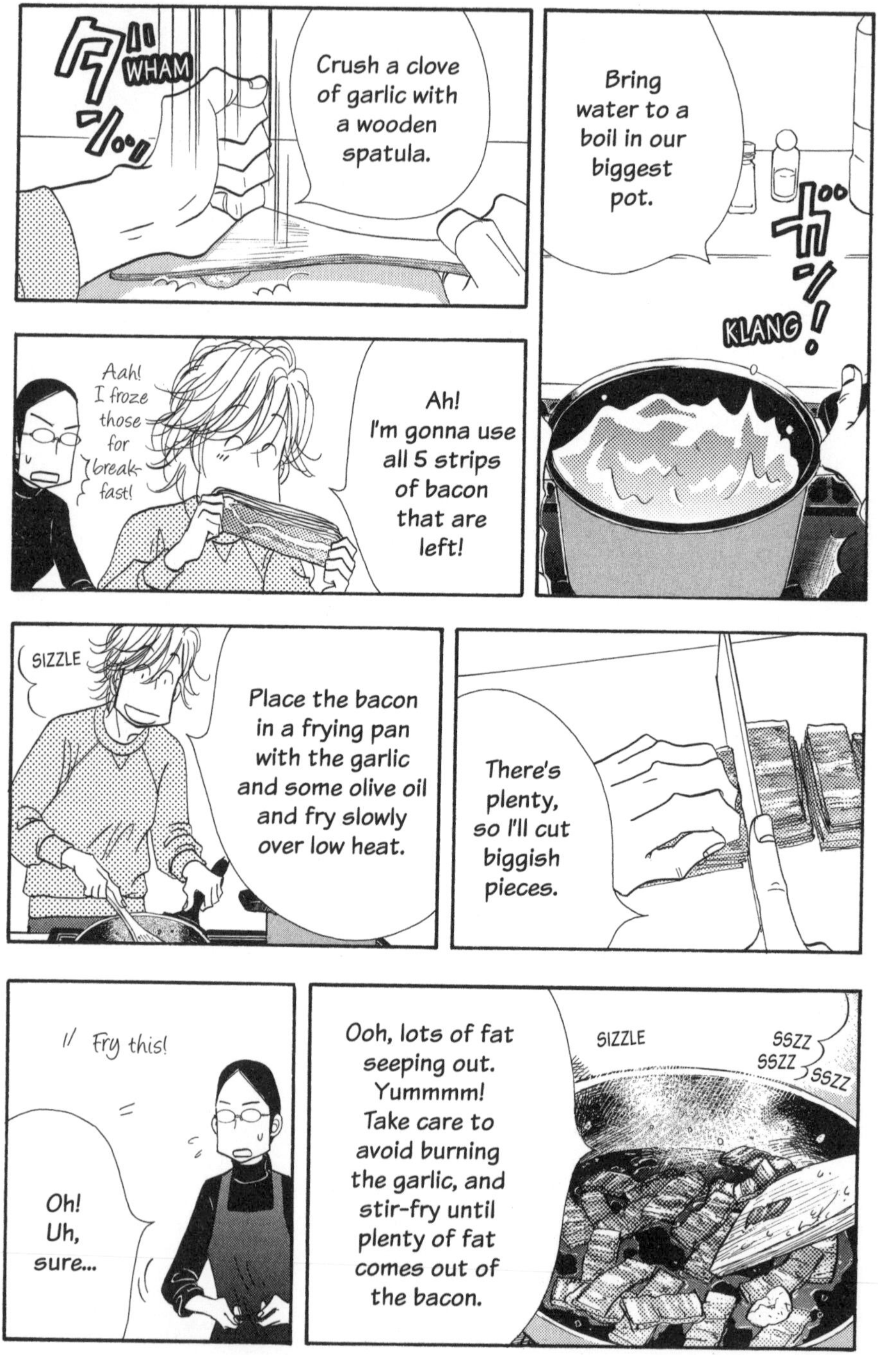
Bring water to a boil in our biggest pot.
KLANG
Crush a clove of garlic with a wooden spatula.
WHAM
Ah! I'm gonna use all 5 strips of bacon that are left!
Aah! I froze those for breakfast!
There's plenty, so I'll cut biggish pieces.
Place the bacon in a frying pan with the garlic and some olive oil and fry slowly over low heat.
SIZZLE
Ooh, lots of fat seeping out. Yummmm! Take care to avoid burning the garlic, and stir-fry until plenty of fat comes out of the bacon.
SIZZLE
SSZZ SSZZ SSZZ
Fry this!
Oh! Uh, sure...

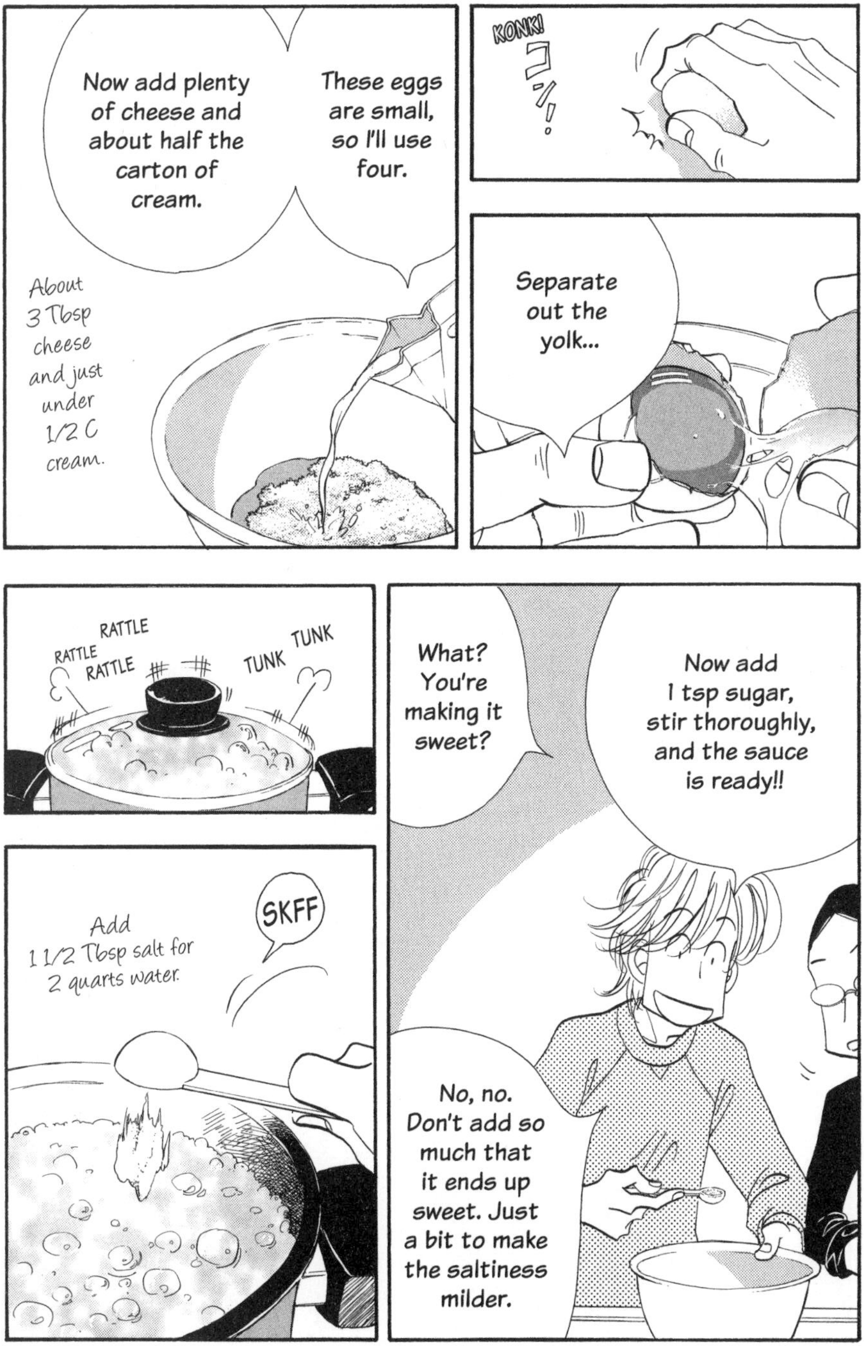
KONK!
Separate out the yolk...
These eggs are small, so I'll use four.
Now add plenty of cheese and about half the carton of cream.
About 3 Tbsp cheese and just under 1/2 C cream.
Now add 1 tsp sugar, stir thoroughly, and the sauce is ready!!
What? You're making it sweet?
No, no. Don't add so much that it ends up sweet. Just a bit to make the saltiness milder.
TUNK TUNK
RATTLE RATTLE RATTLE
SKFF
Add 1 1/2 Tbsp salt for 2 quarts water.

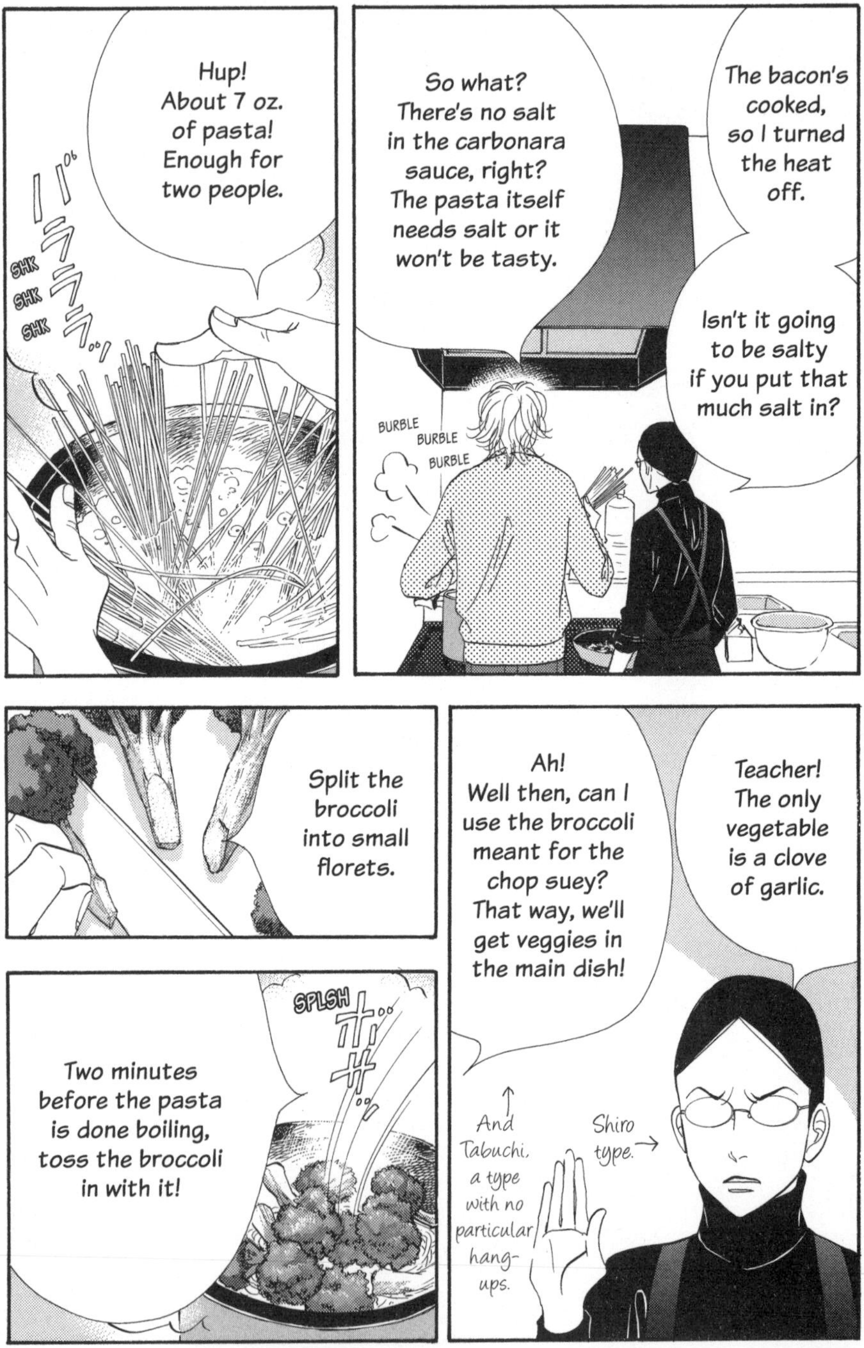
The bacon's cooked, so I turned the heat off.
Isn't it going to be salty if you put that much salt in?
So what? There's no salt in the carbonara sauce, right? The pasta itself needs salt or it won't be tasty.
BURBLE BURBLE BURBLE
Hup! About 7 oz. of pasta! Enough for two people.
SHK SHK SHK
Teacher! The only vegetable is a clove of garlic.
Ah! Well then, can I use the broccoli meant for the chop suey? That way, we'll get veggies in the main dish!
Shiro type.
And Tabuchi, a type with no particular hang-ups.
Split the broccoli into small florets.
SPLSH
Two minutes before the pasta is done boiling, toss the broccoli in with it!

If you don't have any, chicken stock is okay.

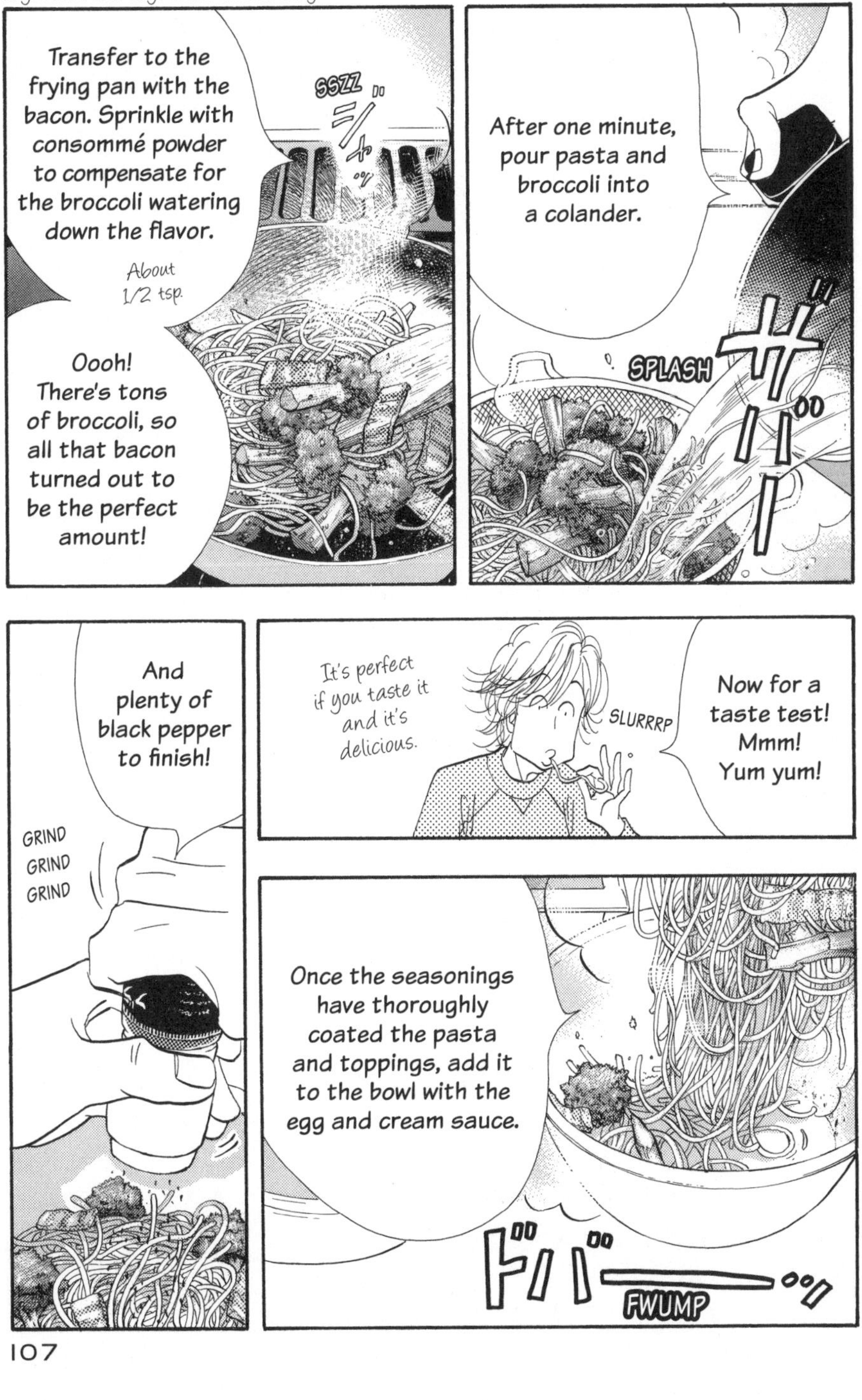
After one minute, pour pasta and broccoli into a colander.
SPLASH
Transfer to the frying pan with the bacon. Sprinkle with consommé powder to compensate for the broccoli watering down the flavor.
SSZZ
About 1/2 tsp.
Oooh! There's tons of broccoli, so all that bacon turned out to be the perfect amount!
Now for a taste test! Mmm! Yum yum!
SLURRRP
It's perfect if you taste it and it's delicious.
Once the seasonings have thoroughly coated the pasta and toppings, add it to the bowl with the egg and cream sauce.
FWUMP
And plenty of black pepper to finish!
GRIND
GRIND
GRIND

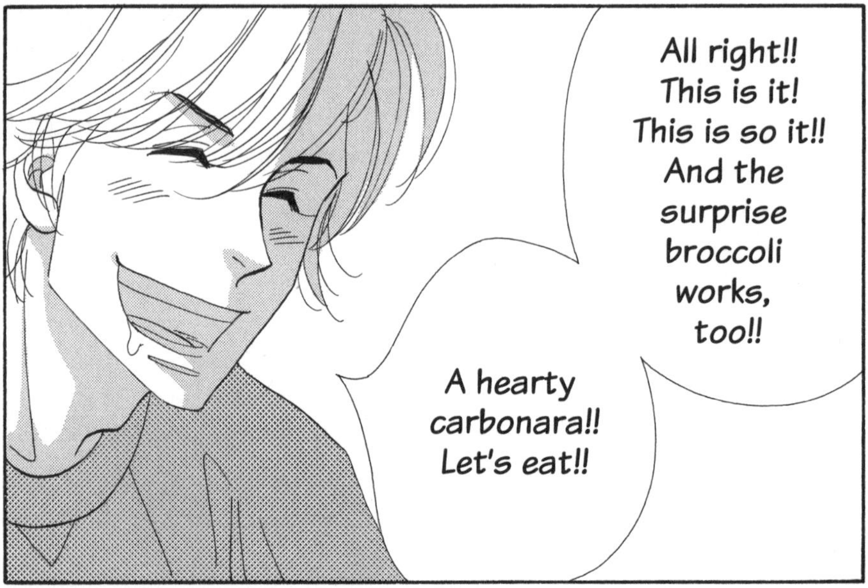
All right!! This is it! This is so it!! And the surprise broccoli works, too!!
A hearty carbonara!! Let's eat!!

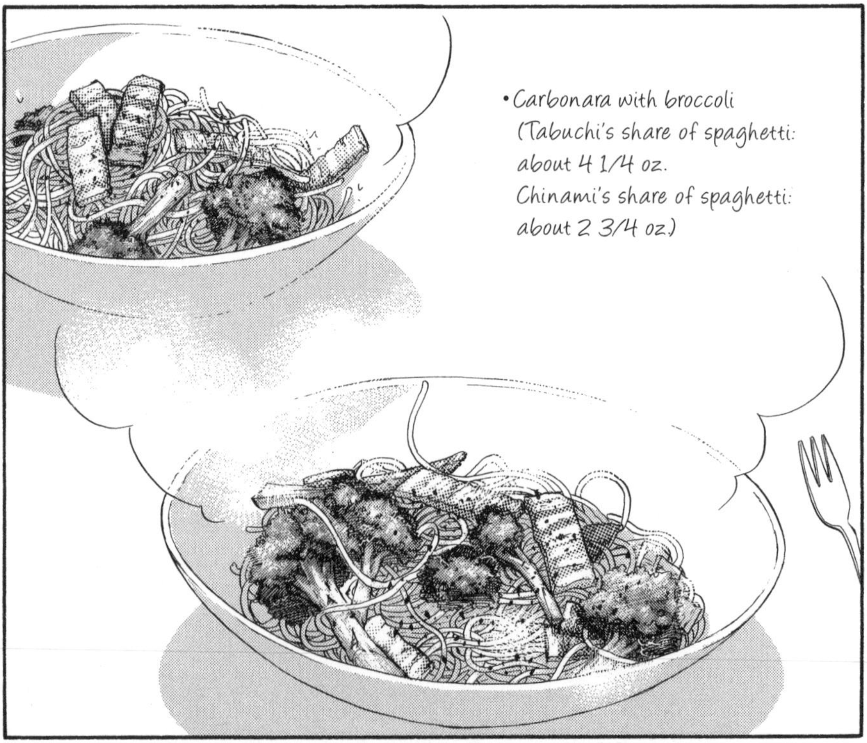
•Carbonara with broccoli (Tabuchi's share of spaghetti: about 4 1/4 oz. Chinami's share of spaghetti: about 2 3/4 oz.)

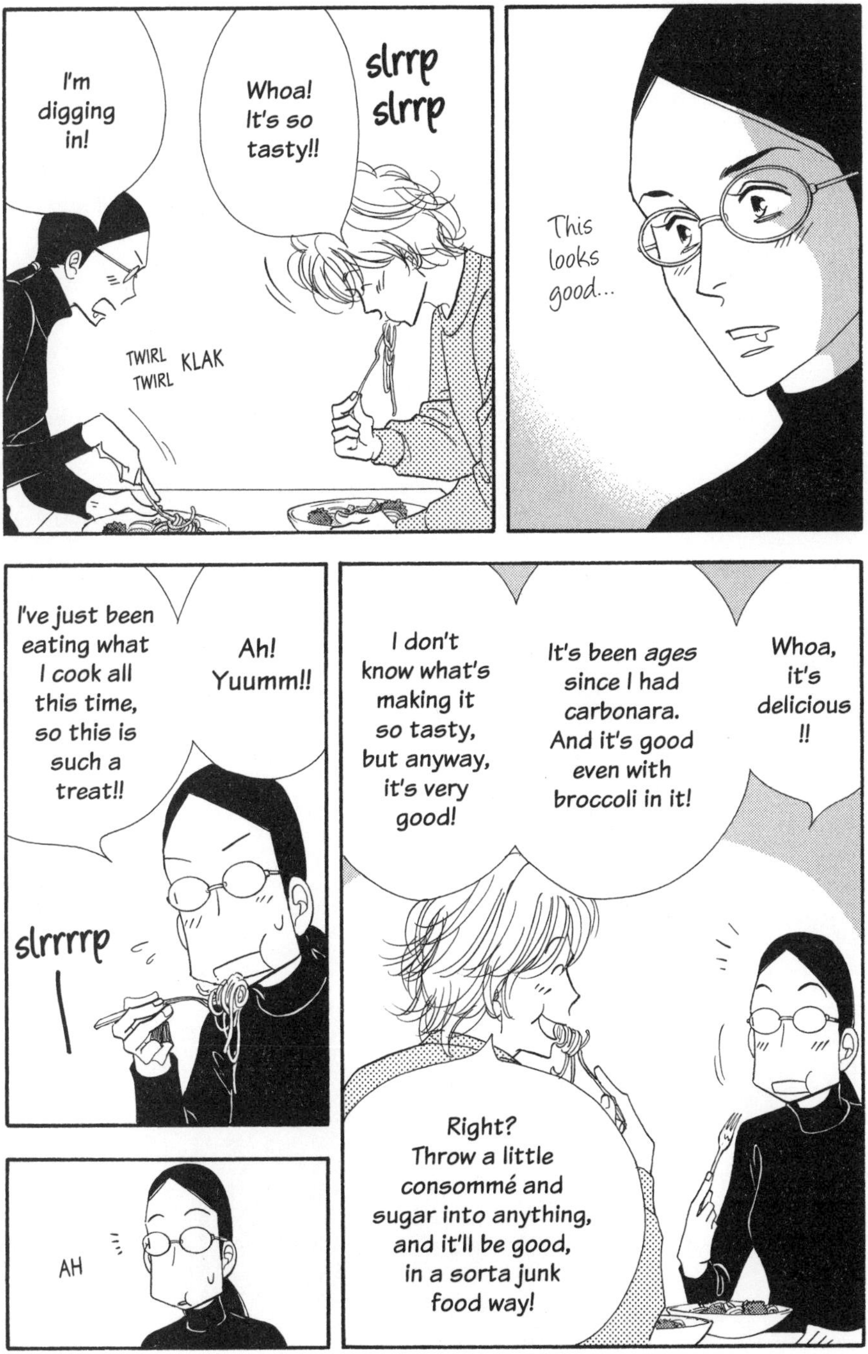
This looks good...
slrrp slrrp
Whoa! It's so tasty!!
I'm digging in!
TWIRL TWIRL
KLAK
Whoa, it's delicious!!
It's been *ages* since I had carbonara. And it's good even with broccoli in it!
I don't know what's making it so tasty, but anyway, it's very good!
Right? Throw a little consommé and sugar into anything, and it'll be good, in a sorta junk food way!
Ah! Yuumm!!
I've just been eating what I cook all this time, so this is such a treat!!
slrrrrp
AH

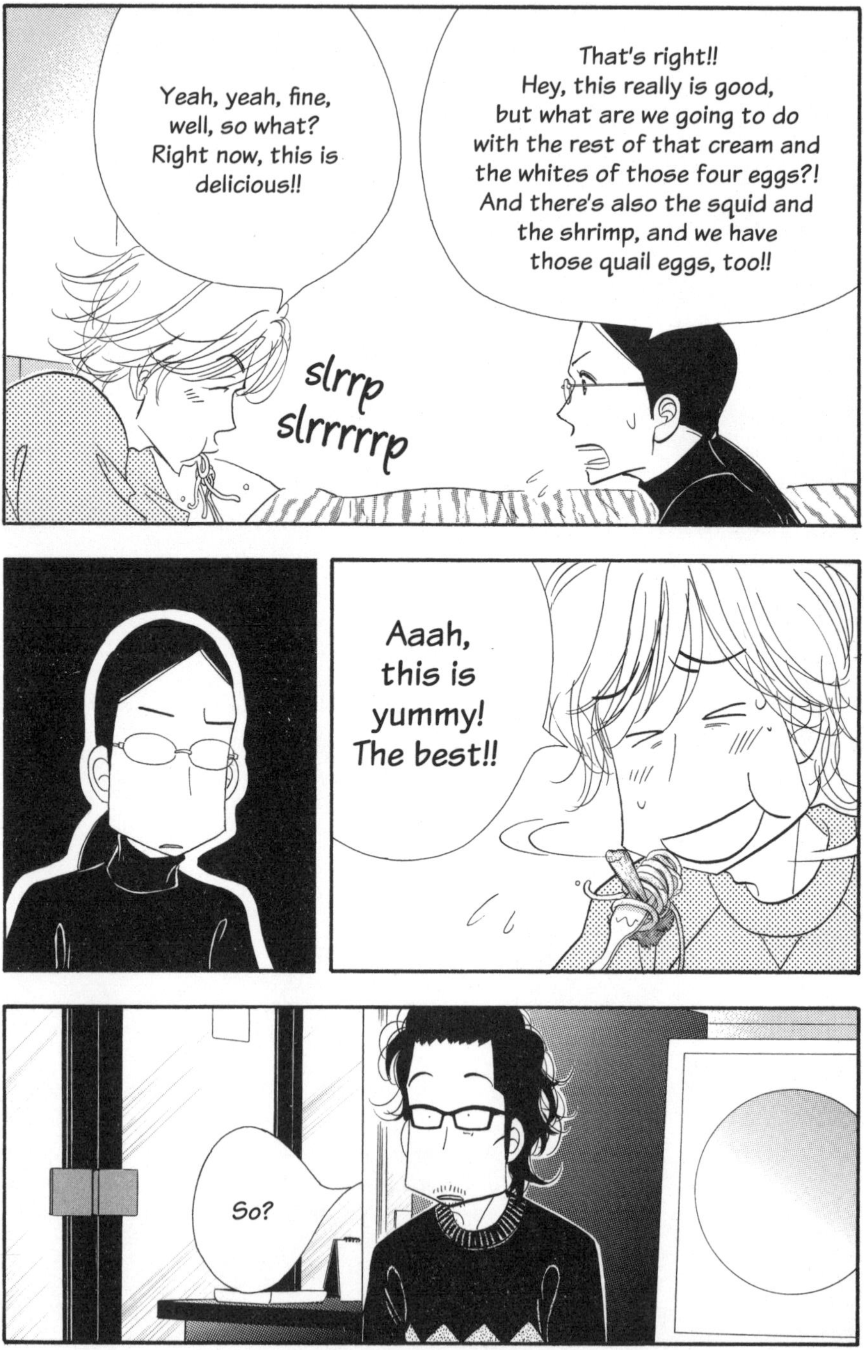
That's right!! Hey, this really is good, but what are we going to do with the rest of that cream and the whites of those four eggs?! And there's also the squid and the shrimp, and we have those quail eggs, too!!
Yeah, yeah, fine, well, so what? Right now, this is delicious!!
slrrp slrrrrrp
Aaah, this is yummy! The best!!
So?

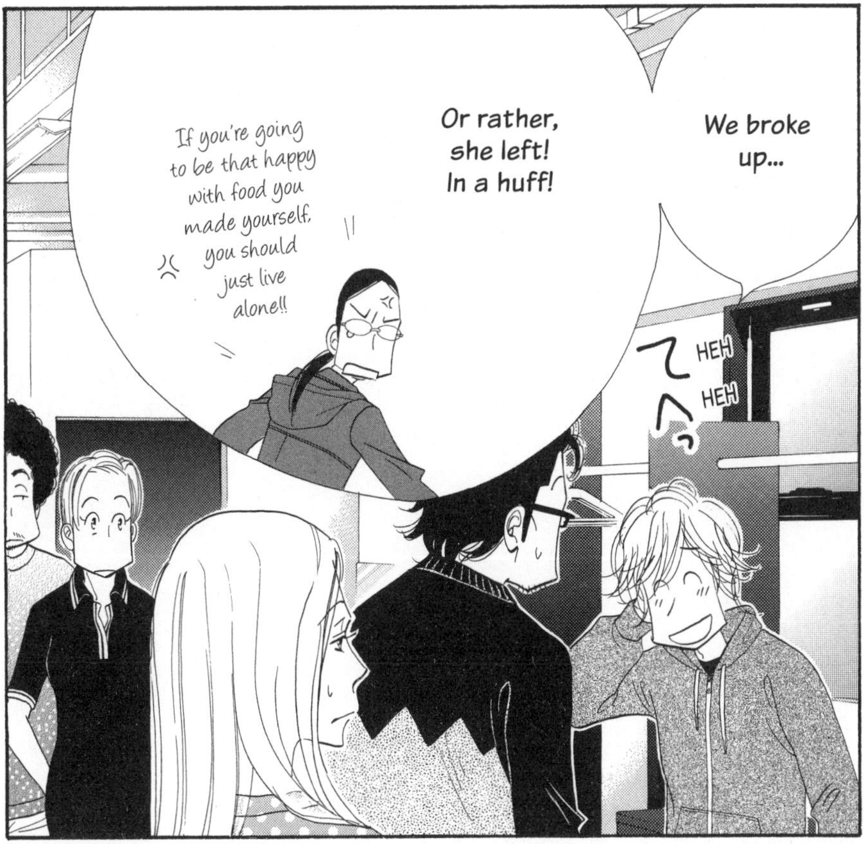
We broke up...
Or rather, she left! In a huff!
If you're going to be that happy with food you made yourself, you should just live alone!!
HEH HEH

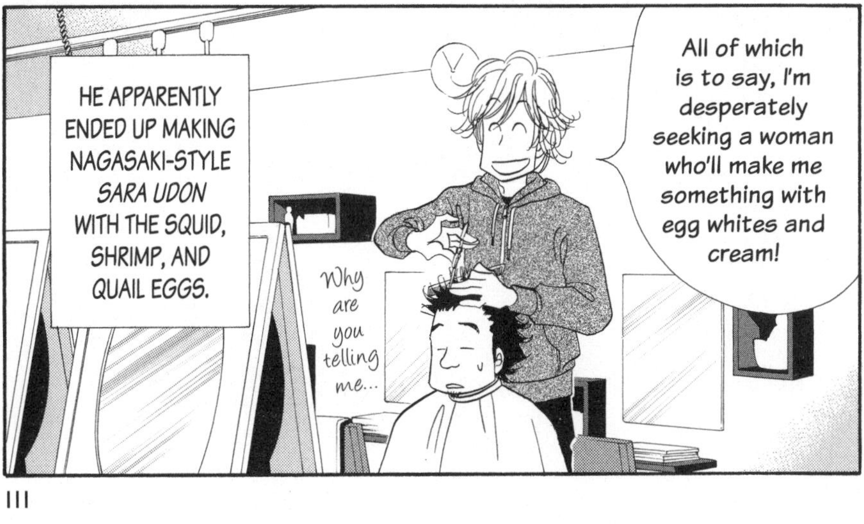
All of which is to say, I'm desperately seeking a woman who'll make me something with egg whites and cream!
HE APPARENTLY ENDED UP MAKING NAGASAKI-STYLE *SARA UDON* WITH THE SQUID, SHRIMP, AND QUAIL EGGS.
Why are you telling me...

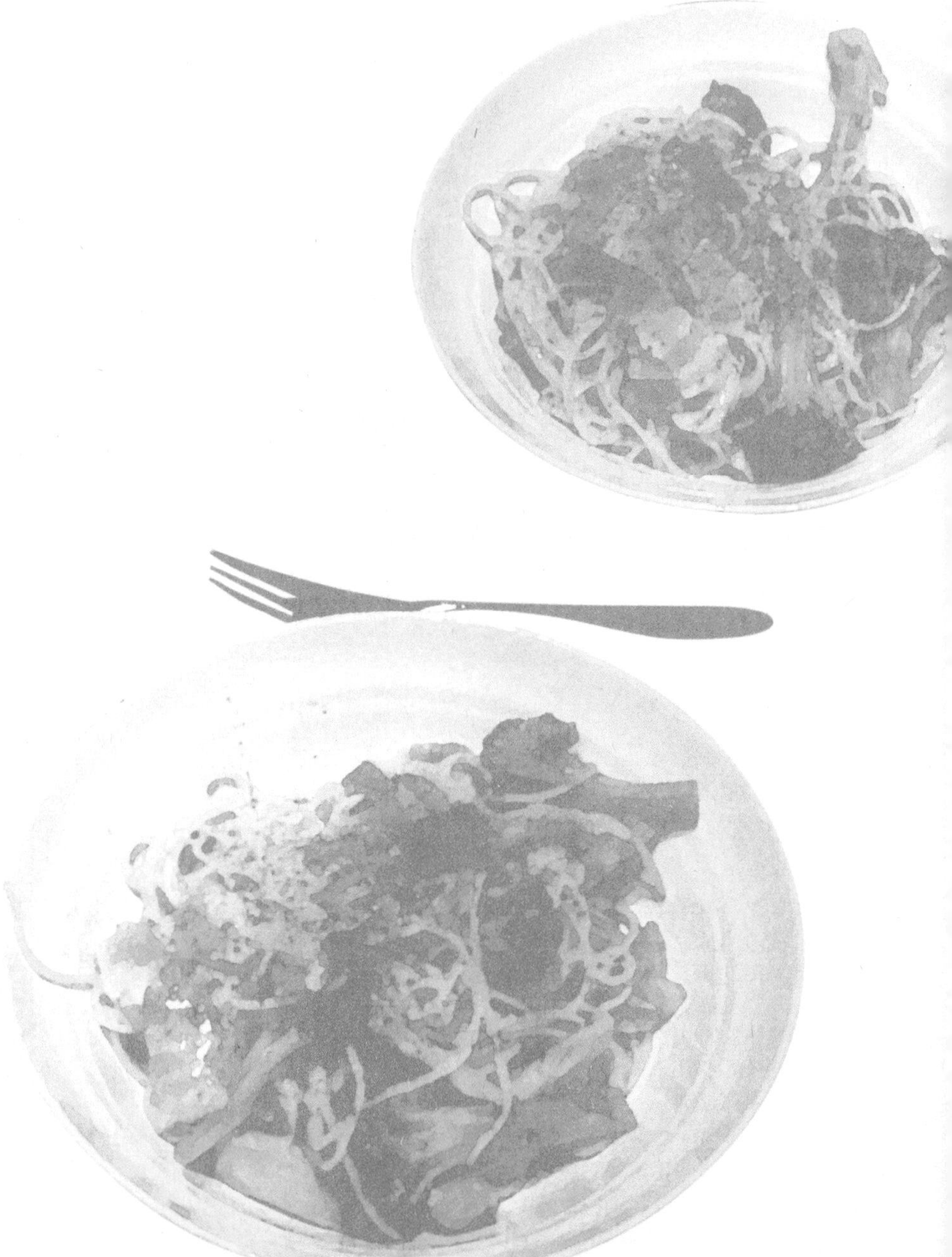

Tabuchi used four eggs, but for the same amount of cream, three eggs is okay, too.
If using four eggs, add another 1/4 C cream, and that will be enough for 9 to 11 oz. pasta.
You can also use *komatsuna* or boiled spinach instead of broccoli.

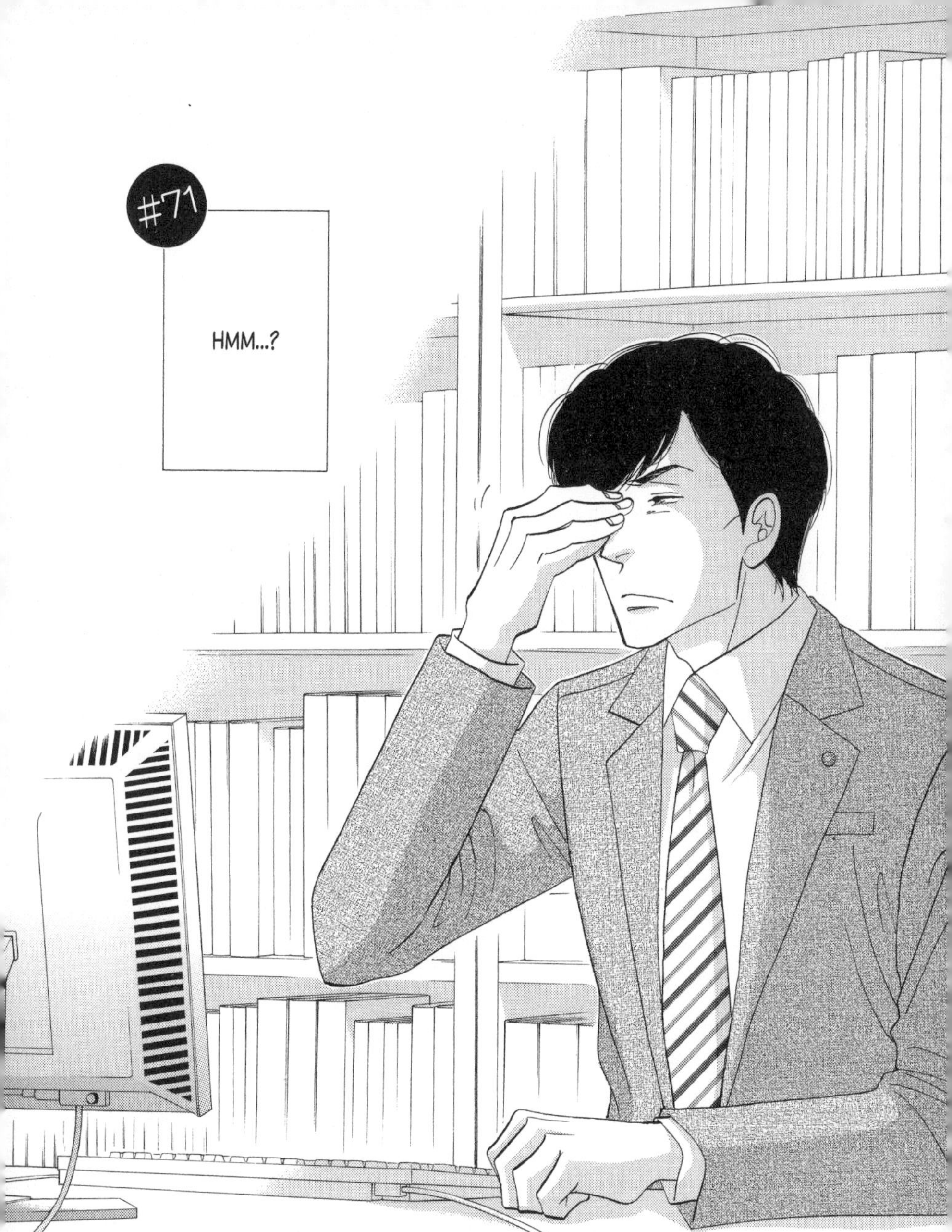
#71
HMM...?

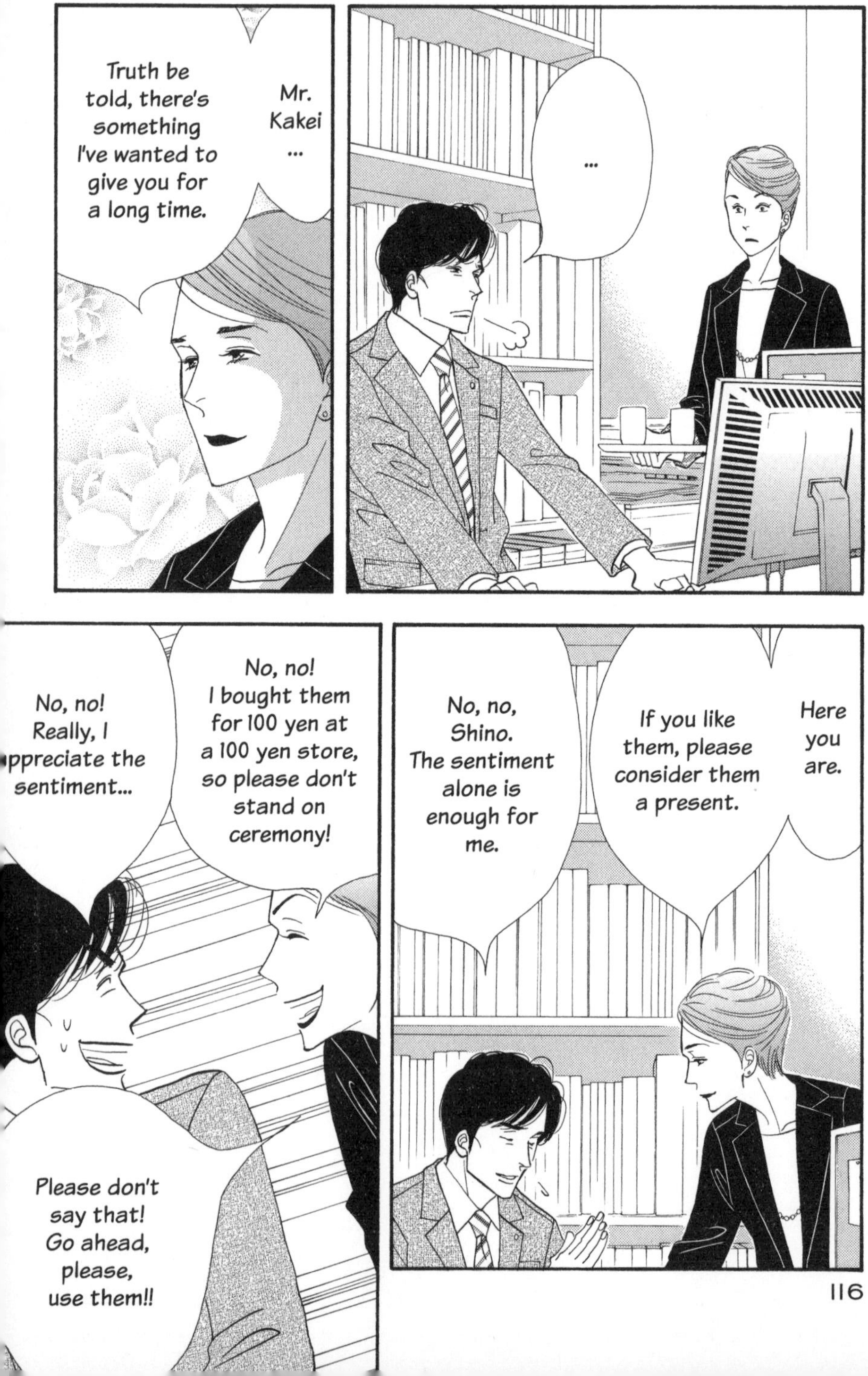
...
Mr. Kakei ...
Truth be told, there's something I've wanted to give you for a long time.
Here you are.
If you like them, please consider them a present.
No, no, Shino. The sentiment alone is enough for me.
No, no! I bought them for 100 yen at a 100 yen store, so please don't stand on ceremony!
No, no! Really, I ppreciate the sentiment...
Please don't say that! Go ahead, please, use them!!

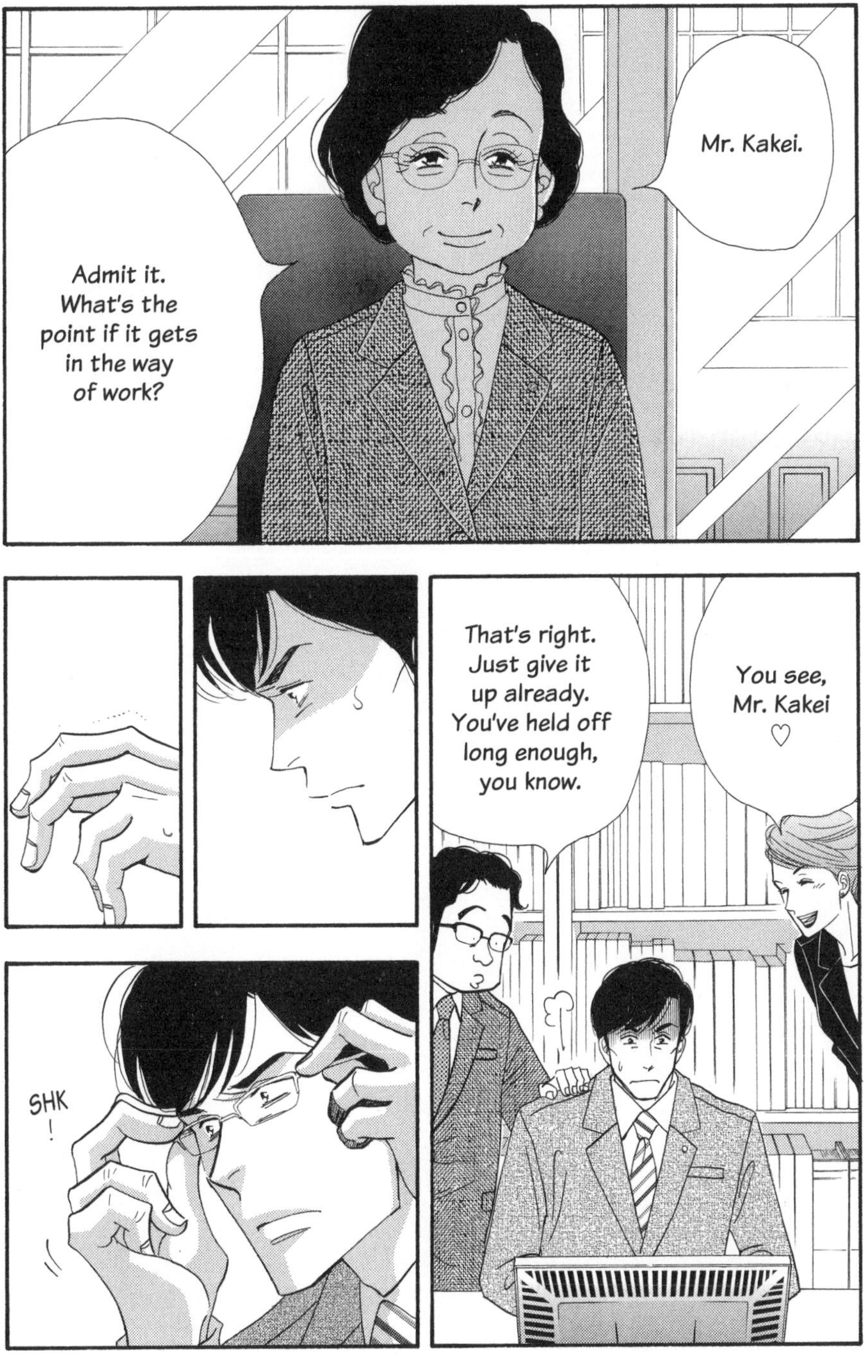
Mr. Kakei.
Admit it. What's the point if it gets in the way of work?
You see, Mr. Kakei ♡
That's right. Just give it up already. You've held off long enough, you know.
SHK !

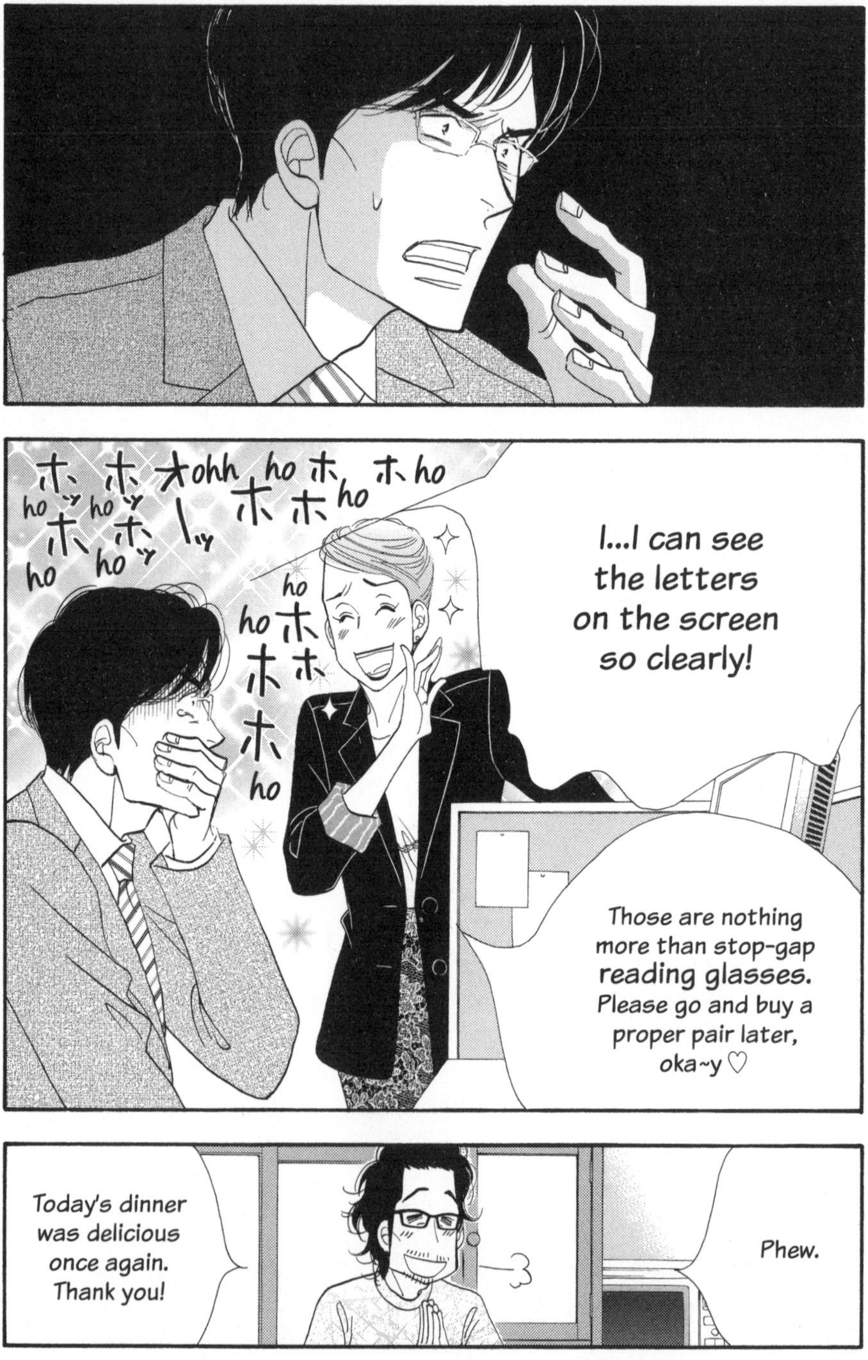
I...I can see the letters on the screen so clearly!
ホ ho ホ ho ホ ho ホ ho オ ohh ホ ho ホ ho ホ ho ホ ホ ホ ho
Those are nothing more than stop-gap reading glasses. Please go and buy a proper pair later, oka~y ♡
Phew.
Today's dinner was delicious once again. Thank you!

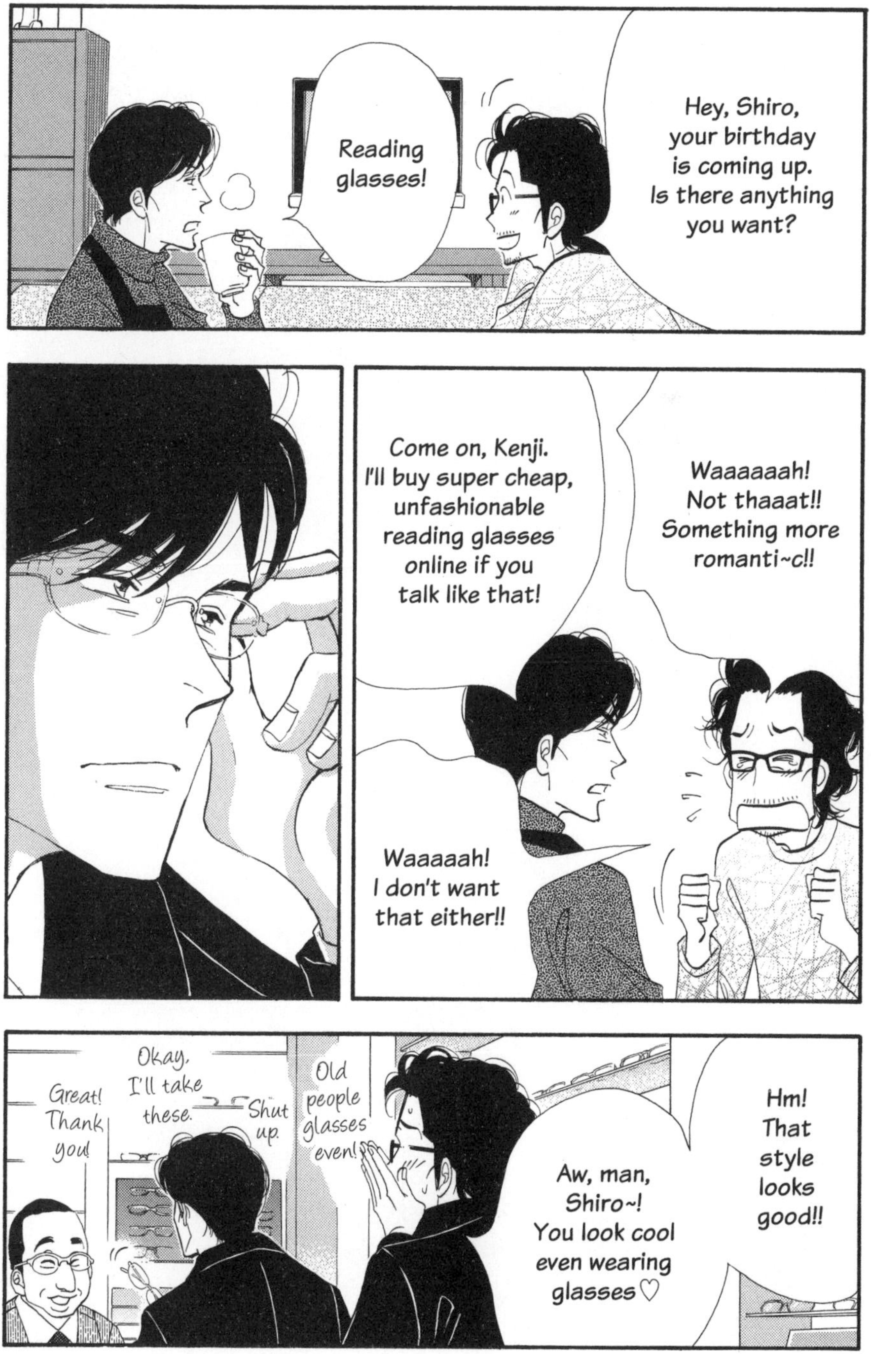
Hey, Shiro, your birthday is coming up. Is there anything you want?
Reading glasses!
Waaaaaah! Not thaaat!! Something more romanti~c!!
Come on, Kenji. I'll buy super cheap, unfashionable reading glasses online if you talk like that!
Waaaaah! I don't want that either!!
Hm! That style looks good!!
Aw, man, Shiro~! You look cool even wearing glasses♡
Old people glasses even!
Shut up.
Okay, I'll take these.
Great! Thank you!

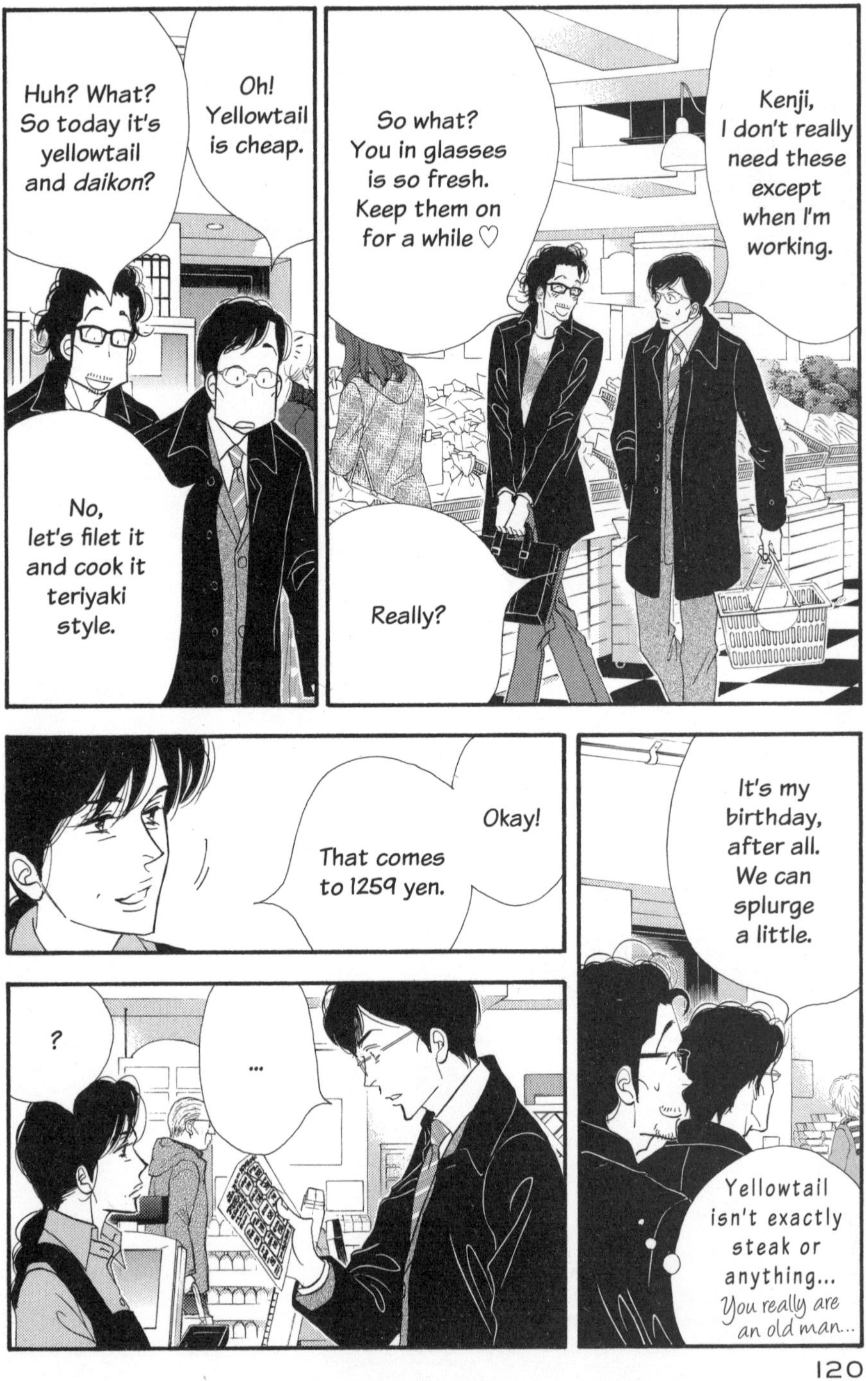
Kenji, I don't really need these except when I'm working.
So what? You in glasses is so fresh. Keep them on for a while ♡
Really?
Oh! Yellowtail is cheap.
Huh? What? So today it's yellowtail and *daikon*?
No, let's filet it and cook it teriyaki style.
It's my birthday, after all. We can splurge a little.
Yellowtail isn't exactly steak or anything...
You really are an old man...
Okay!
That comes to 1259 yen.
...
?

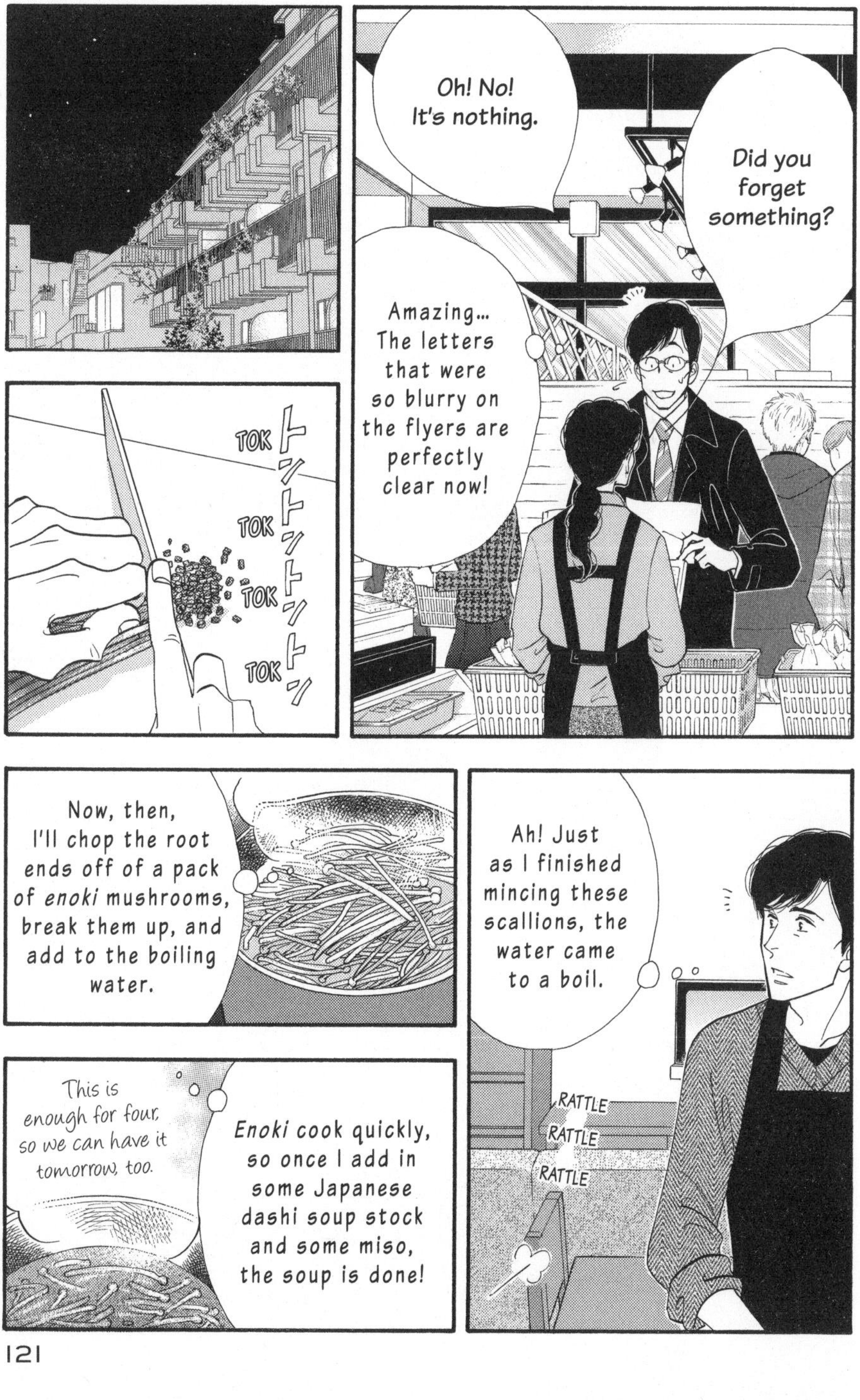
Did you forget something?
Oh! No! It's nothing.
Amazing... The letters that were so blurry on the flyers are perfectly clear now!
TOK TOK TOK TOK
トントントントン
Ah! Just as I finished mincing these scallions, the water came to a boil.
RATTLE RATTLE RATTLE
Now, then, I'll chop the root ends off of a pack of *enoki* mushrooms, break them up, and add to the boiling water.
Enoki cook quickly, so once I add in some Japanese dashi soup stock and some miso, the soup is done!
This is enough for four, so we can have it tomorrow, too.

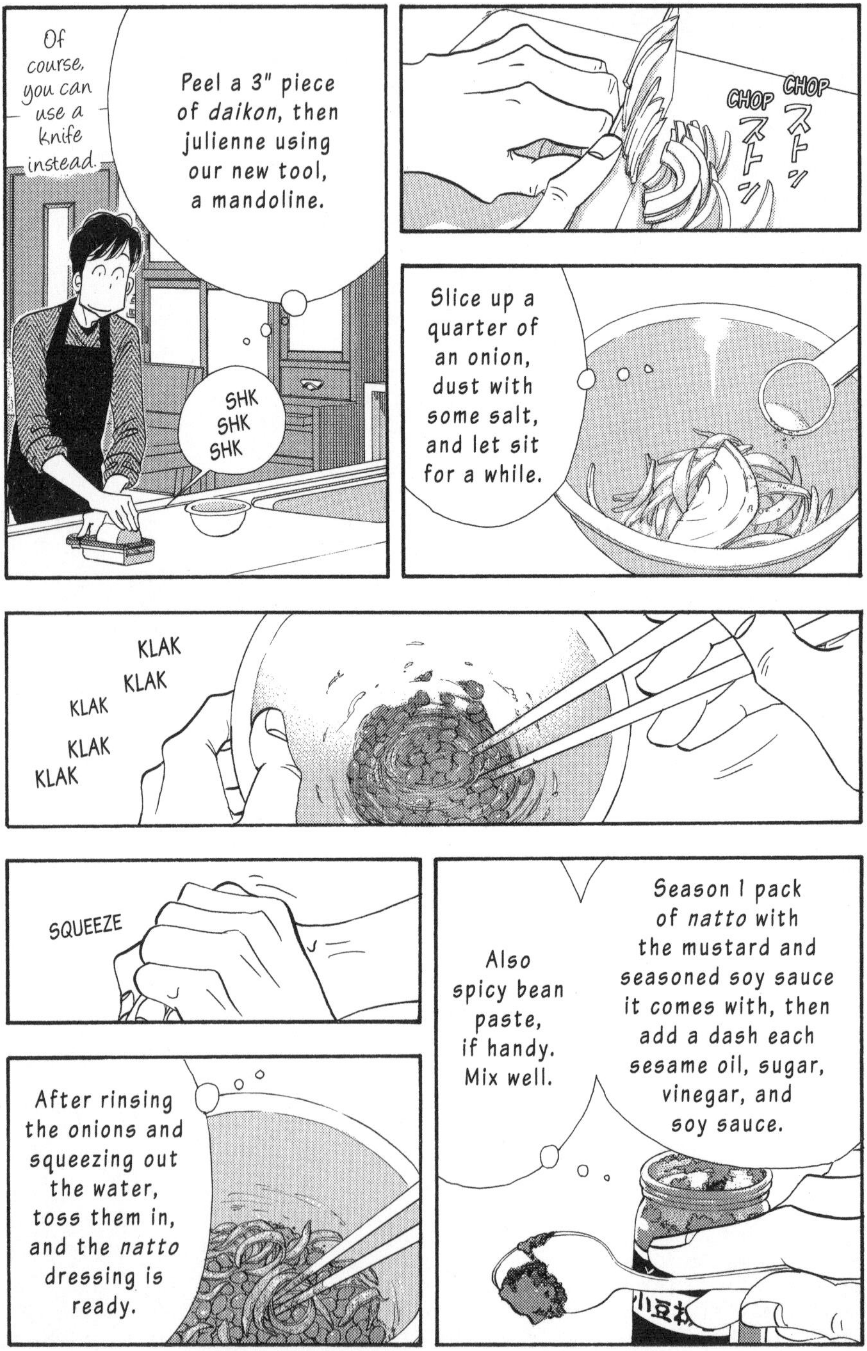
CHOP
ストン
CHOP
ストン
Slice up a quarter of an onion, dust with some salt, and let sit for a while.
Peel a 3" piece of *daikon*, then julienne using our new tool, a mandoline.
Of course, you can use a knife instead.
SHK SHK SHK
KLAK
KLAK
KLAK
KLAK
KLAK
Season 1 pack of *natto* with the mustard and seasoned soy sauce it comes with, then add a dash each sesame oil, sugar, vinegar, and soy sauce.
Also spicy bean paste, if handy. Mix well.
SQUEEZE
After rinsing the onions and squeezing out the water, toss them in, and the *natto* dressing is ready.

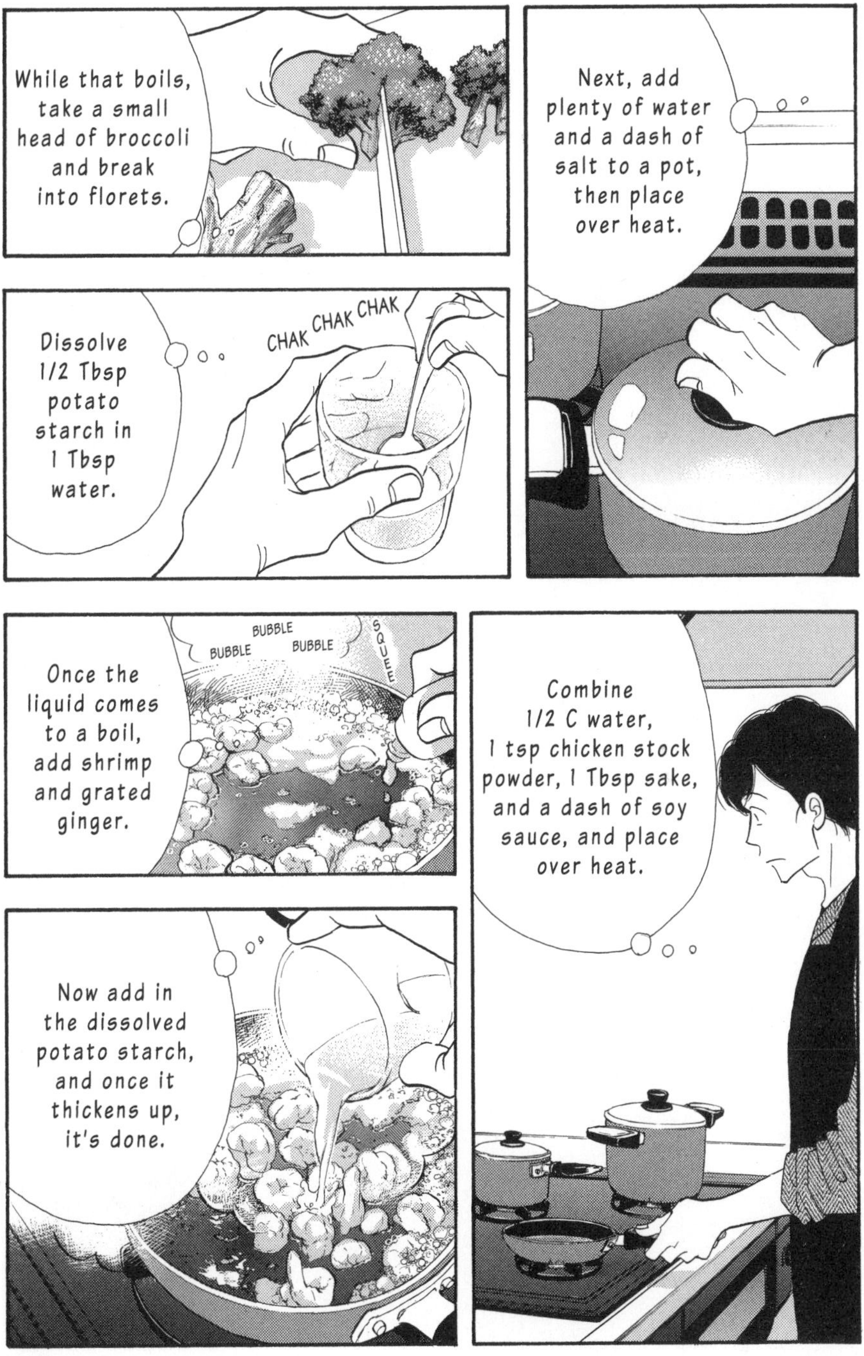
Next, add plenty of water and a dash of salt to a pot, then place over heat.
While that boils, take a small head of broccoli and break into florets.
CHAK CHAK CHAK
Dissolve 1/2 Tbsp potato starch in 1 Tbsp water.
Combine 1/2 C water, 1 tsp chicken stock powder, 1 Tbsp sake, and a dash of soy sauce, and place over heat.
SQUEE
BUBBLE BUBBLE BUBBLE
Once the liquid comes to a boil, add shrimp and grated ginger.
Now add in the dissolved potato starch, and once it thickens up, it's done.

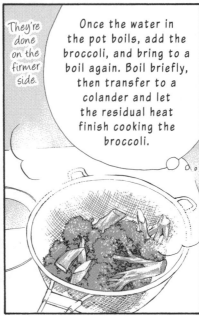

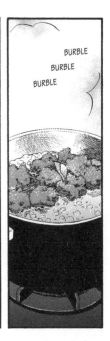

BURBLE
BURBLE
BURBLE
Once the water in the pot boils, add the broccoli, and bring to a boil again. Boil briefly, then transfer to a colander and let the residual heat finish cooking the broccoli.
They're done on the firmer side.
Now for the main dish! Yellowtail teriyaki!
Okay!
First, for the sauce, combine 1 Tbsp each soy sauce, mirin and sake, and 2 tsp sugar, and stir well.
SKFF
SKFF
SKFF
Pat dry 2 filets of yellowtail. Lay in pan, then dust with flour.
Heat a small amount of vegetable oil in a frying pan over medium heat...

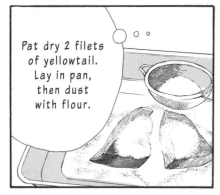

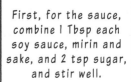

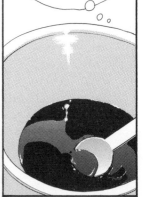

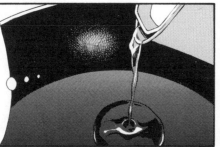

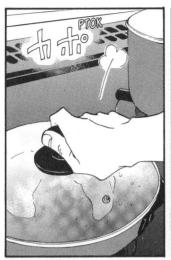

ジュウー
SIZZZZZLE
カポ
PTOK
After a while, the yellowtail will be browned. Once the edges turn whitish, flip them over...
SSZZZ
To make sure the sauce will cling neatly to the fish, siphon off excess oil in the pan with a paper towel or tissue.
Now pour in the sauce stirred together earlier.
Kenji! Dinner's almost ready!
Okay, I'm just finishing up folding the laundry!

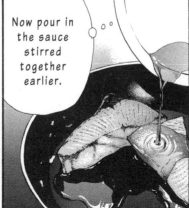

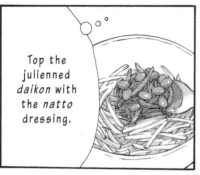

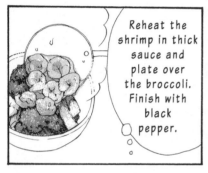

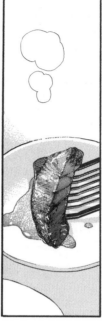

Rock the pan as the sauce cooks down, and the yellowtail teriyaki is done.
SSZZZ
Top the julienned *daikon* with the *natto* dressing.
Reheat the shrimp in thick sauce and plate over the broccoli. Finish with black pepper.
Finally, plenty of scallions for the *enoki* miso soup!
There we go! Perfect!
Oh my! This looks delicious ♡

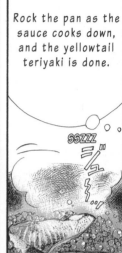

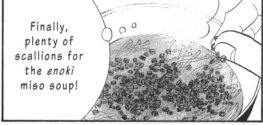

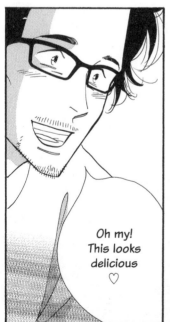

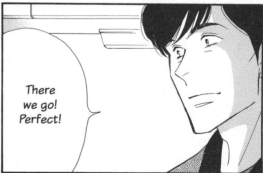

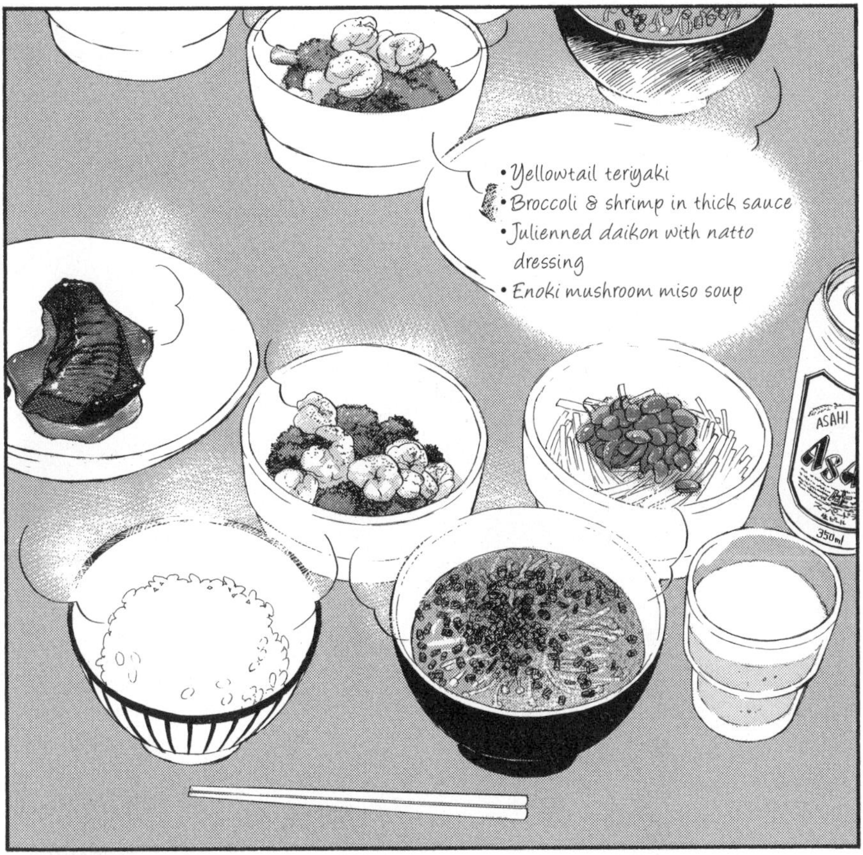
•Yellowtail teriyaki
•Broccoli & shrimp in thick sauce
•Julienned daikon with natto dressing
•Enoki mushroom miso soup
ASAHI
350ml

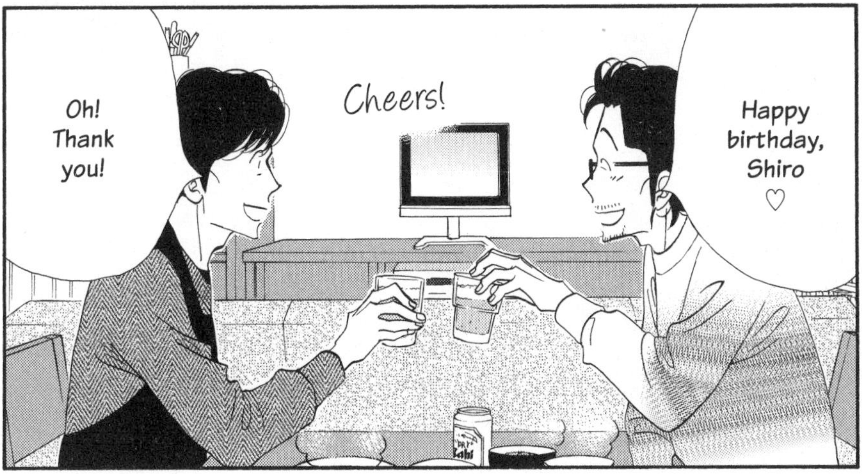
Happy birthday, Shiro ♡
Cheers!
Oh! Thank you!

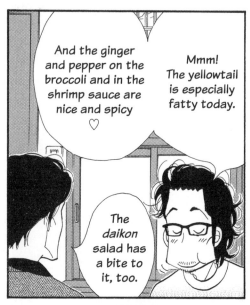

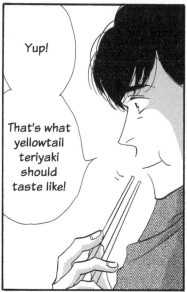

Yup!
That's what yellowtail teriyaki should taste like!
Mmm! The yellowtail is especially fatty today.
And the ginger and pepper on the broccoli and in the shrimp sauce are nice and spicy ♡
The *daikon* salad has a bite to it, too.
Ooh, it really does! Tonight's menu is pub-style, in a way. That's some hot-and-spicy natto dressing!
Aah, I loooove this enoki miso soup ♡
Ah! And then, and then! I bought a cake! Let's have some together later, Shiro!!
ピンポーン
DING
DONG

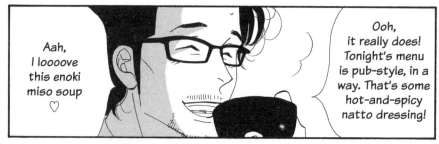

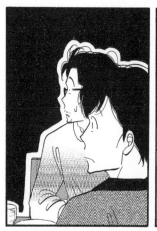

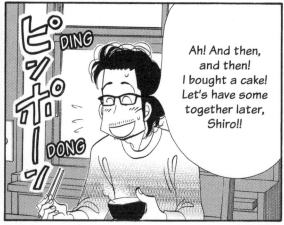

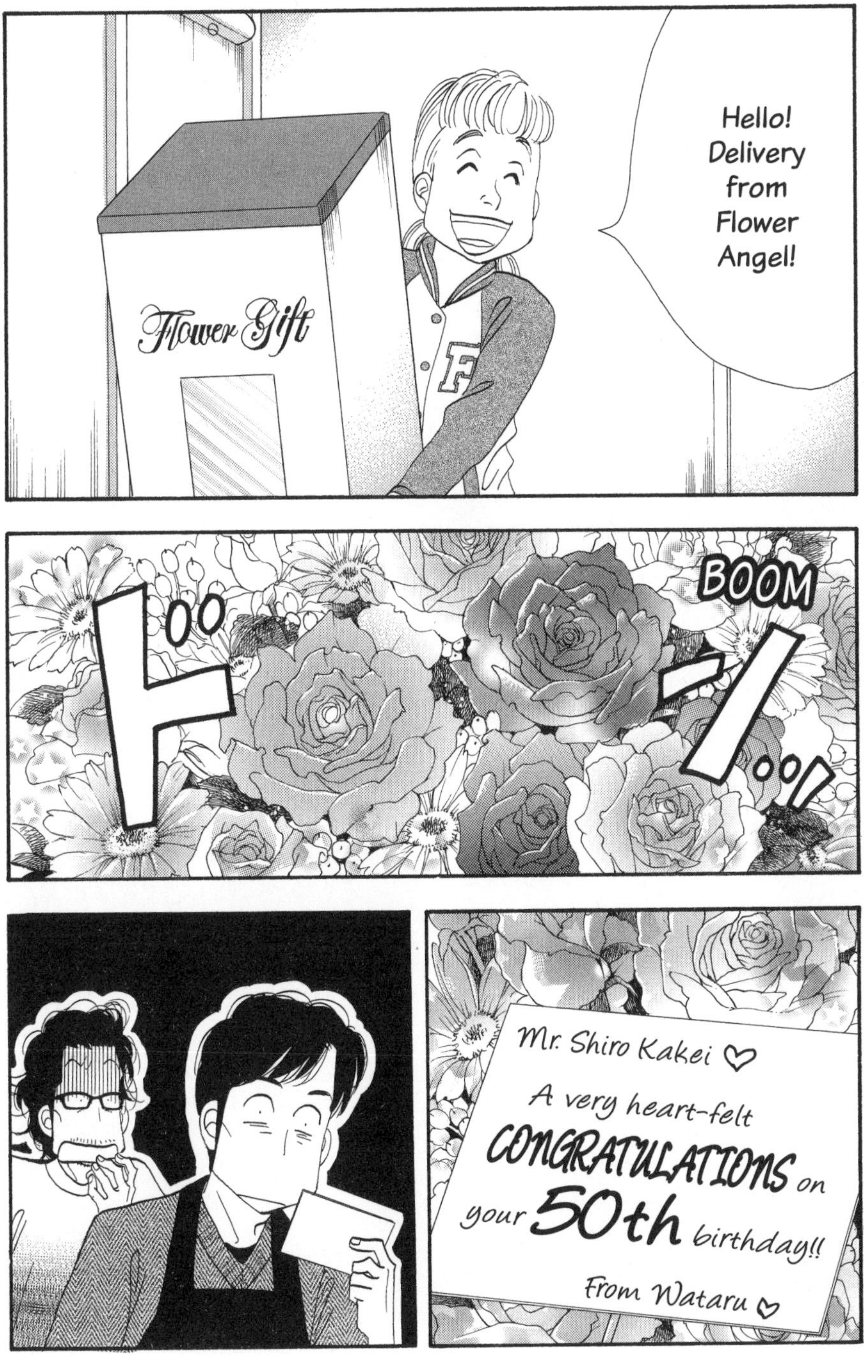
Hello! Delivery from Flower Angel!
Flower Gift
BOOM
Mr. Shiro Kakei ♡
A very heart-felt CONGRATULATIONS on your 50th birthday!!
From Wataru ♡

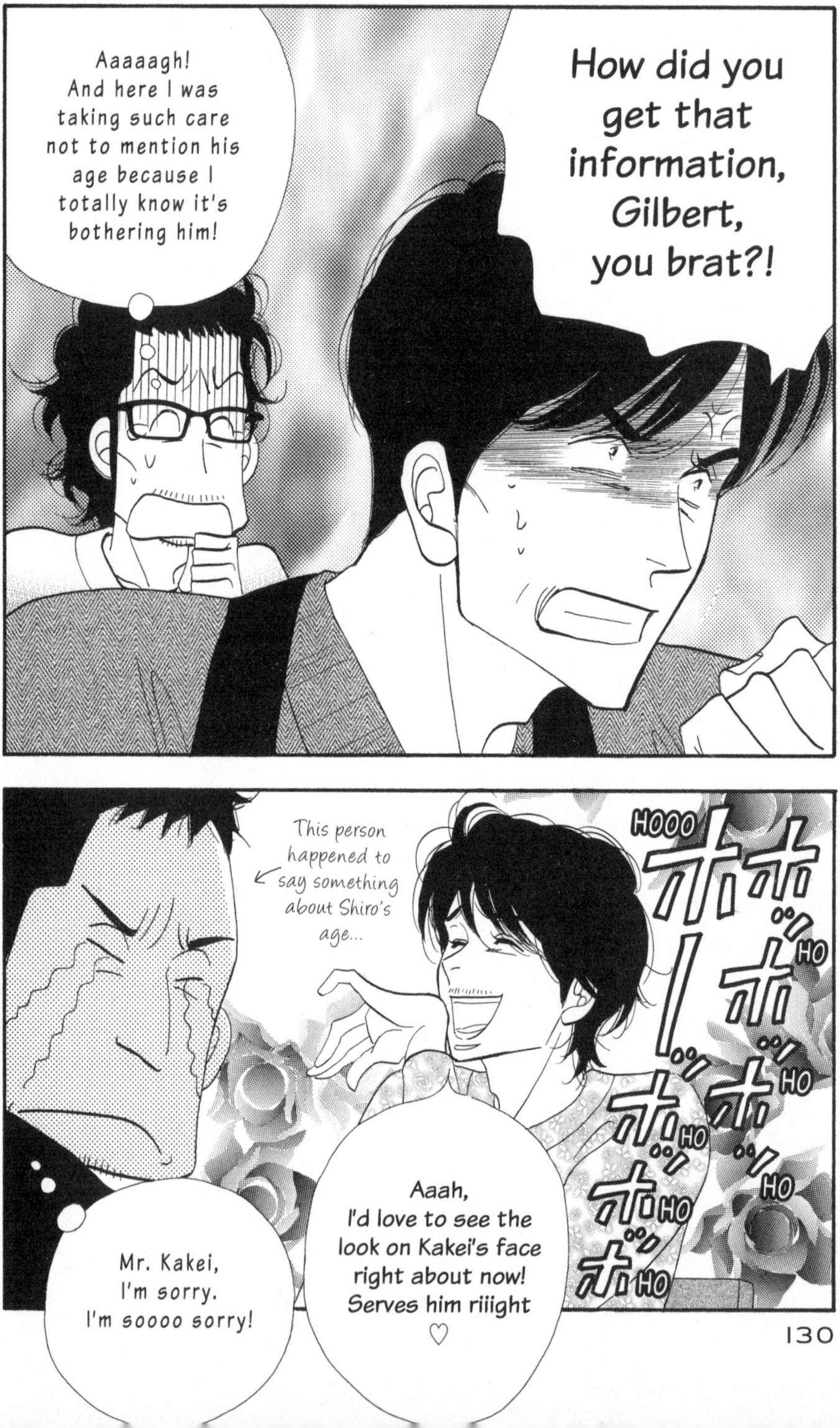
How did you get that information, Gilbert, you brat?!
Aaaaagh! And here I was taking such care not to mention his age because I totally know it's bothering him!
HOOO
HO
HO
HO
HO
HO
HO
This person happened to say something about Shiro's age...
Aaah, I'd love to see the look on Kakei's face right about now! Serves him riiight ♡
Mr. Kakei, I'm sorry. I'm soooo sorry!

The **yellowtail teriyaki** is also very delicious
when served with plenty of grated *daikon* and citrus.
As with the salmon in Chapter 65,
avoid salting the fish first to allow the sauce
to set up the flavors later on.

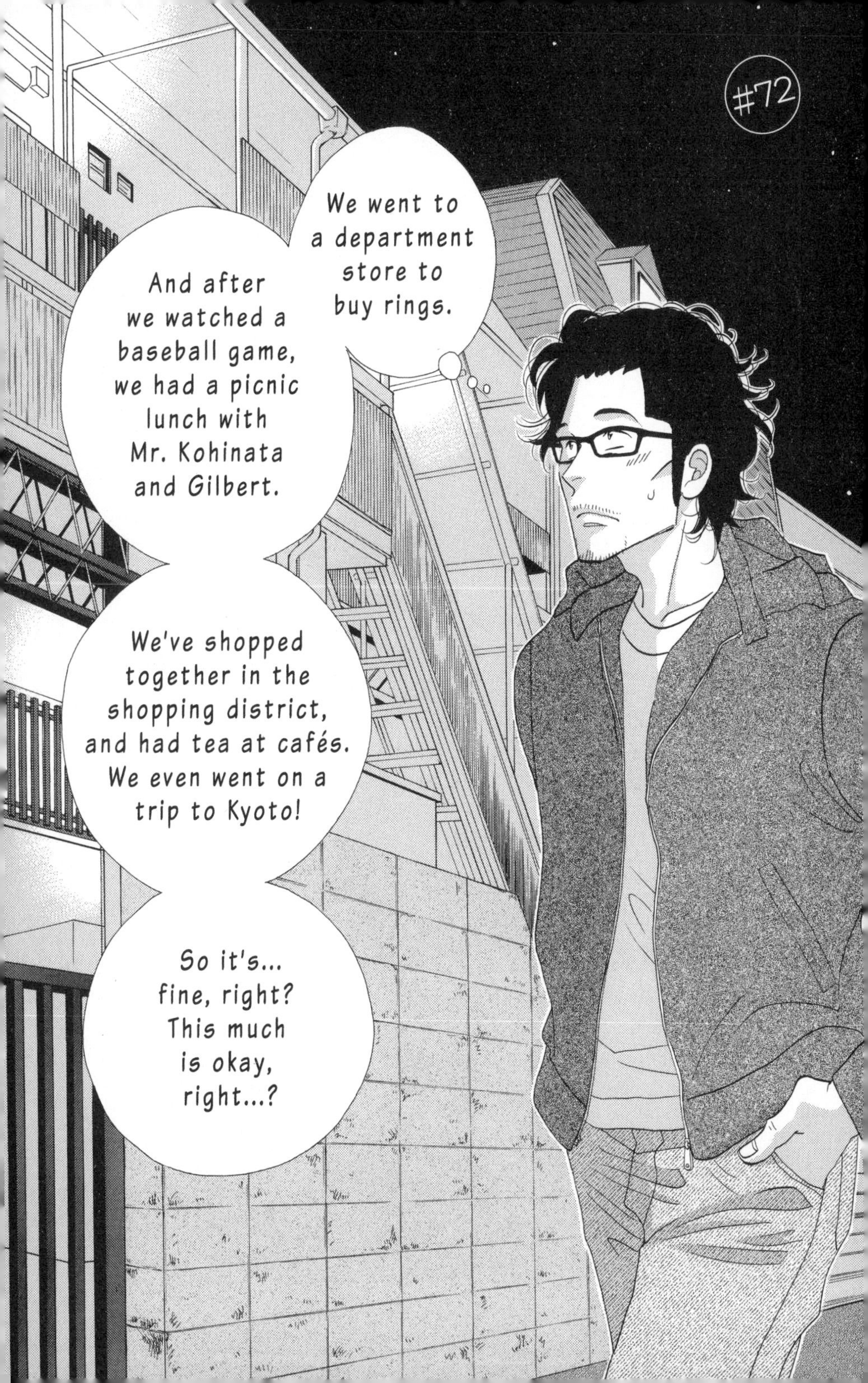
#72
We went to a department store to buy rings.
And after we watched a baseball game, we had a picnic lunch with Mr. Kohinata and Gilbert.
We've shopped together in the shopping district, and had tea at cafés. We even went on a trip to Kyoto!
So it's... fine, right? This much is okay, right...?

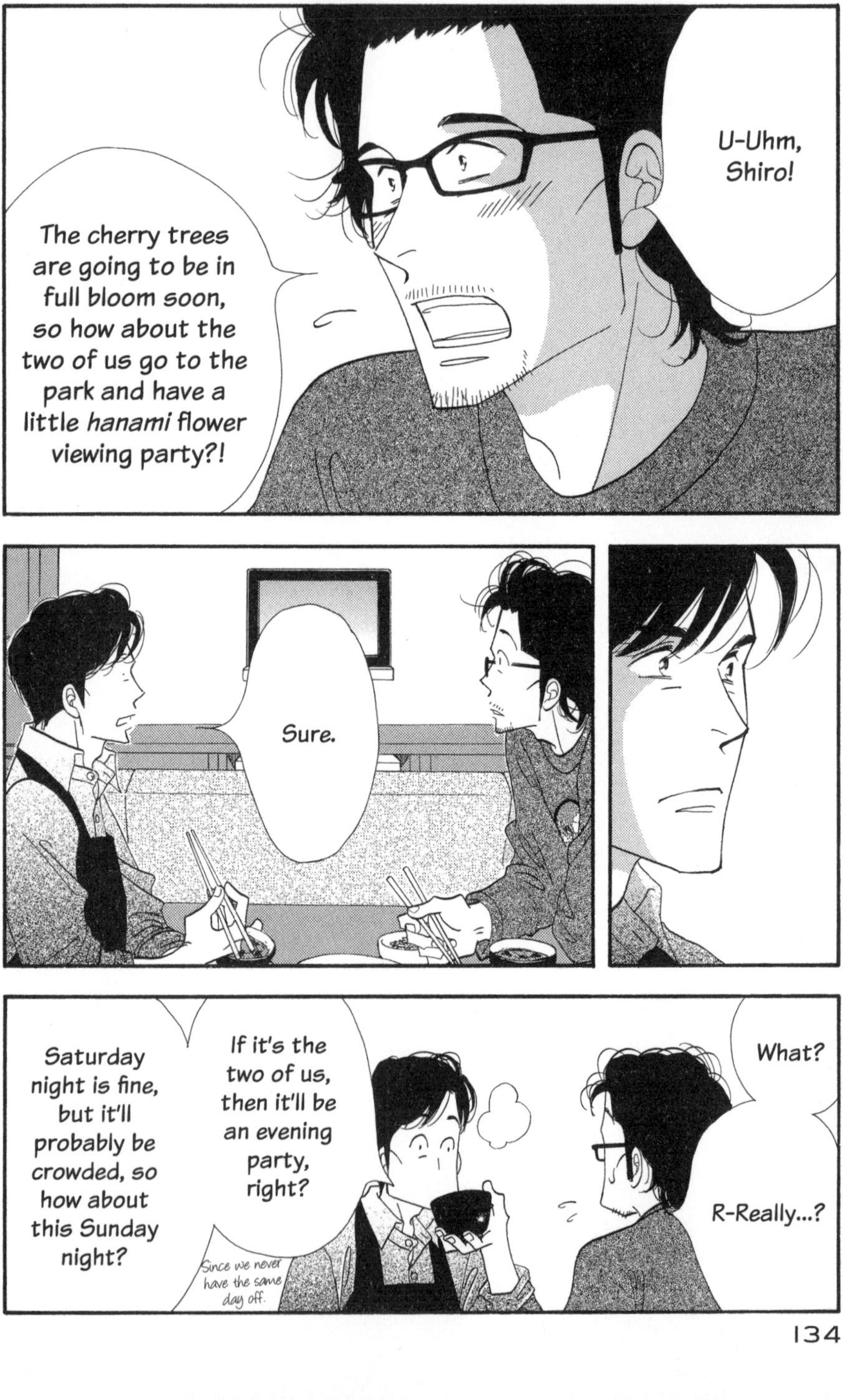
U-Uhm, Shiro!
The cherry trees are going to be in full bloom soon, so how about the two of us go to the park and have a little hanami flower viewing party?!
Sure.
What?
R-Really...?
If it's the two of us, then it'll be an evening party, right?
Saturday night is fine, but it'll probably be crowded, so how about this Sunday night?
Since we never have the same day off.

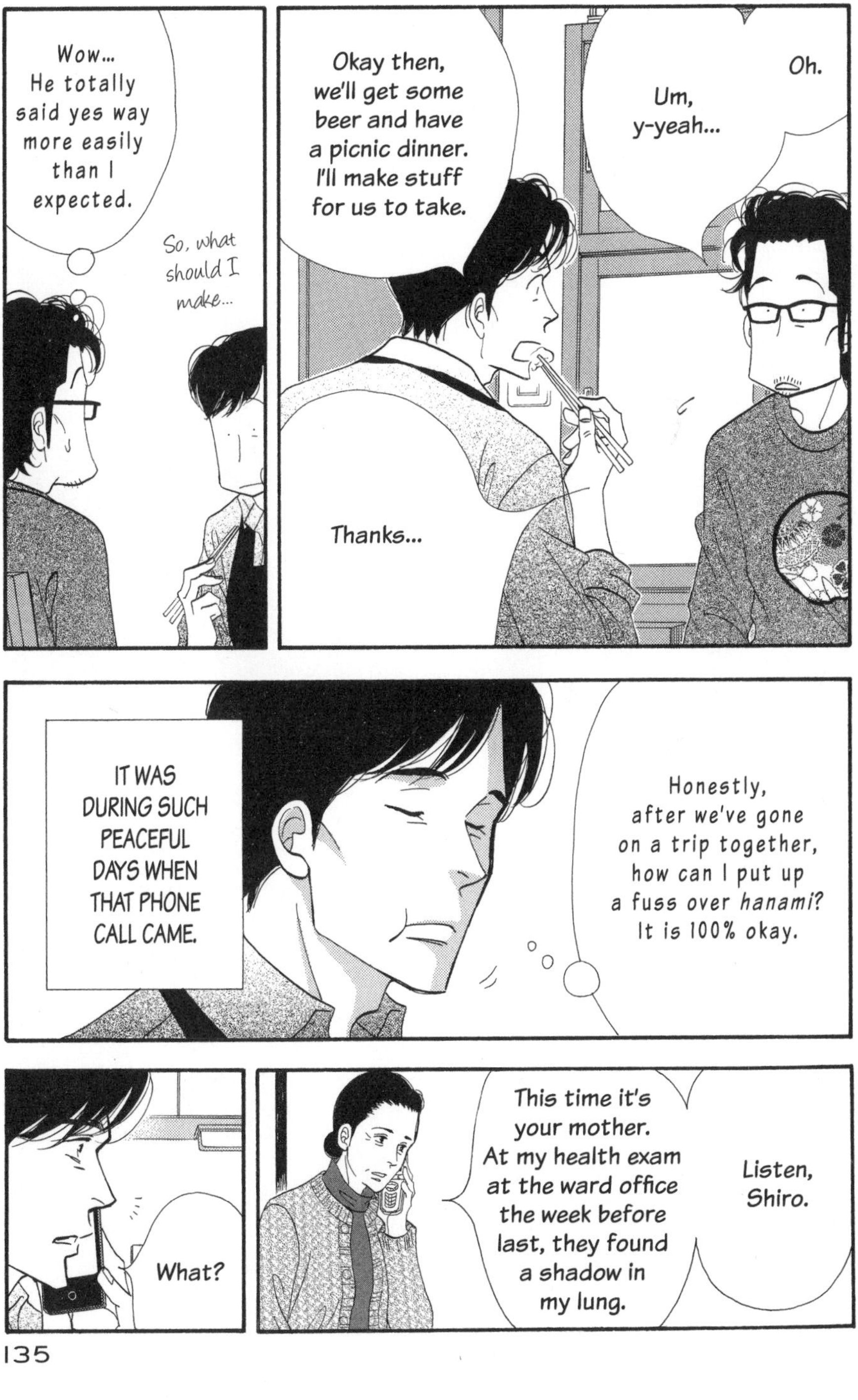
Oh.
Um, y-yeah...
Okay then, we'll get some beer and have a picnic dinner. I'll make stuff for us to take.
Thanks...
Wow... He totally said yes way more easily than I expected.
So, what should I make...
Honestly, after we've gone on a trip together, how can I put up a fuss over *hanami*? It is 100% okay.
IT WAS DURING SUCH PEACEFUL DAYS WHEN THAT PHONE CALL CAME.
Listen, Shiro.
This time it's your mother. At my health exam at the ward office the week before last, they found a shadow in my lung.
What?

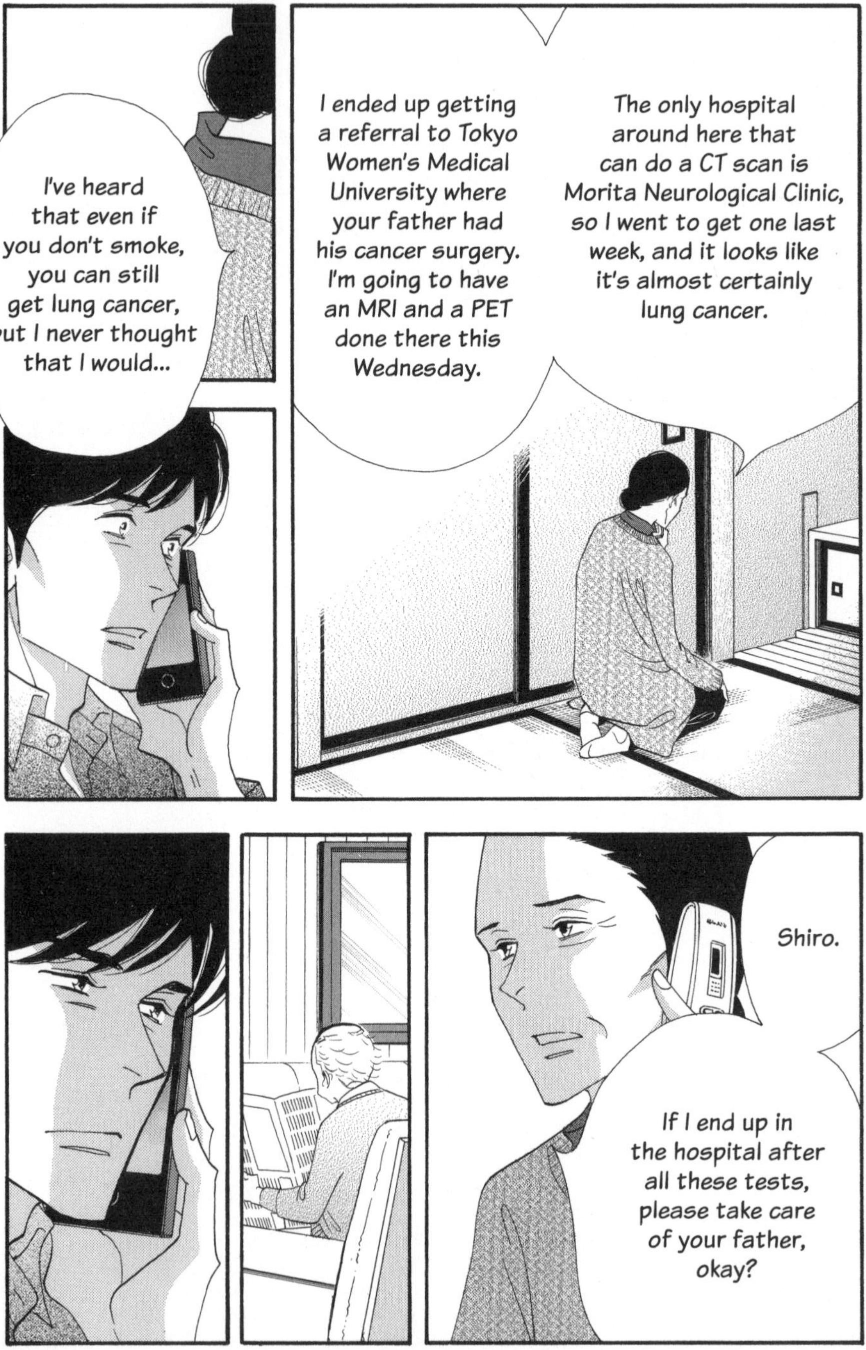
The only hospital around here that can do a CT scan is Morita Neurological Clinic, so I went to get one last week, and it looks like it's almost certainly lung cancer.
I ended up getting a referral to Tokyo Women's Medical University where your father had his cancer surgery. I'm going to have an MRI and a PET done there this Wednesday.
I've heard that even if you don't smoke, you can still get lung cancer, but I never thought that I would...
Shiro.
If I end up in the hospital after all these tests, please take care of your father, okay?

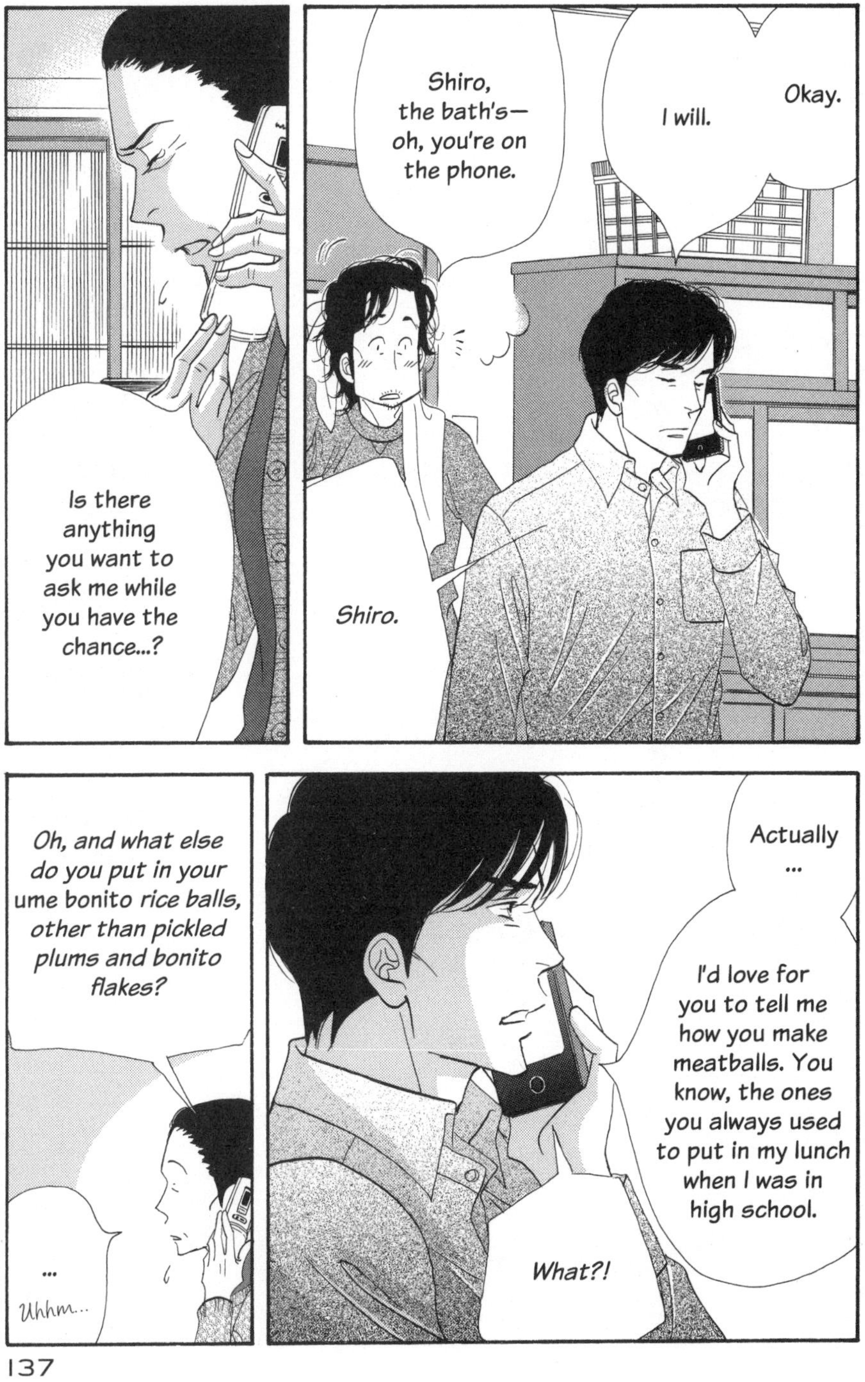
Okay.
I will.
Shiro, the bath's— oh, you're on the phone.
Shiro.
Is there anything you want to ask me while you have the chance...?
Actually ...
I'd love for you to tell me how you make meatballs. You know, the ones you always used to put in my lunch when I was in high school.
What?!
Oh, and what else do you put in your ume bonito rice balls, other than pickled plums and bonito flakes?
...
Uhhm...

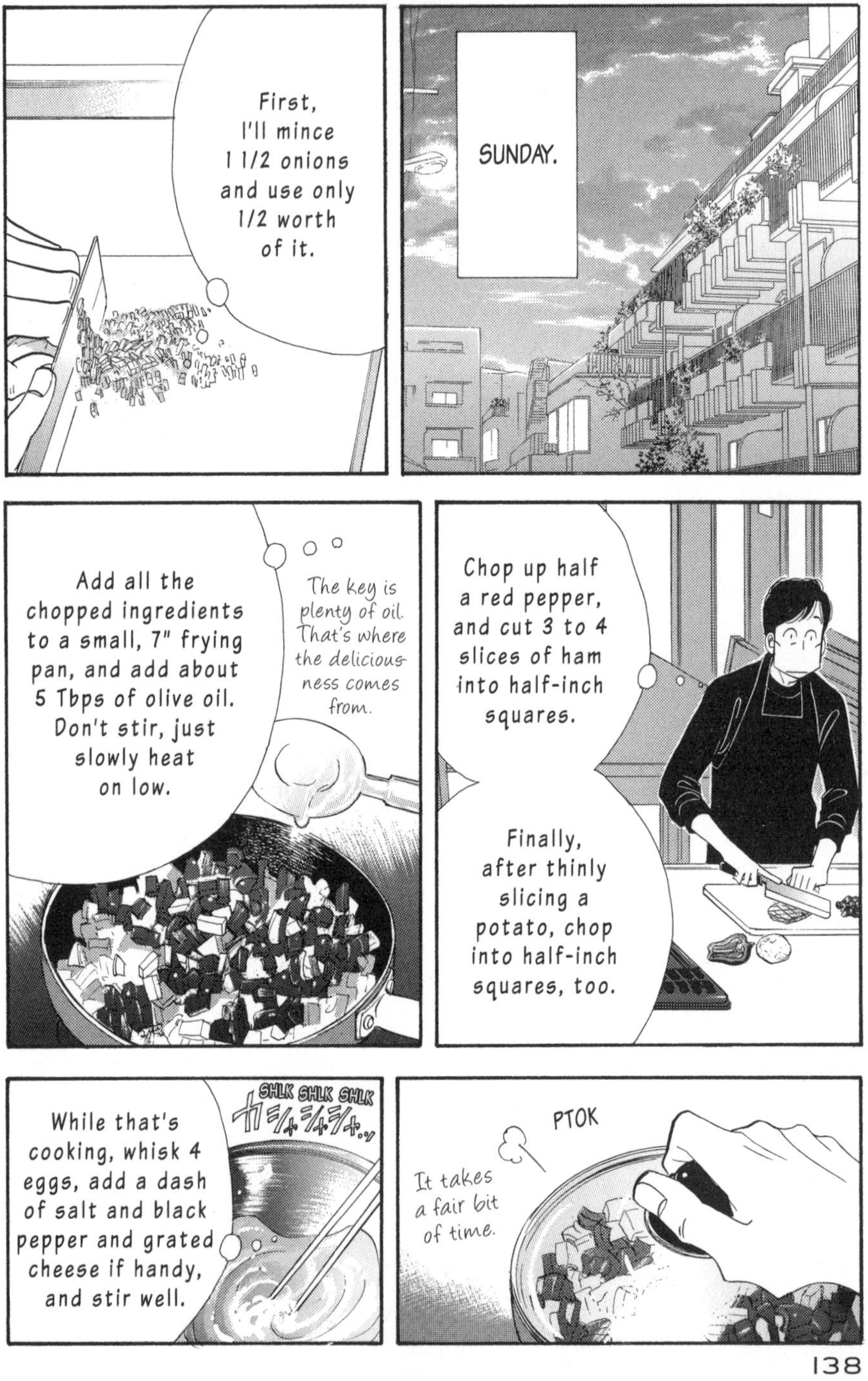
SUNDAY.
First, I'll mince 1 1/2 onions and use only 1/2 worth of it.
Chop up half a red pepper, and cut 3 to 4 slices of ham into half-inch squares.
Finally, after thinly slicing a potato, chop into half-inch squares, too.
Add all the chopped ingredients to a small, 7" frying pan, and add about 5 Tbps of olive oil. Don't stir, just slowly heat on low.
The key is plenty of oil. That's where the deliciousness comes from.
PTOK
It takes a fair bit of time.
SHLK SHLK SHLK
While that's cooking, whisk 4 eggs, add a dash of salt and black pepper and grated cheese if handy, and stir well.

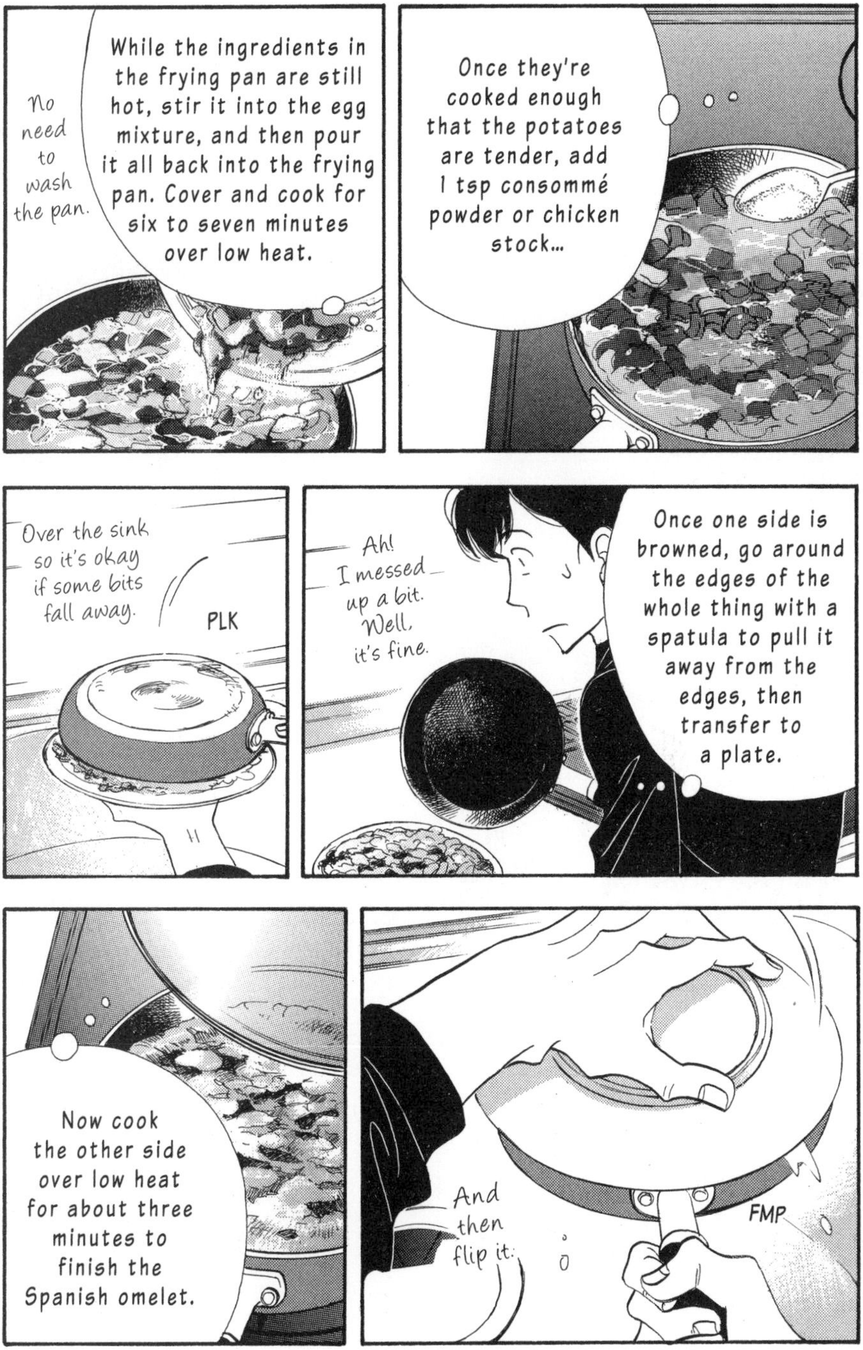
Once they're cooked enough that the potatoes are tender, add 1 tsp consommé powder or chicken stock...
While the ingredients in the frying pan are still hot, stir it into the egg mixture, and then pour it all back into the frying pan. Cover and cook for six to seven minutes over low heat.
No need to wash the pan.
Once one side is browned, go around the edges of the whole thing with a spatula to pull it away from the edges, then transfer to a plate.
Ah! I messed up a bit. Well, it's fine.
Over the sink so it's okay if some bits fall away.
PLK
FMP
And then flip it.
Now cook the other side over low heat for about three minutes to finish the Spanish omelet.

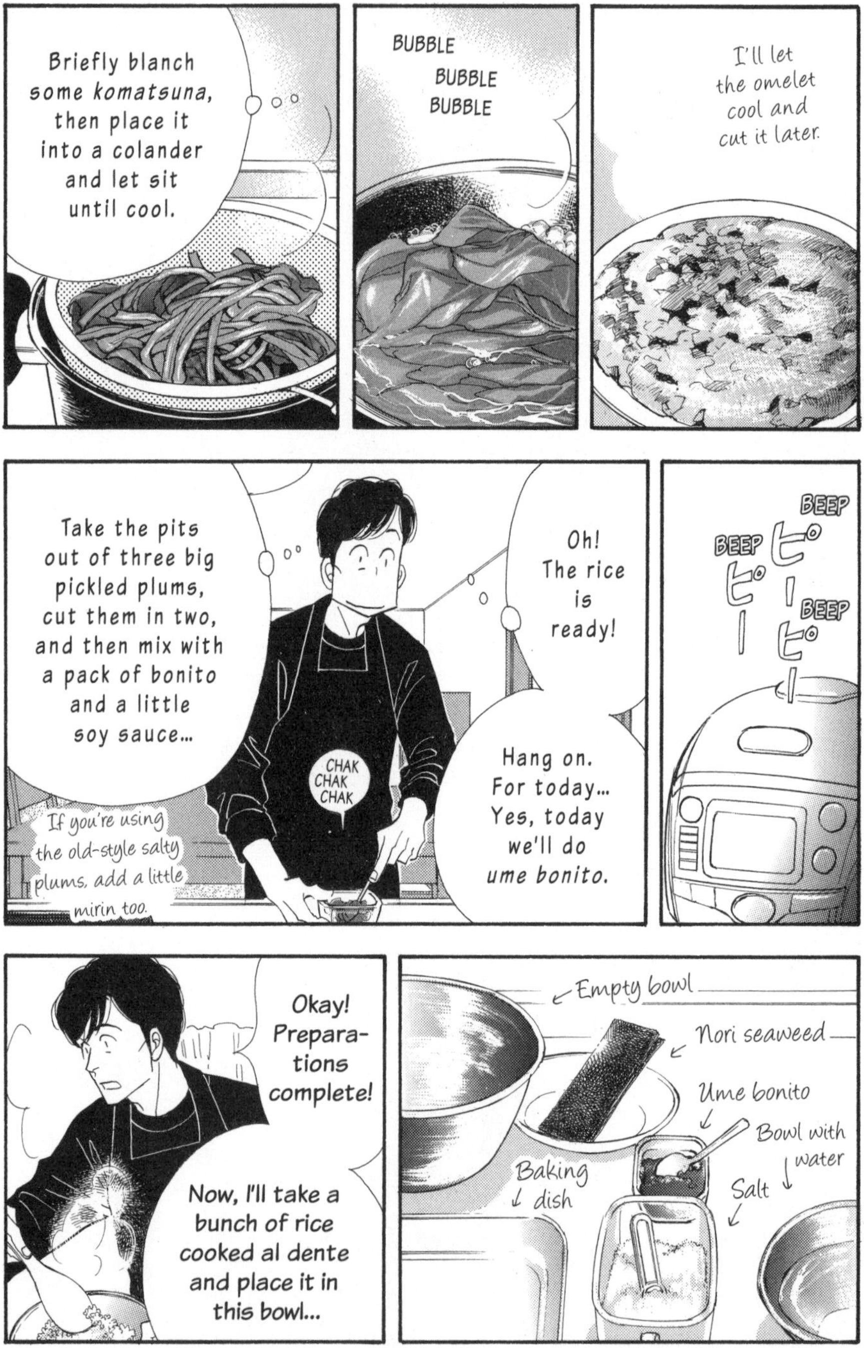
I'll let the omelet cool and cut it later.
BUBBLE BUBBLE BUBBLE
Briefly blanch some *komatsuna*, then place it into a colander and let sit until cool.
BEEP ピー
BEEP ピー
BEEP ピー
Oh! The rice is ready!
Take the pits out of three big pickled plums, cut them in two, and then mix with a pack of bonito and a little soy sauce...
Hang on. For today... Yes, today we'll do *ume bonito*.
CHAK CHAK CHAK
If you're using the old-style salty plums, add a little mirin too.
Empty bowl
Nori seaweed
Ume bonito
Bowl with water
Baking dish
Salt
Okay! Preparations complete!
Now, I'll take a bunch of rice cooked al dente and place it in this bowl...

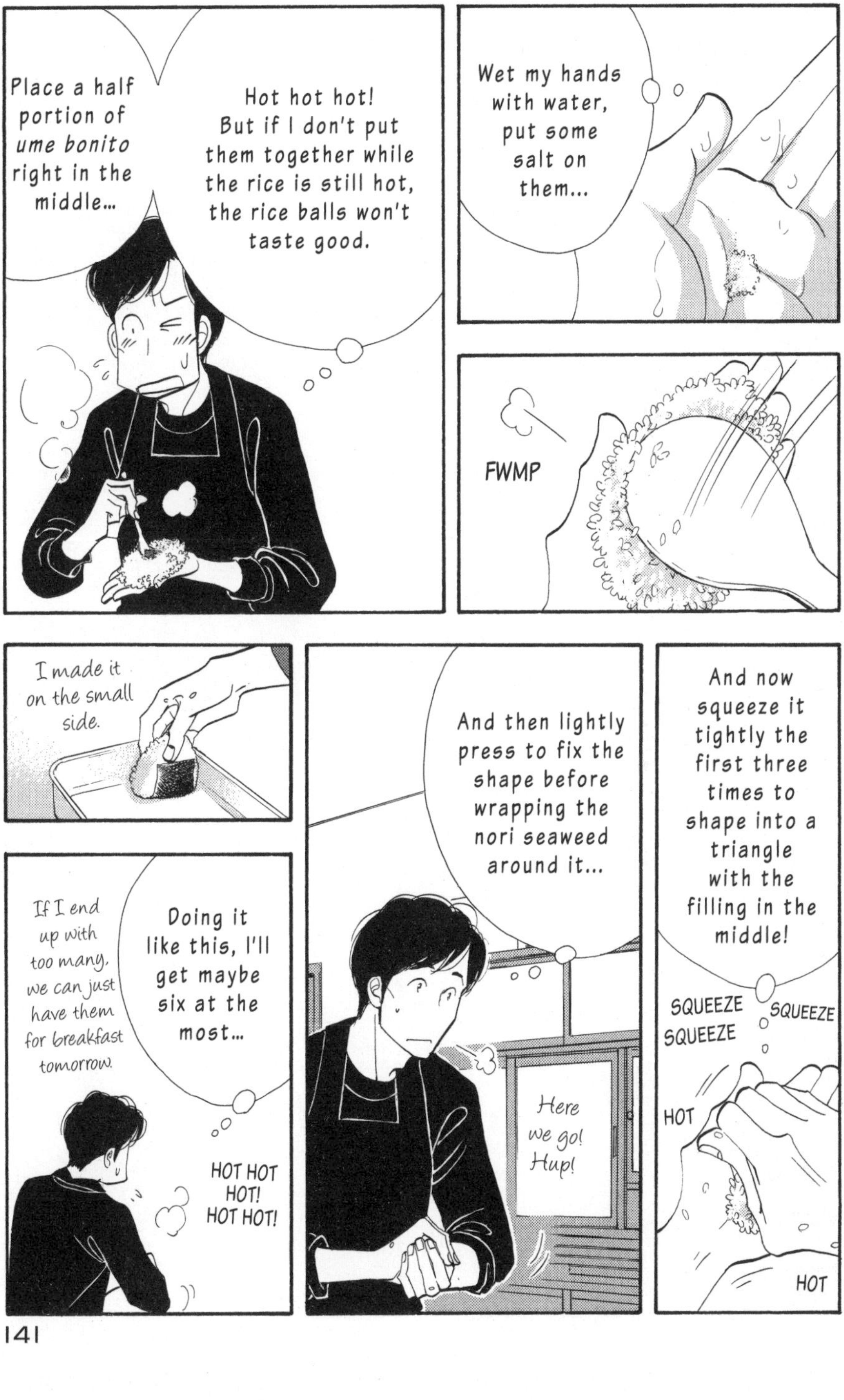
Wet my hands with water, put some salt on them...
FWMP
Hot hot hot! But if I don't put them together while the rice is still hot, the rice balls won't taste good.
Place a half portion of *ume bonito* right in the middle...
And now squeeze it tightly the first three times to shape into a triangle with the filling in the middle!
SQUEEZE
SQUEEZE
SQUEEZE
HOT
HOT
And then lightly press to fix the shape before wrapping the nori seaweed around it...
Here we go! Hup!
I made it on the small side.
Doing it like this, I'll get maybe six at the most...
If I end up with too many, we can just have them for breakfast tomorrow.
HOT HOT HOT! HOT HOT!

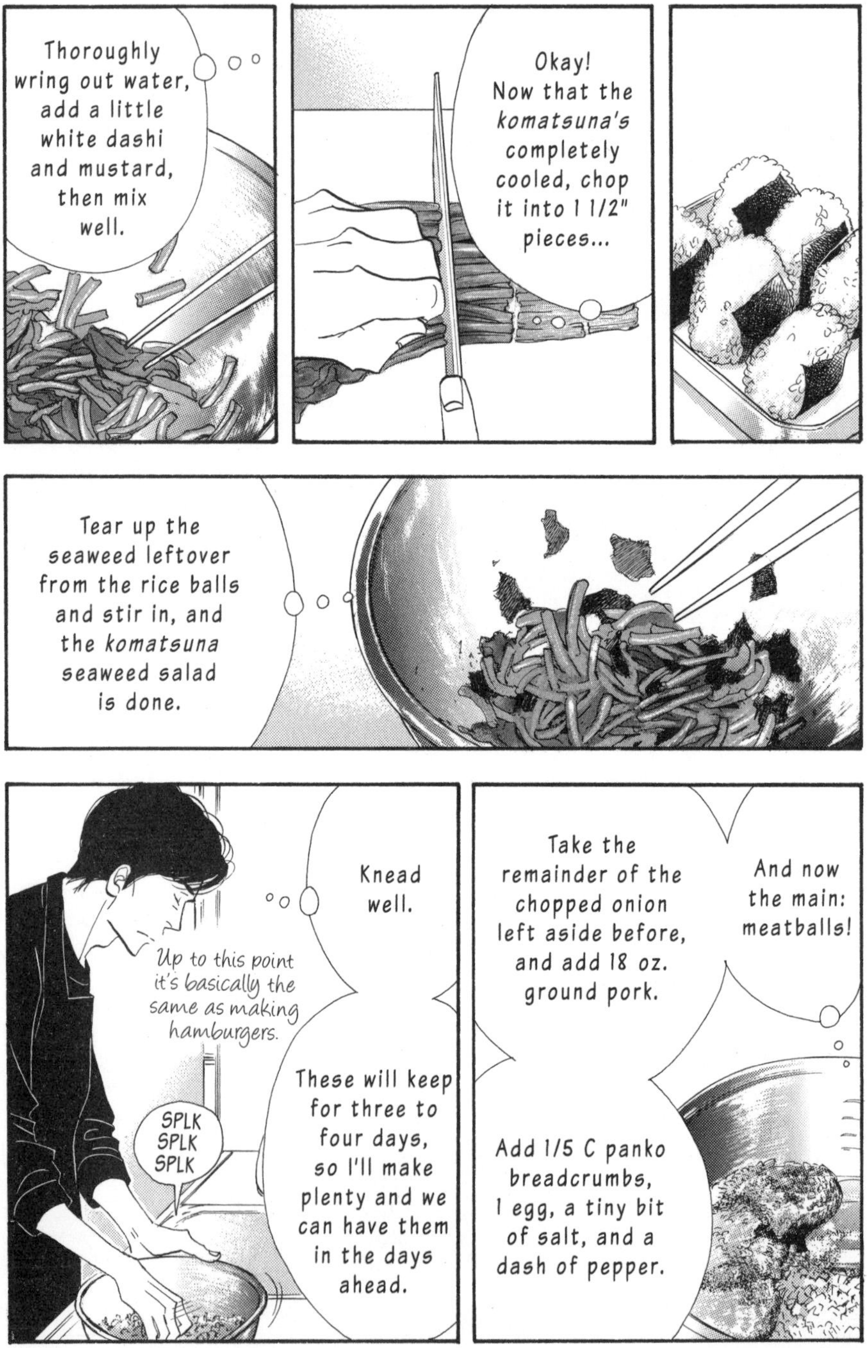
Okay!
Now that the *komatsuna's* completely cooled, chop it into 1 1/2" pieces...
Thoroughly wring out water, add a little white dashi and mustard, then mix well.
Tear up the seaweed leftover from the rice balls and stir in, and the *komatsuna* seaweed salad is done.
And now the main: meatballs!
Take the remainder of the chopped onion left aside before, and add 18 oz. ground pork.
Add 1/5 C panko breadcrumbs, 1 egg, a tiny bit of salt, and a dash of pepper.
Knead well.
Up to this point it's basically the same as making hamburgers.
These will keep for three to four days, so I'll make plenty and we can have them in the days ahead.
SPLK
SPLK
SPLK

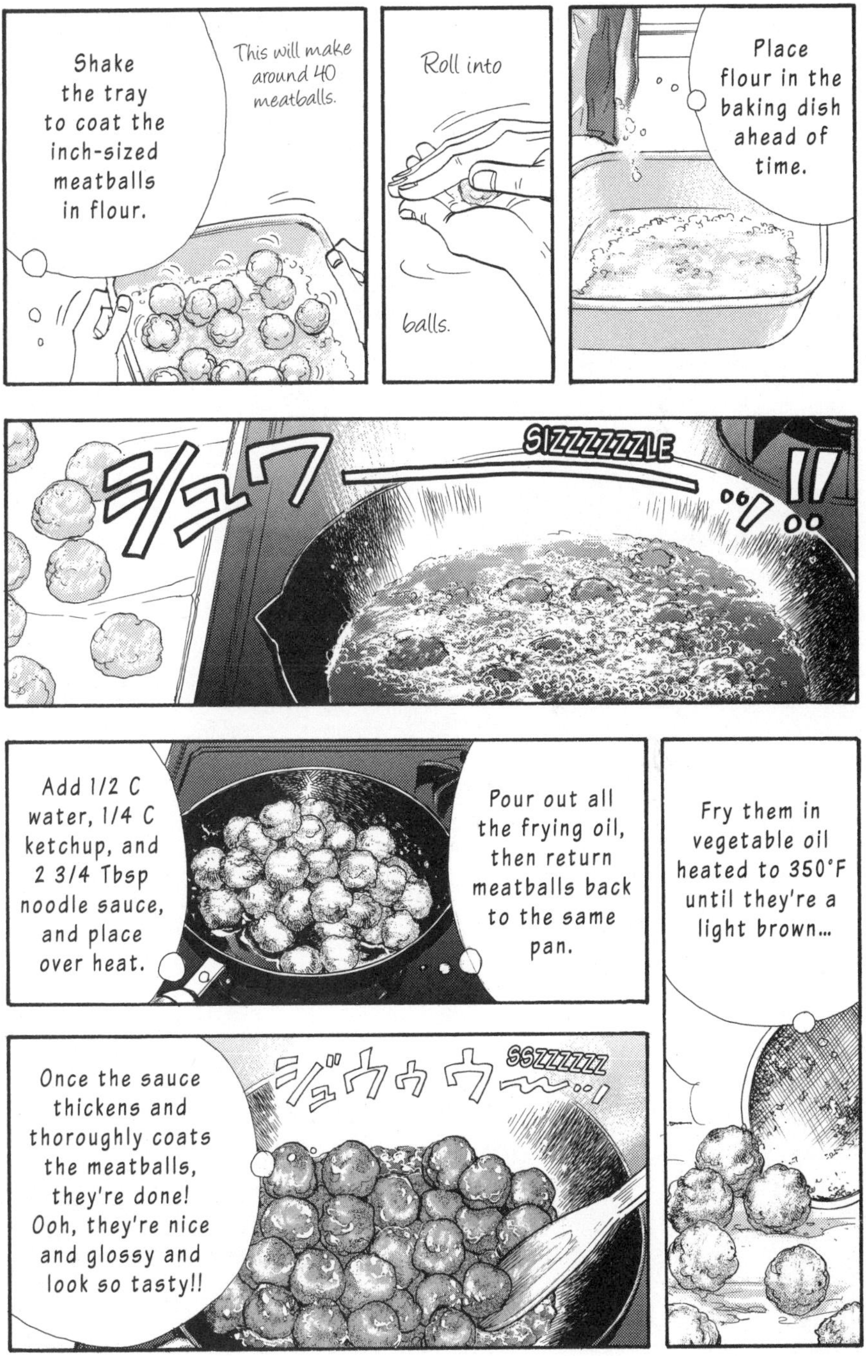
Place flour in the baking dish ahead of time.
Roll into balls.
This will make around 40 meatballs.
Shake the tray to coat the inch-sized meatballs in flour.
SIZZZZZZZLE
シュワーーッ!!
Fry them in vegetable oil heated to 350°F until they're a light brown...
Pour out all the frying oil, then return meatballs back to the same pan.
Add 1/2 C water, 1/4 C ketchup, and 2 3/4 Tbsp noodle sauce, and place over heat.
SSZZZZZZ
ジュウゥ ウ～ッ
Once the sauce thickens and thoroughly coats the meatballs, they're done! Ooh, they're nice and glossy and look so tasty!!

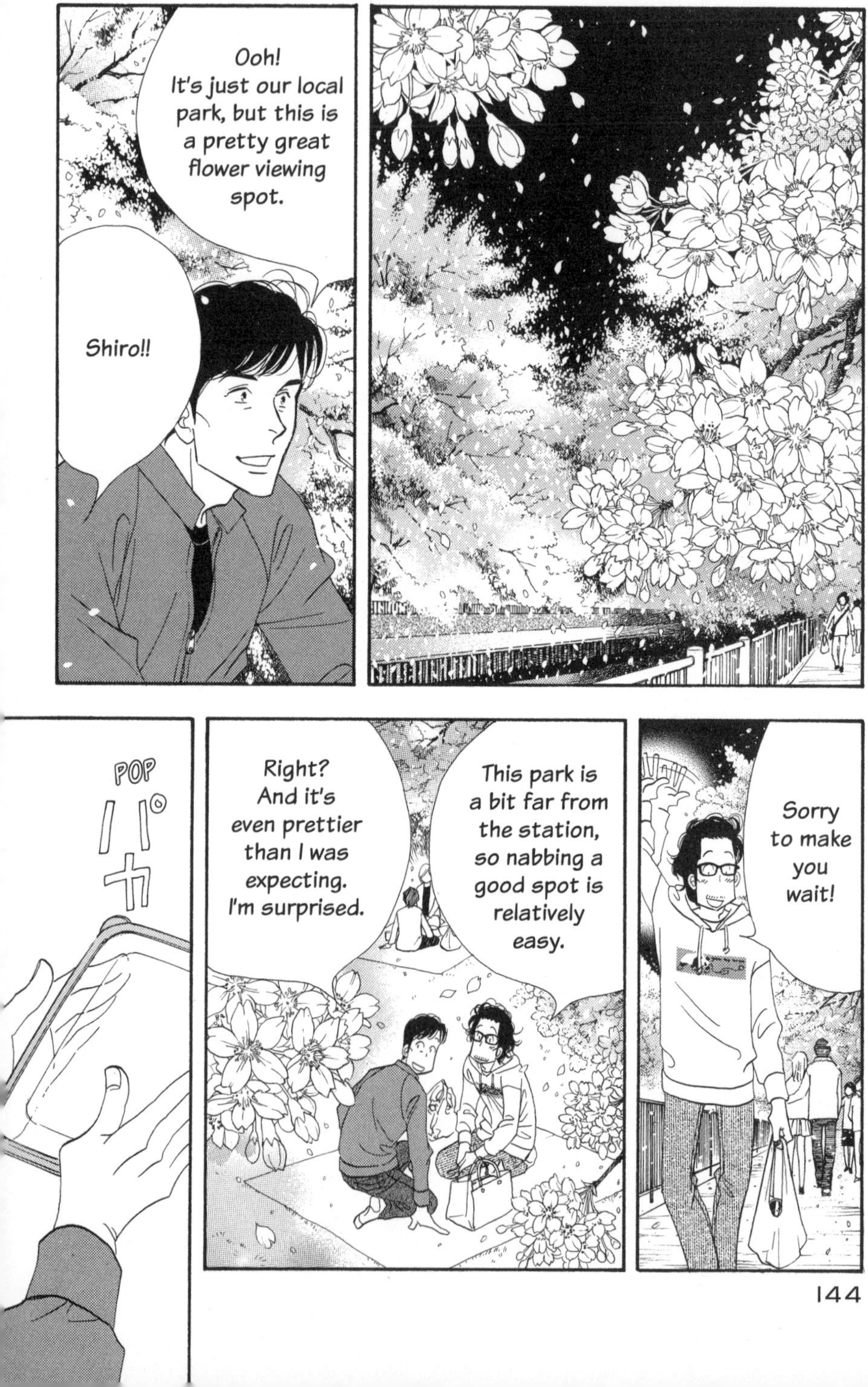
Ooh! It's just our local park, but this is a pretty great flower viewing spot.
Shiro!!
Sorry to make you wait!
This park is a bit far from the station, so nabbing a good spot is relatively easy.
Right? And it's even prettier than I was expecting. I'm surprised.
POP
パカ

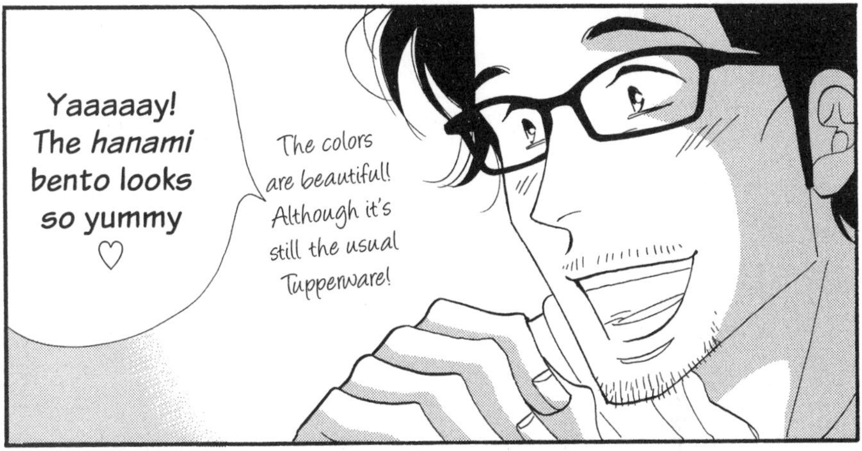
The colors are beautiful! Although it's still the usual Tupperware!
Yaaaaay! The *hanami* bento looks so yummy ♡

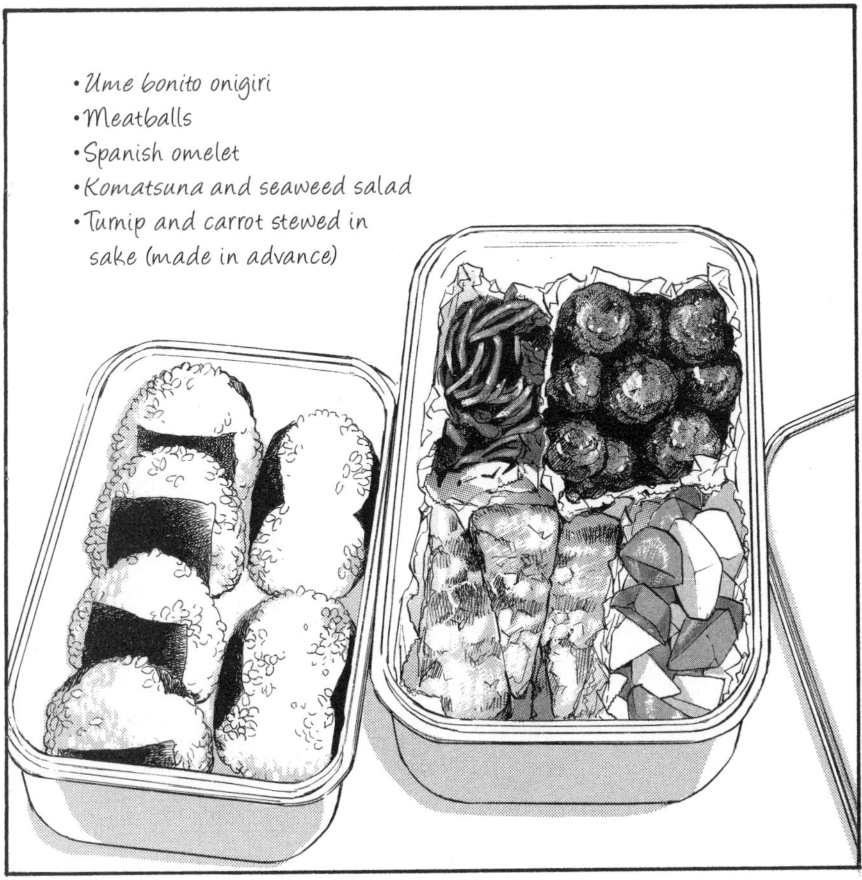
•*Ume* bonito *onigiri*
•Meatballs
•Spanish omelet
•*Komatsuna* and seaweed salad
•Turnip and carrot stewed in sake (made in advance)

Okay, cheers!
Cheers!
Let's eat!
Mm! This omelet is delish!
With the potato in the omelet, there's real volume to it!
Oooh! And the greens mixed with the seaweed is tasty, too!
The seaweed keeps the *komatsuna* from being too watery.
Oh!!
These meatballs are super tasty! Even cold, they're still tender!
They're perfect in a bento with the crowd-pleasing sweet-and-salty ketchup flavor ♡
You're exactly right. These were a packed lunch staple when I was in high school.
They're kind of a pain to make, so while it's belated, it made me appreciate my mother, who made them for me so often.
Mmmmm! And the *ume bonito* rice balls! Somehow you can eat way more rice than usual if it's onigiri!

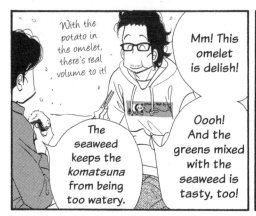

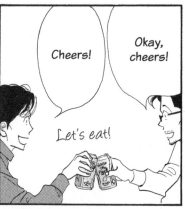

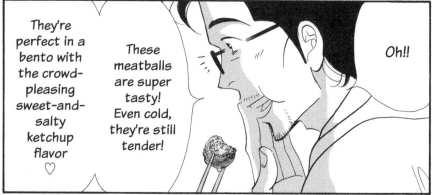

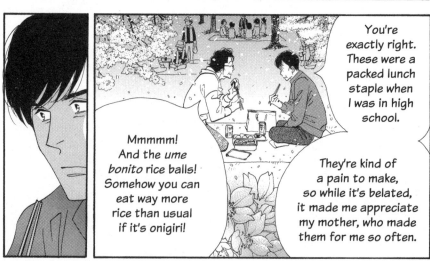

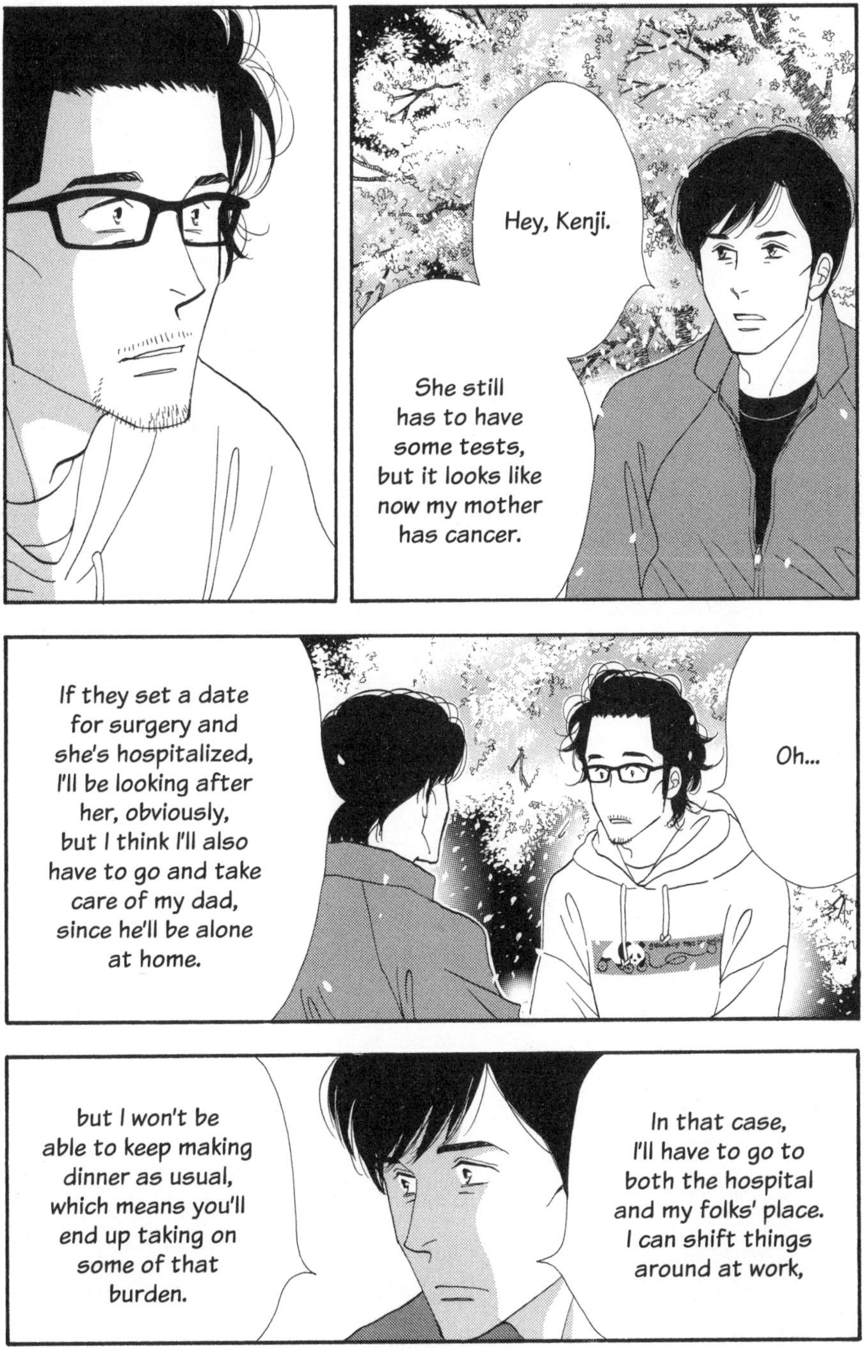
Hey, Kenji.
She still has to have some tests, but it looks like now my mother has cancer.
Oh...
If they set a date for surgery and she's hospitalized, I'll be looking after her, obviously, but I think I'll also have to go and take care of my dad, since he'll be alone at home.
In that case, I'll have to go to both the hospital and my folks' place. I can shift things around at work,
but I won't be able to keep making dinner as usual, which means you'll end up taking on some of that burden.

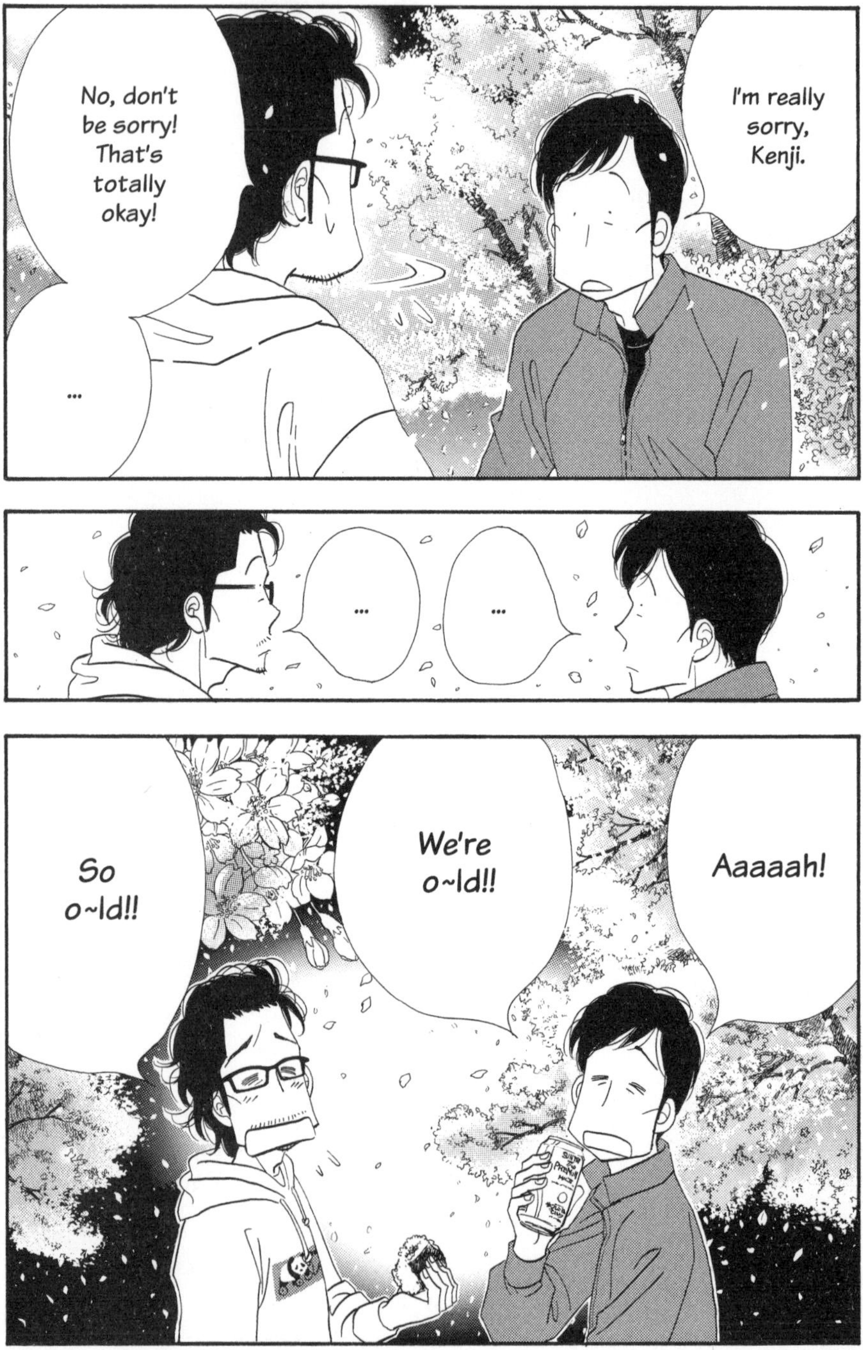
I'm really sorry, Kenji.
No, don't be sorry! That's totally okay!
...
...
...
Aaaaah!
We're o~ld!!
So o~ld!!

The bento fillings introduced here will take up
about a half to a third of the space in a bento box.
The **meatballs** and the **omelet** taste better
cooled rather than piping hot,
so they're suited to being made in advance.

Bonus: Today's Breakfast

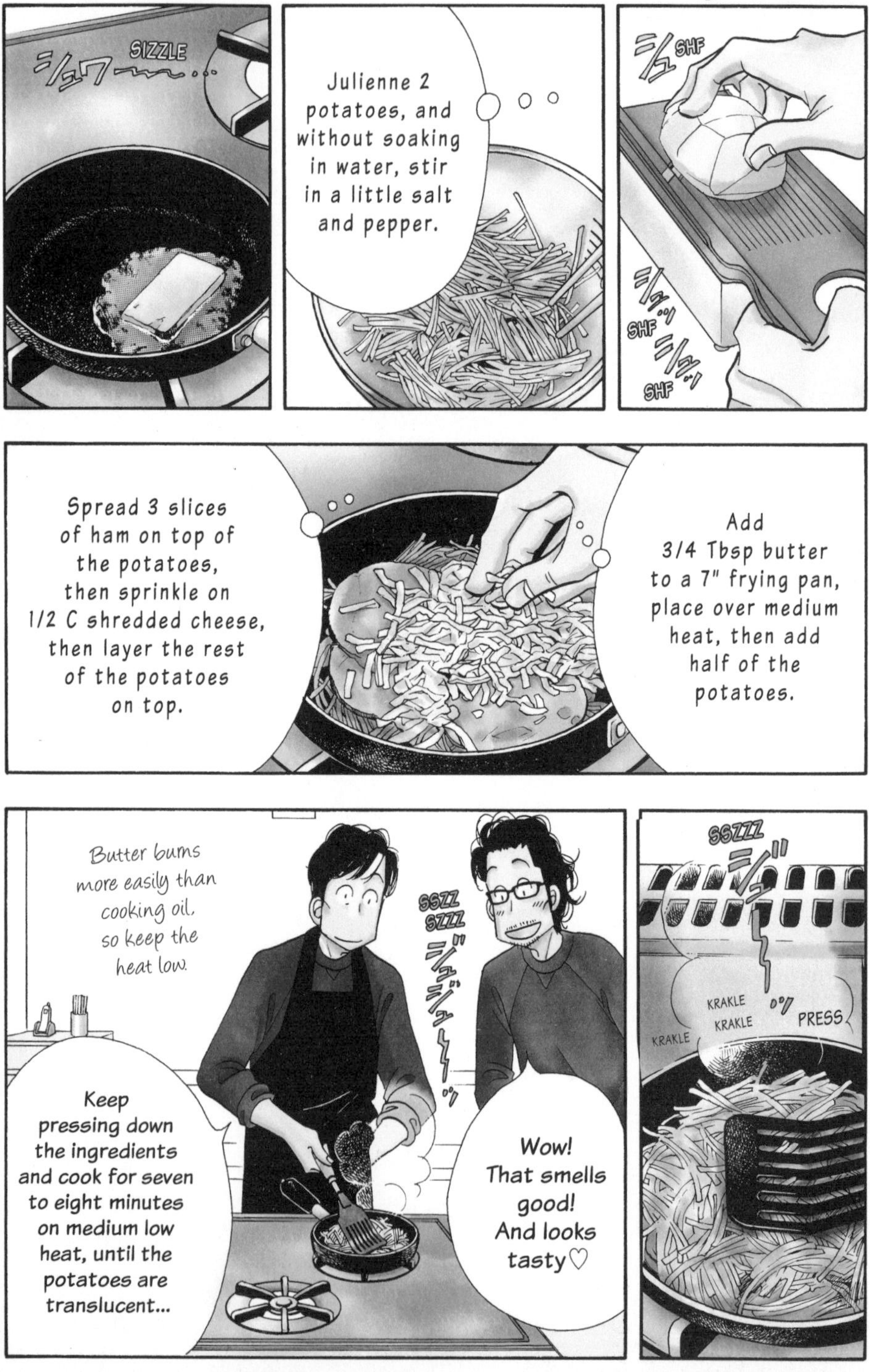
SHF
SHF
SHF
Julienne 2 potatoes, and without soaking in water, stir in a little salt and pepper.
SIZZLE
Add 3/4 Tbsp butter to a 7" frying pan, place over medium heat, then add half of the potatoes.
Spread 3 slices of ham on top of the potatoes, then sprinkle on 1/2 C shredded cheese, then layer the rest of the potatoes on top.
SSZZZ
KRAKLE
KRAKLE
PRESS
KRAKLE
SSZZ
SZZZ
Butter burns more easily than cooking oil, so keep the heat low.
Wow! That smells good! And looks tasty♡
Keep pressing down the ingredients and cook for seven to eight minutes on medium low heat, until the potatoes are translucent...

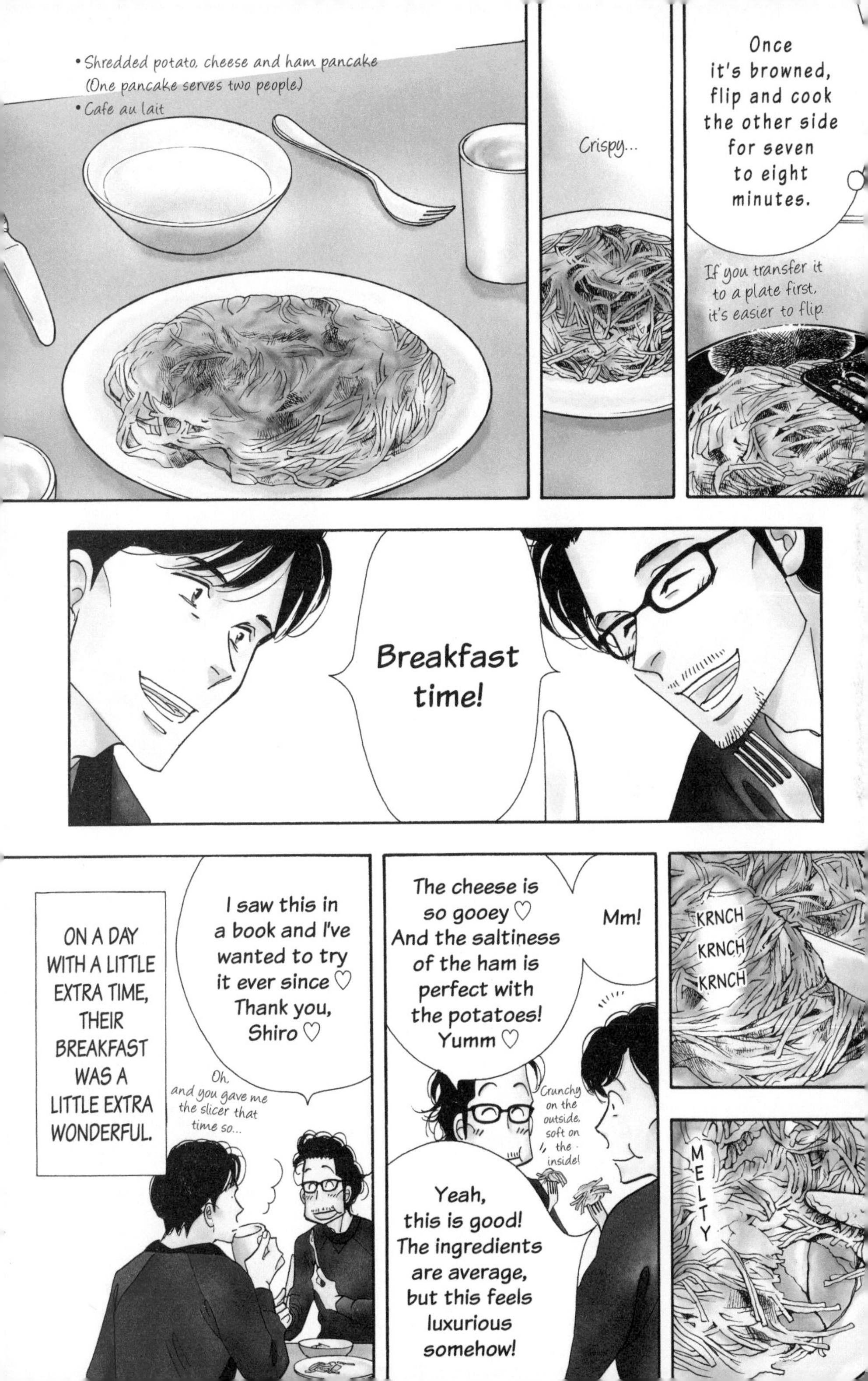
Once it's browned, flip and cook the other side for seven to eight minutes.
If you transfer it to a plate first, it's easier to flip.
Crispy...
• Shredded potato, cheese and ham pancake (One pancake serves two people)
• Cafe au lait
Breakfast time!
KRNCH KRNCH KRNCH
MELTY
Mm!
The cheese is so gooey ♡ And the saltiness of the ham is perfect with the potatoes! Yumm ♡
Crunchy on the outside, soft on the inside!
Yeah, this is good! The ingredients are average, but this feels luxurious somehow!
I saw this in a book and I've wanted to try it ever since ♡ Thank you, Shiro ♡
Oh, and you gave me the slicer that time so...
ON A DAY WITH A LITTLE EXTRA TIME, THEIR BREAKFAST WAS A LITTLE EXTRA WONDERFUL.

Grind black pepper on top of the finished
potato, ham and cheese pancake
for an even more delicious flavor.

what did you eat yesterday?, volume 9

translation: jocelyn allen
production: risa cho
　　　　　　tomoe tsutsumi

© 2015 fumi yoshinaga. All rights reserved.
first published in japan in 2014 by kodansha ltd., tokyo.
publication rights for this english edition arranged
through kodansha ltd., tokyo.
english language version produced by vertical, inc.

translation provided by vertical, inc., 2015
published by vertical, inc., new york

originally published in japanese as kinou nani tabeta? 9 by kodansha, ltd.
kinou nani tabeta? first serialized in morning, kodansha, ltd., 2007-

this is a work of fiction.

isbn: 978-1-941220-50-4

manufactured in canada

first edition

vertical, inc.
451 park avenue south
7th floor
new york, ny 10016
www.vertical-inc.com

is in the air! ♪

In the next volume of What Did You Eat Yesterday? ...

croquette sandwich
spicy miso okra
Tomato soup

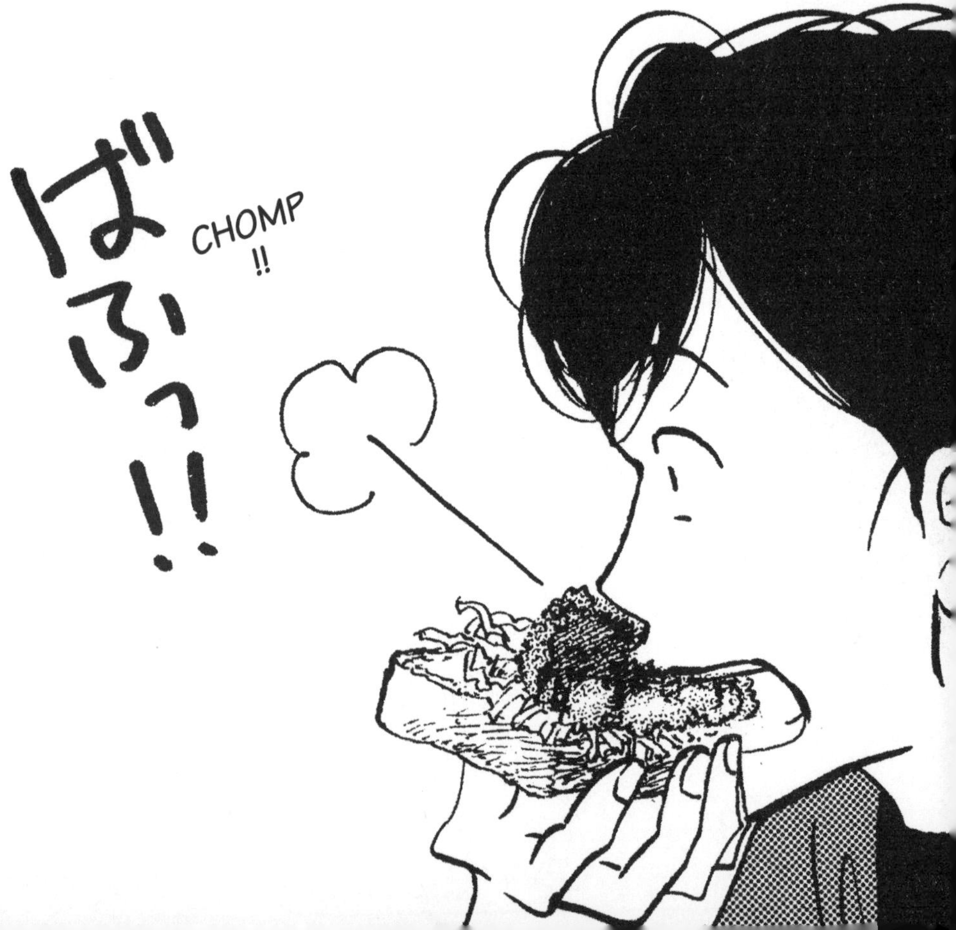
ばふっ!!
CHOMP !!

The sound of happiness

Thai curry
Beef and zucchini stir-fry
shrimp and cellophane noodle salad
And more...

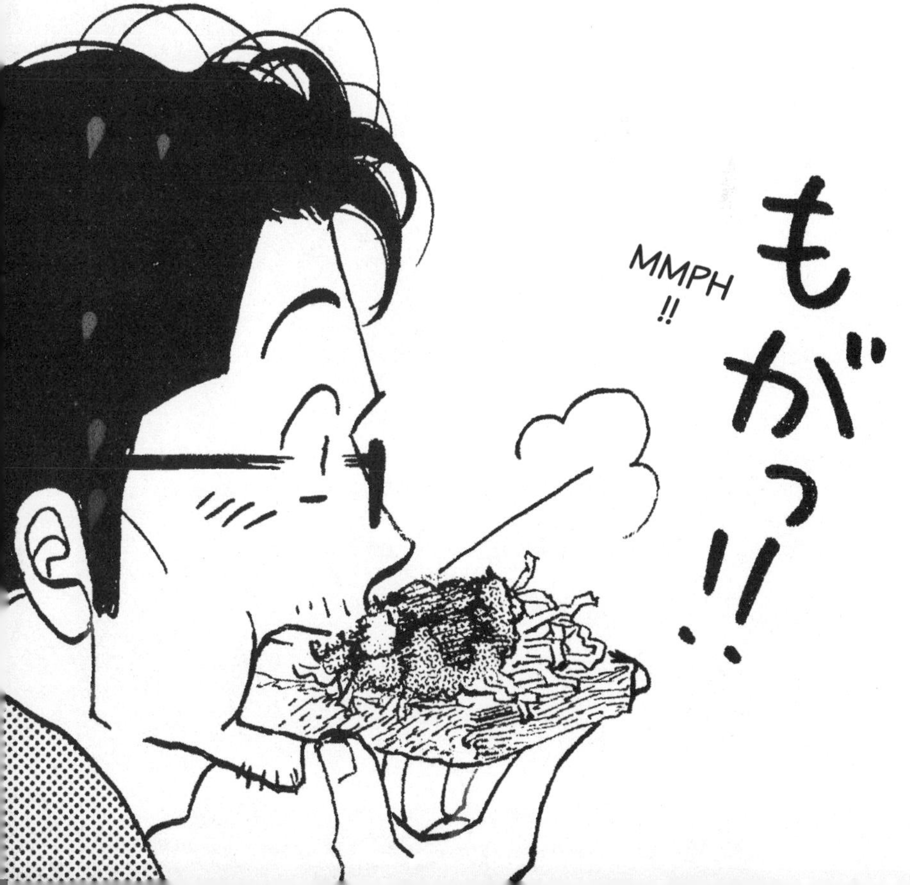
もがっ!!
MMPH !!

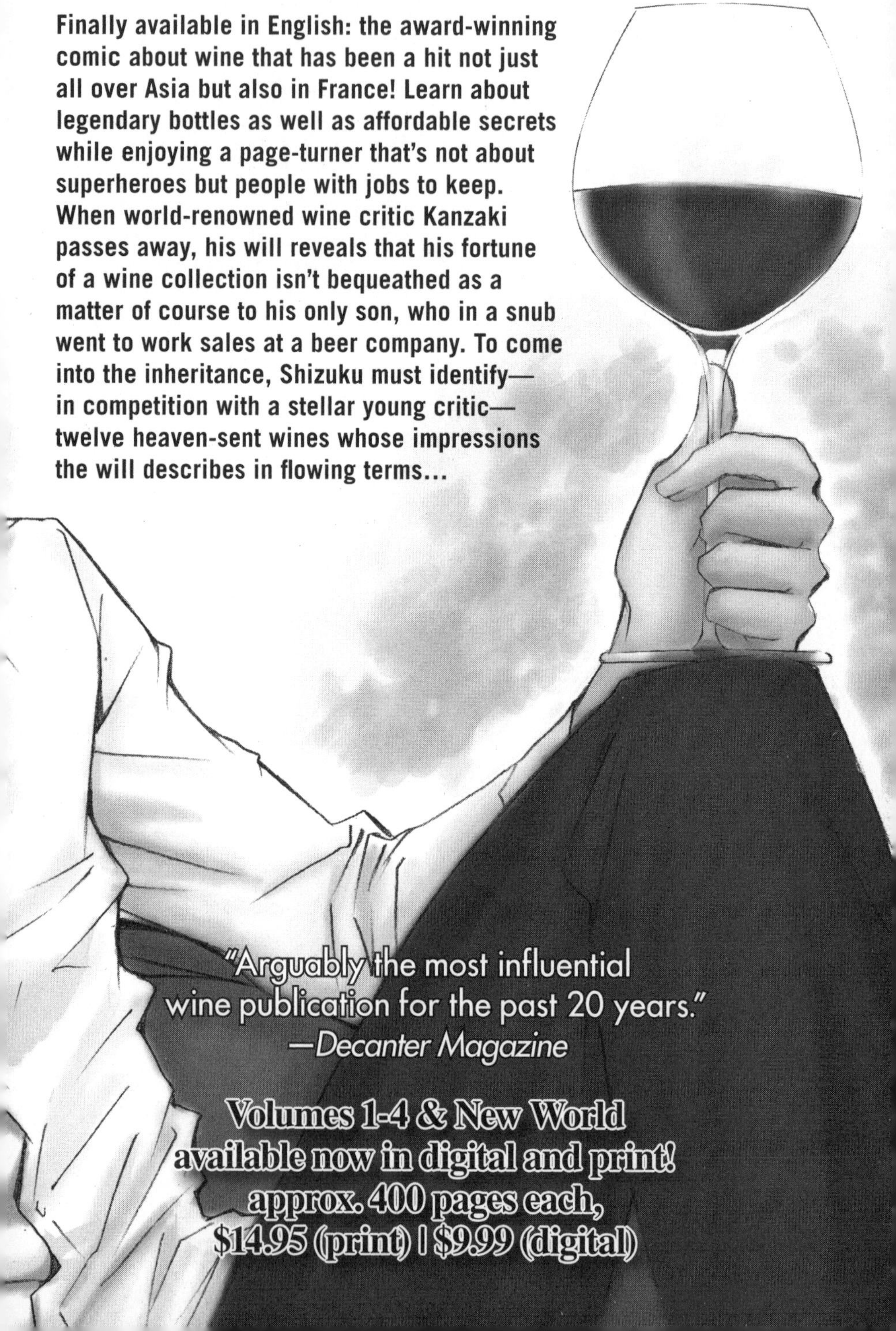
Finally available in English: the award-winning comic about wine that has been a hit not just all over Asia but also in France! Learn about legendary bottles as well as affordable secrets while enjoying a page-turner that's not about superheroes but people with jobs to keep. When world-renowned wine critic Kanzaki passes away, his will reveals that his fortune of a wine collection isn't bequeathed as a matter of course to his only son, who in a snub went to work sales at a beer company. To come into the inheritance, Shizuku must identify—in competition with a stellar young critic—twelve heaven-sent wines whose impressions the will describes in flowing terms...
"Arguably the most influential wine publication for the past 20 years."
—Decanter Magazine
Volumes 1-4 & New World
available now in digital and print!
approx. 400 pages each,
$14.95 (print) | $9.99 (digital)

WINNER
GOURMAND COOKBOOK AWARDS
2009

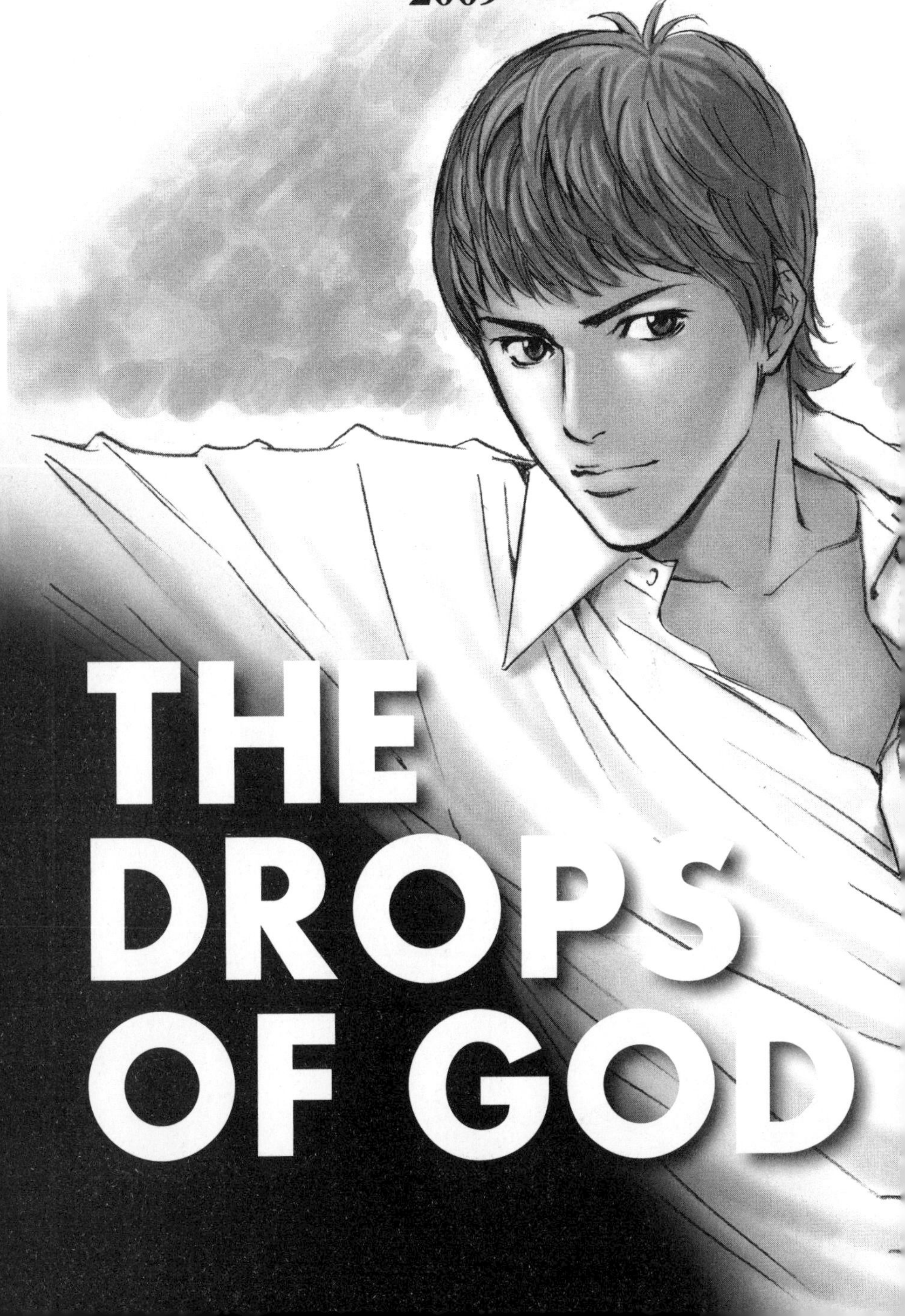
THE
DROPS
OF GOD

INSUFFICIENT DIRECTION

Read this energizing comic and feel proud (or simply unashamed!) of your geeky hobbies. Although manga artist Rompers (*Sakuran*, *In Clothes Called Fat*) doesn't consider herself too far gone, she's gotten married to a towering figure of the otaku persuasion, Director-kun (*Neon Genesis Evangelion*, *Cutey Honey*). Includes copious annotations on Japanese pop culture and an interview with Hideaki Anno.

176 pages | US $14.95 / CAN $16.95

WRONG WAY

Japanese books, including manga like this one,
are meant to be read from right to left.
so the front cover is actually the back cover, and vice versa.
To read this book, please flip it over
and start in the top right-hand corner.
Read the panels, and the bubbles in the panels,
from right to left,
then drop down to the next row and repeat.
It may make you dizzy at first, but forcing your brain
to do things backwards makes you smarter in the long run.
we swear.